Awaken

One people · One planet · One spirit

FIRST PRINCIPLE – FIRST NATIONS ACKNOWLEDGEMENT

It is with a deep sense of gratitude One acknowledges and recognises the First Nations Peoples of the world as the traditional custodians of Country (land, sea* and sky) on Earth. One openly, generously and humbly offers One's respect to First Nations People's living cultures, affirms One's special connection to place and celebrates One's adaptive vibrant communities, as well as One's spiritual ancestors and Elders past, present and emerging. One honours the spirit in One and all sentient Beings on the planet and in the universe.

*Throughout this book, all references to 'sea' include all bodies of water.

Everything is connected – all is One

First published in Australia in 2021 by
Shawn Wondunna-Foley
Innerway
PO Box 2141
Hervey Bay QLD 4655
Australia
www.innerway.com.au

Copyright © Shawn Wondunna-Foley 2021

All rights reserved. This book is copyright. Apart from any fair dealings for the purposes of private study, research, criticism or review permitted under the Australian Copyright Act 1968, no part may be stored or reproduced by any process without prior written permission. Enquiries should be made to the publisher.

ISBN: 978-0-646-82428-4

 A catalogue record for this book is available from the National Library of Australia

Front cover design: Lorna Hendry and Shawn Wondunna-Foley
Editing and layout: Lorna Hendry
Typeset in A-Space and Born
Printing: IngramSpark

AWAKEN
One people • One planet • One spirit
Co-create the best version of oneself now

Shawn Wondunna-Foley

STATEMENT OF ACKNOWLEDGEMENT

One gratefully acknowledges the financial assistance from the Regional Arts Development Fund (RADF) by the Queensland Government and Fraser Coast Regional Council for this publication.

The Regional Arts Development Fund (RADF) is a partnership between the Queensland Government and Fraser Coast Regional Council.

DISCLAIMER

The information contained in this book is for general guidance on matters of spiritual enlightenment and mindful living interest only. While the author has made every attempt to ensure that the quotes and information contained within this book have been obtained from reliable sources and are correct at the time of printing, the author and the publisher are not responsible for any errors or omissions or for the results obtained from the use of this information.

All information in this book is provided 'as is', with no guarantee of completeness, accuracy or timeliness, or of the results obtained from the use of this information, and without warranty of any kind, expressed or implied, including, but not limited to, warranties of performance, merchantability and fitness for a particular purpose.

In no event will the author or publisher, its partnerships or corporations or the partners agents or employees thereof be liable to you or anyone else for any decision made or action taken in reliance on the information in this book or for any consequential, special or similar damages, even if advised of the possibly of such damages.

ABOUT THE AUTHOR

Butchulla (*Badtjala*) First Nation Australian independent author, Shawn Wondunna-Foley is a public speaker, positive thought leader, streetscape/visual/installation artist, creative designer, spiritual lifestyle coach, cultural advisor and ideas–wellness philanthropist. Currently working as a public servant, Shawn has a great love of Country (land, sea and sky). He values the arts, culture and the community (Hervey Bay) where he lives, works and plays on the Fraser Coast in regional Queensland, Australia.

Shawn is the author of several cultural heritage publications – *The Badtjala People, I on Country* as well as mindfulness and spiritual consciousness books on wellness and wellbeing – *One, Two* and *Three*. His self-published quotes book *One* was sold out twice and the series continues to be a fantastic resource and awesome gift for people seeking inner guidance and a more enlightened inner way to live One's life in this modern world and on Earth.

Shawn acknowledges and aligns to the universal idea that: *Everything is Connected – All is One. Everyone is spiritually entangled in an ocean of conscious existence with all other sentient Beings in the universe.*

Awaken, Shawn's first major nonfiction work, is an amazing, shared journey of inner spiritual awareness and a profound awakening experience.

Read Shawn's blog and connect with him on his website www.innerway.com.au. One is also invited to click on the elearning course at www.innerway.com.au, which has been specifically designed to accompany this book.

DEDICATION
Many spirits – One consciousness

This book is dedicated to 'the One' who dares to imagine a better future for all people and planet Earth. A future 'Now', where the currency of ideas for prosperity, abundance and awakening is freely traded around the planet daily. Where all Earth citizens operate at a higher level of consciousness and practice mindfulness in every aspect of One's life. Where people operate in global communities of interest, knowing that everyone has the ability and capacity to freely access information to improve One's mind and body with the support and guidance of spiritual light warriors, mentors, Masters, ambassadors, teachers, healers and life coaches. A place that values paying it forward rather than an electronic funds transfer at point of sale (EFTPOS). A world free of imprisoning people in a life of virtual endless debt, desperation and depression. A global community that is as invested in collective wellness and individual positive wellbeing as much as it is in co-creating the 'right' conditions to enable and ensure the smooth succession and custodianship of Earth to the seventh generation. A vision that begins with the end in mind, approximately 200 years or more from this point in time.

One's intention for this book is to shine a light on raising the vibration of spiritual literacy through focusing on a point of unity and oneness on planet Earth. Infinite positive possibilities already co-exist that have the potential to significantly improve the world today. One need only meditate on this eventuality and align One's life (mind–body–spirit), vibration and actions to manifest it in One's life. Be sure to welcome and enjoy this living experience today. What One imagines in One's mind, One manifests in reality with the cooperation of other sentient Beings on Earth and the universe. Today is the day to change the way that One looks at things, so that the things One looks at also change now.

Know that the hero of One's life story is the person reading this book – there can be only One. No superior cosmic intelligence or Divine Being is coming to save One from One's life. If this were the case, this Supreme Being would have already done so. This is the way it has always been done since the dawning of humankind on planet

Earth. One must fearlessly face One's ego and become its Master. It is time to rediscover One's true divine nature and realise One's awakened path in life. One is the captain of One's ship. One's ultimate inner destiny will not be found by staying in the safe harbours of One's mind and life. One must journey across the uncharted ocean of existence with only the stars and One's inner spirit to guide One. Believe in One's spirit, One's inner way in this world, and know that the universe is always on One's side.

Be 'the One' who dares to imagine a better life and future today – so be it now!

Know that One is going to be okay. It may not seem like it in this moment. But everything will all work out for One in the end.

Love, light and oneness.

Shawn
Hervey Bay, Queensland, Australia

BE ONE NOW

One simple moment of spiritual realisation.
One divine awakening for all of humankind.

Shawn Wondunna-Foley

Important note 2
Useful terms 4
Introduction 7
Mission for Humankind on Earth 15

EARTH MISSION LOG

January 20
February 52
March 82
April 114
May 145
June 177
July 208
August 240
September 272
October 303
November 335
December 366

Acknowledgements 398
Affirmation for life 400
Circle of mindful and conscious existence 401
Final note 402

IMPORTANT NOTE
Language of spirit or 'One'

Throughout the pages of this book, a new language of spirit or 'One' has been used and incorporated to enable the reader to realise a new way of perceiving, thinking, feeling, living and being in the world today.

The Sapir-Whorf hypothesis of linguistic relativity states that the language One speaks influences, limits and determines how One sees or perceives One's world and the universe. This book is written in an English 'spiritual language style', which uses the term 'One'. It reflects a non-dimensional and non-linear view of space–time. Every spiritual thought takes the form beginning with or inclusive of 'One', where 'One' is spirit, soul or cosmic consciousness.

'One' is an inclusive term referring to spirit, soul, cosmic consciousness, Source, the Creator, God, Allah or Divine Supreme Being. It has been written in this way to reflect an intimate conversation between the spiritual source for all things in the universe and One's spirit.

The terms 'I', 'you' and 'your' have been deliberately omitted in order to provide greater clarity, spiritual unity and global inclusiveness. This distinction is key and fundamental in shifting One's mindful perception to a more profound inner knowing and divine sense of oneness within One's spirit or Being. It is about intentionally and purposely co-creating a space with 'no self' to know oneself. To undertake One's ultimate spiritual journey in this life, it is best to: *Remove oneself from the equation of One's life.*

Where there is no 'I', there can be only 'One'. Where there is no 'You', there can be only 'One'. In the absence of 'I', 'me', 'mine', 'you' or 'your', there is only ever One's divine spirit, soul or cosmic consciousness. This is One's eternal presence in the universe. One has co-created this new language and the opportunity to inspire One's way of living and being through One's realisation and awakening of One's spiritual truth – here and now. Know that there is no space or distance between oneself and One's spirit. When One looks inwards, One will know One's inner way and direction in life.

There has never been a more perfect moment in One's life to journey deeply within oneself and awaken to One's own divine existence and living reality on Earth.

All that ever was and will ever be in the universe is present within One's infinite divine presence 'Now'. Wherever One goes on planet Earth, or in any other part of the known universe, One is already home – *Be Here Now.*

USEFUL TERMS

Bright
An enlightened awake spiritual sentient Being.

insanity
Being a sane person who tries repeatedly to 'fit' into a world where most people's minds are operating a stream of egoic unconscious mindless memes or thoughts.

light hole
A state of non-dimensional existence having an infinite presence of source consciousness so intense that all spiritual consciousness is drawn to it.

meme
An element of a culture or system of behaviour passed from one individual to another by imitation or other non-genetic means. Also an image, video or piece of text, typically humorous in nature, that is copied and spread rapidly by internet users, often with slight variations.

sacred space
An embodied emptiness by a particular individual within One's mind–body–spirit holding a great respect, openness and alignment to co-create a new manifested reality or experience.

self-organising theory
The capacity of a system to change itself by creating new structures, adding new negative and positive feedback loops, promoting new information flows and making new rules. It is a process where the organisation (constraint, redundancy) of a system spontaneously increases, without this increase being controlled by the environment or an encompassing or otherwise external system.

seven key states of consciousness
Knowing, awareness, oneness, joy, free will, peace and presence.

seven key virtues
Compassion, helpfulness, acceptance, generosity, simplicity, patience and openness.

sol
A solar day on Earth. The interval between two successive returns of the Sun to the same meridian (sundial time) as seen by an observer on Earth.

spiritual entanglement
A phenomenon whereby source consciousness is present in such a way that the individual spiritual states of consciousness exist independently until aligned, and the act of conscious alignment of one influences that of the other, even when at a distance from each other in space–time within the universe.

spiritual singularity
A state of non-dimensional conscious reality where states of consciousness exist in infinite or endless beingness.

the way
'The way' is a term used in Buddhism or Zen teachings that, in its simplest definition, means an approach to life that flows in harmony and alignment with nature or the natural synergy of the universe in the present moment.

Type 1 civilisation
The Kardashev scale categorises a civilisation's level of technological advancement based on the amount of energy it is able to use:

- a Type 1 civilisation can use and store all of the energy available on its planet
- a Type 2 civilisation can use and control energy at the scale of its planetary system
- a Type 3 civilisation can control energy at the scale of its entire host galaxy.

A Type 1 civilisation has been able to harness all the energy that is available from a neighbouring star, gathering and storing it to meet the energy demands and needs of the population.

NAMASTE

One's spirit honours every other spirit in the universe.

One honours the place within oneself where the entire universe resides.

One honours One's mind, body and spirit, soul or cosmic consciousness.

One honours the light, love, oneness, truth, beauty, kindness, compassion and inner peace within others – because it also exists within oneself.

In sharing these divine virtues and qualities, everyone is united.

Everything is Connected – All is One.

Shawn Wondunna-Foley

INTRODUCTION

On 1 January 2020, One began writing this new Earth Life Journal not knowing how the year may unfold, including the impact of COVID-19 on work–life relationships, social habits and people's daily lives around the world. It was a time to self-isolate, maintain physical distancing and align with One's inner Being. This alone time allowed One to look deeply into One's spirit, soul or cosmic consciousness and come to terms with this changing world that One lives in now. In these moments of stillness, it gave One time to clear One's mind of old paradigms, dysfunctional egoic thought patterns and outdated ways of thinking.

Now is the time to cleanse a new path towards manifesting a new future reality today. There has never been a more profound moment in One's life than now to embrace a new way of living and being on planet Earth. Every person's behavioural algorithm or personal operating system for living life on Earth requires a serious upgrade. One needs to decommission One's old and outdated egocentric personal operating software version 1.0 and install a completely new alternative spirit-centred version 2.0.

Know that it is One's responsibility to change oneself from within and share this divine spiritual greatness with the world. Time is an illusion, so One's moment always lives in the now of One's existence.

Looking back over the years, One has consistently felt like One was living on a planet with mindless strangers where One does not belong. One has felt like One was trying to continually repurpose oneself to fit into lifeless cultures – a community, social network and world that basically makes no sense at all. As One now understands One's place in the universe, One has come to the inevitable conclusion that countless people, communities, societies and nations have created a world that enshrines egoic values, anti-virtuous living principles and the non-existence of spirit into every aspect of living life. Governance structures, statues, social systems, institutions and lawful democratic expressions try to propagate this egoic truth as 'moral, ethical, just and normal', but it is definitely not **'the way'** of the universe at all. It never has been and never will be.

The spiritual ecology of living a 'free life' on Earth, in balance with nature, has been seriously disrupted and distorted over several generations by people who have uploaded and reinforced an egocentric culture of conditional, controlling and fear-based principles, processes and practices. It is widely recognised that this egoic way of living is now completely out of date. It has passed its use-by date on the planet and needs to be discarded or recycled into something useful.

As One reflects upon One's place, purpose and path in life, it is important to take the time to honour the passing of the 'old ways' of living and allow the emergence of 'new ways' of being in this world. It is time to come together in a united oneness and recognise that everyone has a shared responsibility to co-create the new Earth and enable a spiritually awakened **Type 1 civilisation**.

The beginning of the year is always an optimistic time for oneself. One looks to the future with confidence, positivity and a deep sense of knowing that the universe is on One's side and that everything will work out okay. One often finds that One is nudging oneself back into the present moment when One drifts away due to the normal distractions of living life. It is all part of the ongoing process of realigning One's balance and harmony with 'the way' and the natural rhythm of life in the universe.

As One joyfully entertained the idea of this book, One reflected upon One's present life and made a clear, conscious decision to do something different and unique this year. So began this new path of writing about One's positive prosperity and intentional inspiration on planet Earth.

Today is the right time to begin something new in One's life. This is the right moment and the right day to do so. As One begins this new journey and starts to co-create this journal, One knows that great people do not fear time. One did not come to Earth to accumulate mountains of money or 10,000 things, chase after the illusion of being a celebrity or important person, or indulge oneself in manipulating others to serve One's ego's insatiable fear, separateness, insecurity, power and control. One is here on Earth for a higher purpose.

One is filled with joyful excitement, inspiration and an overflowing belief of positive optimism for this coming year and decades. One is completely confident that this year and decade will be awesome and, at times, beyond One's wildest imagination.

One's mind–body remains completely receptive and open to being guided by One's spirit through this process. It is One's desire to leave a living legacy for those conscious 'spirit walkers' who are following a similar path and choose to be here now. While the initial intention is clear, what is not certain is the infinite life outcomes for those who are reading this book now. It is One's intention to co-create these words, thoughts and ideas to be a guide and 'inner light gift' for future truth-seekers. It will serve as a trail of thoughtful breadcrumbs for all sentient Beings who choose to come to Earth in this present moment.

One's spirit reaches out across time and space to One now.

One's spirit invites One to align to 'the way' and be all that One can be in this infinite moment of 'Now'.

Know that One is spirit, soul or cosmic consciousness. As a divine Being of the universe, One can never be created or destroyed. One exists within an infinite continuum of beingness – beyond any human construct or limitation. One's human form, be it male, female or transgender is only a temporary expression of the universe unfolding and manifesting itself within this space–time continuum.

Change is a time of pain, disruption and growth. Know now that it is the year of change and planet Earth is in a time of inner and outer transformation. It is a struggle that has been going on for the best part of the last 2000 to 3000 years and in some First Nations cultures for many thousands of years more. Most citizens on the planet choose to remain ignorant or simply socially blind to the patterns of personal misalignment, resource conflict or social injustice. Many humans prefer to mindlessly walk the earth in a state of unconscious living. One could refer to these people as the 'unawakened' – drifting through One's life like a seed pod yet to open floating on a river flowing effortlessly to the ocean.

There is no single legal entity that governs the entire planet. Egocentric systems of governance across the world are inherently unstable, politically self-consumed, coercively corrupt or disruptively dysfunctional. Most current modern Western systems of governance exist to maintain a subtle system of economic, social and cultural compliance of the population to benefit the wealthy's sense of civil economic entitlement and ongoing social certainty. The Earth has no single unified planetary vision, system of inclusive governance, shared belief or common goal of how to co-exist in harmony with all living entities on the planet.

People who consciously choose to be mindful, prosperous and abundant or show any kind of unifying leadership and act in the best interests of all Earth citizens tend to be vilified and labelled as extremists, or insane. There are many people whose only job is to silence those who seek and speak the truth about what is happening on Earth. With the growth of multinational corporations and global media industries, there has also been a rise in the creation of artificial intelligence systems, and interactive algorisms to manufacture fake news to flood social media platforms in an effort to promote misinformation and misdirection by way of fear and addictive sensationalism. The purpose of this approach is to dilute any and all real discussions about global human wellness and personal wellbeing. This is 'the great silence' of inconvenient truths trying to spread across the world. But not everyone believes the messaging of this irrational, egoic, human psychosis. There is a rising trend in global discussions about asserting individual responsibility and collective mature action in the best interests of all citizens of Earth.

Leaders are emerging with every new generation and, along with them, more innovative and disruptive technologies to change egoic-dependent living systems into more socially responsible, adaptive, flexible, agile and spiritually centred lifestyles that promote collective wellness and individual wellbeing on Earth. People are beginning to see the value and vitality of investing in a global culture that promotes prosperity, abundance and an awakened life for One and all. When people care, the planet naturally benefits.

While the exact future may be unknown, what is certain is that change is constant. All this prolonged human pain and suffering will only lead to One inevitable outcome – inner evolution. As more and more disruptive technologies and algorithms are invented to challenge the status quo of control and command within communities and nations across the planet, physical borders will become less important. What will arise and begin to emerge is a clarity of awareness. Intentional aspirations and virtual visions will be created to shape a new reality and manifestation of it on Earth or elsewhere in the solar system. One will begin to see edges of dramatic evolutionary change appearing on the horizon, moving closer and with increasing speed like a tsunami approaching the shore. This will most likely have the greatest impact in the next decade and continue to evolve exponentially, particularly as it relates to people engaging in life through adopting healthy habits like meditation, conscious practices of being mindful in One's daily decision-making processes and being aligned to inner spirit, soul or cosmic consciousness.

In 100 years, Earth citizens will operate from a vastly different point of reference. The population will function and operate in new unimaginable ways, within:

- global communities of interest/s involving all Earth citizens
- self-organised diverse eco-social-cultural local living communities
- networks of applied ideas, inspiration and excellence
- the rise of digital intelligence and its own technologically advanced applied coded machine language
- innovation and investment creators for all of humankind (on-world and off-world)
- mindful healing, healthy living and spiritual enlightenment universities
- prosperity, abundance and awakening transition centres
- meditation, learning and positive practice spaces (mind–body–spirit)
- personal wellbeing and whole-of-life wellness centres
- digital, design and development spaces for creators
- hubs of creative-artistic-cultural expression across the planet.

This global change will lead to a cascading effect within all social systems, businesses and existing governance models. It will also be the catalyst for the emergence of a new, unifying global spiritual **meme**, language and spiritual way of thinking.

The population of the entire planet will come to a point of realisation about pre-existing thoughts patterns and false assumptions regarding individual human personhood and identity. There will be a significant shift in the modalities of planetary lifestyles, living–being on Earth and elsewhere in the solar system.

At the beginning point of this change will be a paradigm shift in the two most basic and fundamental questions most humans ask:

- Who am I?
- What is my purpose in life?

Know that if One desires to change One's life, living outcome and thus the entire planet, One must first change the level of One's consciousness by asking two different questions:

- Who is 'One'?
- How does 'One' co-create an awakened, mindful and spiritual life on Earth?

When One changes the questions, One completely shifts the starting point and direction of One's life.

Through co-creating this simple change in One's life, One entirely alters One's life trajectory, living outcomes and the future of planet Earth.

Do not underestimate One's ability to be part of the change process to co-create a new Earth.

Human beings will undergo an inner transformation as part of a spiritual evolution to a new age of 'conscious enlightenment' on the planet. All paths are leading to this point of singularity. This divine outcome is undeniable and inescapable for the entire population on the planet. This is the path that will lead to all citizens becoming part of a new united, spiritually based Type 1 civilisation. This change is already on its way and already here – 'Now'. The most challenging thing for all of humanity is not to destroy itself during these moments of realisation, transformation and awakening.

To resist this divine outcome will only lead to One's ongoing personal suffering. The universe is guiding all humans to this place of self-realisation, self-transformation and self-awakening. One's divine destiny already exists now. Believe ... so it will be.

As the older generations gradually pass away, the limitations of the inherited social systems of order will eventually begin to become outdated and obsolete. There will be an emergence of new ways of perceiving One's place in the world and changed ways of making an effective and meaningful contribution to One's family unit, personal partnerships, friendships and peer groups as well as global communities of interest on the planet. The networking of human interaction across the planet will increase more and more. It will grow synergistically, naturally and organically. These web-based connections and relationships will shape a new wave of thinking at an accelerated and exponential rate, although actual 'real-life' experiences will lag behind this 'thought front' of global change and adaptive integration. People will continue to question 'the system or matrix of governance' and seek real answers and solutions to a shared global prosperity and abundance for all citizens on Earth. Conscious conversations between all humans will ripple across the planet like a silent euphoric virus of enlightenment or shared divine oneness.

The question will not be if it is happening, but how One will accept and embrace this new wave of change when the moment arrives in One's life. Look not outside oneself, but within oneself for the wisdom that One seeks now. One cannot hide from One's divine destiny or this spiritual evolution. One cannot blind oneself with ignorance in the hope that this moment or day will never come. It will arrive in One's inbox or on the latest app or in conversation with a friend or on social media in One form or another. One may be already experiencing it here and now. It is already changing the existing mindscape and social landscape of the modern world. As this meme grows within friendship networks, groups and online–offline communities, so too will people's awareness change as well. One will notice a paradigm shift in divine consciousness that will expand exponentially in every direction on the planet.

When enough people believe in One's inner divine oneness, this oneness will reach a critical mass or tipping point of global awareness and cause a ripple effect within the consciousness of all people living on the planet. No border patrol, razor wire fence, remote island detention centre or immigration policy will be able to keep this change or thought catalyst out.

No single person, corporation or single nation on Earth will be able to deny a person or communities the right to express One's divine nature, living wellness and positive wellbeing in the interests of current and future generations of humans living in harmony and balance within the natural environment.

Many great spiritual leaders have long echoed the idea of 'be the change that One seeks to see in this world'. This statement is as true as it ever was.

The idea of a spiritual evolution is not a radical thought, it is simply a natural consequence of a divine living system self-correcting by aligning current thought patterns with 'the way' of the universe. It may have taken some 2000 to 65,000 years to arise out of various human cultures and spread globally on Earth, but it is here now. It is about individual alignment of One's inner awareness of One's spirit, soul or cosmic consciousness and the universe. It is also about acknowledging the detrimental impact of continuing ego centric dysfunctional thought patterns of the past, such as greed, power, separation and control in favour of spirit-centric mindful practices, meaningful meditation and intentional virtuous actions.

One needs to align to the awakened wisdom of the Elders, Masters and thought leaders and apply it in this present moment to One's daily life for the benefit of all future generations.

A new future begins the moment One consciously decides to embrace a new vision and mission for oneself and humankind.

MISSION FOR HUMANKIND ON EARTH

When One chooses to accept this Mission, One will be acting in the best interests of One's higher self and be able to benefit all of humankind on planet Earth.

The Mission Framework is intended as a spiritual light traveller's guide for living and being on Earth. The Mission Framework includes:
1. Mission Parameters
2. Mission Priorities
3. Mission Directives
4. Mission Outcomes

In order to maximise the experiences of this book or Mission Log, it is best that the reader become familiar with the Mission Framework. The structure of the Mission Framework is key to co-creating the best version of oneself 'Now'.

Mission Parameters

1. To utilise all available resources to enable One to consciously awaken to One's higher enlightened spiritual self within One's Being and intuitively live life in peace, balance and harmony on planet Earth.
2. To mindfully adapt, continually improve and co-create to be the best version of oneself.
3. To unconditionally gift One's love, presence, knowledge, experiences and wisdom to One and all future generations.

Mission Priorities

1. To realise that One is and will always be an infinite, immortal and eternal spirit, soul or cosmic consciousness of the universe.
2. To awaken within and be One with One's divine spirit and the universe.
3. To be completely present and mindful in all that One thinks, says and does on Earth.

4. To cultivate a mindful practice and healthy habits of applying all seven key virtues in every aspect of One's daily life (compassion, helpfulness, acceptance, generosity, simplicity, patience and openness).
5. To guide others on One's path and purpose in life by living One's life in alignment with 'the way' of the universe – here and now.
6. To raise a higher level of awareness and vibration for all of humanity to change and transform from the inside out, which will enable a new prosperity and abundance mindset, a new way of living and being, and the co-creation of a new Earth experience for all future generations.
7. To continue to spiritually evolve within a continuum of infinite beingness.
8. To intuitively align with all seven states of One's spiritual Being (knowing, awareness, oneness, joy, free will, peace and presence) in this life.

Mission Directives*

Directive One
To live a prosperous, abundant and awakened life that serves and honours One's spirit, oneself, other humans, animals, planet Earth and the universe in a virtuous way without harm or through inaction allow harm to come to these living entities.

Directive Two
To act consciously and mindfully with the First Directive.

Directive Three
To protect and express One's existence in alignment with the First and Second Directives.

Mission Outcomes

An awakened, unified, spiritually based Type 1 civilisation on Earth that is diversely expressed by:

- spiritually conscious and mindful human beings co-existing in peace, harmony and balance on the planet
- a prosperous and abundant living and being culture held in trust by every Earth citizen for all future generations in perpetuity.

* Adapted from *The Three Laws of Robotics* by Isaac Asimov – a set of rules that govern the ethics of his fictional robots.

ns, so one is.

EARTH
MISSION LOG

SOL DAYS 1-366

JANUARY
Sol day 1-31

One believes that we are all on the precipice of great change and spiritual awakening on planet Earth. It is an inescapable and undeniable truth that, as humans evolve, this new living experience will manifest into reality. One is excited at the possibility of a global shift in higher consciousness across the world. A personal transformation and divine realisation for a new age of mindful and spiritual enlightenment will change the face of living and being on Earth for the next 1000 to 10,000 years.

One believes that anything is possible in this present moment. One believes in oneself (mind–body–spirit) and One's future life now on Earth. One will co-create the right conditions with other sentient Beings, which will enable wonderful, harmonious, kind, caring and compassionate relationships. One will add to the collective intuitive intelligence of awake people on the planet through mindfully cogniforming or reconfiguring One's own inner mindscape, thoughts and beliefs. One's way of life will be to cultivate and practice habits of mindful meditation, positive wellbeing and spiritual alignment. One knows that One can live joyfully and peacefully, and at the same time align to One's inner virtues and spirit, soul or cosmic consciousness. One believes in a world where every citizen of Earth lives in prosperity, abundance and balance with Country (land, sea and sky).

As this year begins, One believes in a circle of spiritual oneness or unconditional love consciousness that will envelop all human beings and the entire planet. One's mind is free and One's spirit is open to receiving divine wisdom and spiritual guidance from all sources to co-create the best version of oneself. One takes full responsibility for One's life, mindful living existence, divine spiritual presence, awakening and positive action to enable experiencing this new Earth reality today – so be it now.

SOL DAY 1

1 January

Today is a brand new day on planet Earth. It is an exciting opportunity to embrace One's spirit and look to the future with unconditional positivity and overflowing optimism. Do not revisit the mistakes of One's past. It is time to live and be in the present moment – here and now. This is the moment to deeply connect with One's spirit and water the seeds of courage to change and transform One's life completely to benefit oneself and all of humankind.

With every ending comes a new beginning. This new day, new year and new decade brings with it the potential to co-create something amazing in One's life and thus the lives of all other Beings on planet Earth. One only has to look inside oneself for the key to One's future. One need only realise that One is a divine Being of the universe and that One's time here on planet Earth is limited, so embrace One's fear and shine a light on it that will illuminate One's path. One is exactly where One needs to be to co-create the best version of oneself now. Nothing is fixed in this world; all relationships are impermanent. Everything is a great illusion from which One can manifest any reality that One so chooses – so be it now.

One knows that what exists within One's spirit, soul or cosmic consciousness is greater than any issue, circumstance or condition that One will ever encounter in this life.

Now is the time to trust One's inner spirit, path and the universe. Take a leap of faith into the unknown and discover what may be. Whatever it is, One knows that One will be okay. Afterall, One's silent partner in all things is the universe. There is nowhere to go and nothing to escape from in this world other than One's own imagined fears and failures.

Let's make an unconditional commitment to oneself to live mindfully this year and make this decade the best of One's life.

SOL DAY 2
2 January

Know that One can face anything in life, including death, because One's spirit is free.

Imagine and visualise the best thing that One could possibly experience today and this year. Sit quietly in meditation with this vision in mind. Allow oneself to be in the moment, as if this manifestation has already occurred. Feel the experience as if One were living this reality now. In a world of infinite possibilities, One could go here or there. Be guided by One's spirit in every aspect of One's life. Be the solution to everything in One's life. One has infinite capacity and immeasurable capability to be the best version of oneself right here, right now.

On this day, take a moment to pause and flow with life. Do not rush into things, simply allow the morning and evening to unfold as it is meant to be. Allow oneself to relax and let life flow in its own way. Resist trying to direct the river of people's lives and personal experiences. Let go of the idea that One must force, manage or manipulate a particular outcome if One seeks to be successful in life. Life is life. People will come and people will go. Be grateful for One's presence in One's life. Be thankful for the opportunity to share One's positive qualities and living experiences.

Life and living it is a series of simple and interconnected moments, flowing effortlessly like a leaf floating on top of the water as the current of the river moves it naturally along and downstream. Be open, be free and be welcoming of the journey as it unfolds. Move with the cosmic rhythm of life as One works, plays and rests.

Look for the gift in each moment and One will surely find it. Be virtuous and act in alignment with One's mind–body–spirit and the universe. Simply breathe and lean into life.

SOL DAY 3

3 January

On this day and in this year, One has the chance to co-create anything that One desires to manifest in this world. While many humans scuttle about for the external scraps of personal validation of who One thinks One is, or material things, with the thought that it will improve One's status and success in life, One needs to move beyond this limited mindset and thinking. One needs to realise that One, as spirit, is more than One's human form or representation of One's achievements in life. One is a great Being of the universe. Nothing and no-one can ever erase this greatness within One. No other person can make One feel small and insignificant without One's permission.

Realise that One is not human, but a divine spirit that is host to a time-limited human form.

Know that One does not own a single atom within One's body. They are simply passing through One's manifested human form on Earth for a limited period of time and then returning to the cosmos. One's form is composed of stardust from the cosmos. Celebrate this freedom, rejoice in this knowledge and embrace this wisdom that One exists beyond the daily illusion of life, which so many humans are preoccupied with at this present moment.

Use today as a launch point to set One's mind free of concern, worry or fear for the future and live in the present moment of 'Now'. Wherever One is and whatever One may be doing, know that One is and will always be a Being of light, love and oneness in the universe.

Learn to let go of all attachments, judgements and resistance in One's life. One must realise that One is the student, the teacher and the Master of One's life on Earth.

SOL DAY 4
4 January

When One wakes on this day, remember that One is truly an awesome spirit and that all is here for One's awakening and experience as a sentient Being. Do not be distracted by fear, anger, hate, jealousy, envy or comparison of One's life to any other living person. Take the time to prepare and cultivate a practice in One's mind to be virtuous and mindful in all aspects of One's life. Practice meditation and mindfulness so it becomes as natural and as effortless as breathing.

Set an intention for this day to enjoy it and flow with it in a loving, kind and peaceful way. All is as it needs to be – accept it and move on. Flow with life and life will flow within oneself.

Whatever One thinks about the most, One will attract into One's life. Be patient, be focused and then act without expectation, knowing it will be so. Create the space to visualise the best image within One's mind for One's life and living experiences. Then act on this path, knowing that One is exactly where One needs to be now.

The key to living a wonderful life is to simply manifest and experience wonderful moments each and every day of One's life.

Know that to manifest any experience in One's life requires the cooperation of other sentient Beings and the universe. The founding belief which supports this is that the universe is always on One's side and has One's best interests at heart for One's higher self and living purpose. Whatever happens today will be just right for One on One's life journey on Earth.

SOL DAY 5
5 January

On this magnificent day, create the intention to be open, accepting and welcoming of good, positive people and experiences in One's life today. Allow One's mind–body to receive prosperity and abundance in all forms in One's life as easily as the rain falls on the ground or the sun shines in the sky.

Overflow with love, gratitude and graciousness for the simple things in One's life, like being alive on planet Earth. Give thanks for the clean air One breathes, the fresh water One drinks, the healthy food One eats and One's warm clothes, friends, kinship networks, family, partners and lovers as well the safe shelter One has in One's life. Radiate this feeling of thankfulness into the world and the universe. Today is a wonderful day to be alive now – celebrate this joy from the inside out.

Do not be overly concerned about world issues. Simply focus on what One can think and do where One is now with One's thoughts and mind–body (altered consciousness) energy. Know that whatever vibrational frequencies One is choosing to emit into the universe, the universe will align with it and give One more of the same. This is how prosperity and abundance works in the universe. It is all part of the divine principle of **'self-organising theory'**. Has One ever noticed how similar people are naturally drawn to each other in a crowd or function? It is all about energy harmonising with similar energy.

One's spirit is a gateway to infinite states of consciousness such as knowing, awareness, oneness, joy, free will, peace and presence. Find a way each day to move closer to One's spirit and align with One's true higher self. This is One's best fit for One's best life on Earth.

SOL DAY 6
6 January

Look forward to today with excitement as things begin to positively change in One's life. It is another glorious day on planet Earth. Recognise the true beauty of One's divine Being and One's capacity to shine a light for others to see One's way in this world.

Never underestimate One's gifts, abilities and power to influence the energy of people in One's life and others across the world by simply being One's best. Some may see obstacles and challenges, but One's perspective now is to see opportunities and the chance to operate in a unified field of infinite possibilities. Anything can be achieved if One focuses One's mind, works in alignment with oneself, others and the universe, and allows One's energy to flow in the direction of One's vision. After all, direction is much more important than speed.

From little things, big things grow, change and evolve. It is time to move beyond any limiting beliefs, ingrained thought patterns and old habits. There is a change on the horizon and One is part of this change. One need only step into the light and immerse oneself in this new reality of manifested living and being on planet Earth.

Like most great things, this begins small, like a raindrop, but eventually turn into a gentle stream, a flowing river and then a vast deep ocean of pure potentiality and infinite possibilities. Be like the oceans on Earth, which nurture and sustain a diversity of life.

Know that great things are happening in One's life. Prepare the way for these things to manifest and so will it be now.

SOL DAY 7
7 January

Light a spiritual spark to ignite One's inner joy to fill One's mind and body on this morning. Always embrace an optimistic outlook that everything will always work out for One. Now, in deep stillness and mindful silence, set One's intention to experience peaceful, loving and positive moments today. One knows that all big things are accomplished in small ways. Little by little, everything is formed and reformed from matter and energy or altered consciousness on planet Earth. Keep things simple and great things will be achieved. This is often the path that leads to amazing outcomes. Great change happens in nature through simple humble actions, and success is accomplished the same way in One's life.

Anything is possible when One believes – so believe and be it now.

The future is fluid and being continually shaped in 'the Now' by what One believes, thinks, says and does in this moment. As a cosmic co-creator, One can significantly shift and shape One's reality into any experience that One chooses to perceive and manifest. One is truly a Being of infinite potential, existing beyond any limiting human belief or constructed space–time boundary. One is powerful beyond measure. One is unique and incredibly special.

As One moves effortlessly throughout the day, stay focused on the task at hand and complete one thing at a time. Then rest, review and refocus One's energy for the next task until whatever One is working on is finally completed, or the day has come to an end. Take care of One's mind and body. Nurture and nourish it with care, kindness and compassion.

Move through today and this world without attaching oneself to any fixed expectation. Know that One is perfect, whole and complete in One's current Earthly human form and spiritual existence.

SOL DAY 8

8 January

Today is a wonderful day to centre One's life and align with One's spirit now. The sun has risen again to signal the beginning of a brand new day and generously shines its radiant light on planet Earth. Use this morning time to go for a walk, do a yoga session or some other form of exercise, and connect with One's inner spirit and nature. Feel the sun's rays or the breeze upon One's face and give thanks for this brand new day in One's life.

With every breath and step One takes in life, be mindful of where One is now.

One may look upon the world with One's eyes, but One sees with One's mind. One may sense the world with One's body, but One's spirit is pure awareness itself. Learn the difference and One will be able to negotiate the various paths One needs to move forward from moment to moment and day to day throughout this year and decade.

Take the time to pause, rest and reflect in meditation before One begins One's day. It is perfectly okay to sit in silence and make space to calm One's mind and clear One's thoughts. Allow One's mind to be empty of everything. Now be with One's spiritual presence only.

Spaciousness is an asset in One's life. It has the unimaginable potential that something wonderful can happen or manifest if only One chooses it. Where there is space, there is opportunity to co-create anything One dares to imagine. This is why One is so appreciative of space in One's life. The other thing that naturally co-exists with space is freedom – freedom to choose how to live One's life and freedom of how to be in this world.

Choose to be free of all that does not serve One's life. Declutter One's life of all negative energy and meaningless attachments. Invite freedom to be present in One's mind and life – so be it now.

SOL DAY 9

9 January

Train One's mind to observe One's thoughts, habits and life. Each day, cultivate a living practice that aligns with One's mind–body–spirit and commit to One's inner purpose.

Set aside adequate time in One's daily life for One's individual wellbeing. Create space for time to meditate, time to plan and organise, time to work, time to play, time to rest and sleep, time to reflect, renew and refresh One's mind–body. Live One's life as a journey, not a destination where One must arrive at the speed of light. All good things take time and time is always available for good things.

The more One can slow down and create space in One's life, the more One will be able to see new ways to live an alternative way in this modern world. Less stress – more patience and prosperity. Less conflict – more peace and harmony. So on and so forth. The universe can only respond to One's inner vibration. It is important to know that things begin to change when One changes how One perceives and thinks about things.

Most people want the world to change to suit One's current desire or perception of how things should be. In fact, the change that One seeks must begin within oneself.

Ask oneself a question today. How will One change the way One experiences this beautiful, amazing, wonderful day? Write it down in a journal or on a sticky note and put it on the fridge or bathroom mirror. Complete this statement: One will be … (compassionate, helpful, accepting, generous, simple, patient and open) with oneself and to other people in every situation One experiences on this easygoing, beautiful day.

SOL DAY 10
10 January

Express confidence in oneself, that One is truly capable of achieving great things through simple acts of care, kindness and compassion in One's life. Everything is revealed to oneself at the right moment. Be patient and move confidentially along the path of One's life today.

Let go of the struggle to be a particular type of person or play a certain role in the world. These are just characters on the stage of life. Realise that One is the director of the play and that One is the main character in One's own personal real-life story. As a co-creator, One can shape One's living story into a tale of great adventure, love and success, or misery, hate and failure. Be the hero of One's own story. Be the person who uses One's bumps, bruises and breaks as motivation to succeed in life. Cultivate an attitude of gratitude and relentless resilience to live life and be present in this moment.

It does not matter whether One gets knocked down by the slings and arrows of misfortune and misadventure, it matters what One does when One gets back up.

When One holds an unshakable faith that everything will work out for One, guess what happens – it does! Whatever the situation or challenges in One's life, One will figure it out. This will be done with the support of other sentient Beings. Know that the universe is always listening to One's intentions and is on One's side.

Anything is possible in this world – One's belief in oneself and the universe makes it so.

SOL DAY 11
11 January

When the opportunity presents itself to change and transform One's mind-body and life, embrace it with open arms. Challenges in One's life are a chance to learn, grow and change. All spiritual paths in life are a personal journey along the road of awakening from within. One's best and most purposeful work is done on the inside – be here now. Know that One can begin One's inner way at any moment in time.

Use this day to look within and realise that what One truly seeks has and will always be within oneself now. One's inner spirit is a gateway to cosmic consciousness, the source and every other sentient Being in this vast universe.

One's mind-body is living dynamic cosmic energy (altered consciousness). In addition, One has limitless ability to heal oneself and, through One's mindful actions and presence, heal planet Earth too. One need only imagine it to be true and so it will be. As a co-creator of One's life and living experiences, One has the potential to manifest anything in One's life now.

Meditate on One's inner spirit and the infinite abyss of pure divine consciousness within. This internal presence is the eternal presence of One's Being. It is the light, the path and 'the way' to One's divine destiny. Believe in One's spirit, soul or spiritual consciousness. Know that what will be revealed to One will be immeasurable and beyond One's imagination. Simply create the space and time to look deeply inside oneself now.

SOL DAY 12
12 January

The future is best lived in the present. This is the day that One co-creates One's destiny by living it 'Now'. Move with joy when One is transforming and reconfiguring One's mind and One's way in this world. Many will not be able to see One's awakened path or understand One's way. These unconscious minds are trapped within One's own ego matrix and are yet to become free of this illusion. It is a virtual prison of self-limiting beliefs, thoughts and reality.

There will come a time when all citizens of Earth will be guided by spiritual thought leaders in 'the way'. This is not about the global uptake of any individual national tribalism or particular religion, faith or culture but the sharing of a new perspective of mindful living and being in this world. Living with an open mind and awakened consciousness. The day is coming when people will finally see One's ego and choose to align with One's spirit. This awareness will enable a new way of living life on Earth. One unified consciousness on One living planet. It is inevitable that humankind will consciously evolve – this is the next step in human evolution. Time is irrelevant – only the awakening of humanity is important now. This will set the direction for the next 1000 to 10,000 years or more on Earth and in this solar system.

The more that this message is shared across the planet, the more individual people will naturally align One's consciousness to a new way of thinking that will give rise to a new way of living and being in this world. The process has already begun. There is an unquestionable thirst to change the old habits, dysfunctional egoic mindsets and archaic systems of governance from previous generations and co-create a new future today.

One's time is 'Now'! Co-create the space to enable these changes within One's life.

SOL DAY 13
13 January

The less One resists change in One's life, the more One will be free of attachment. Whatever One is holding on to now is also a form of virtual imprisonment. This simply means that it is important to continually remove the clutter from One's life on a daily basis.

Let go of all the things that One does not require or that do not serve One anymore. It is going to be okay – trust the process and 'the way' of the universe. Everything is always working out for One on Earth. All things happen for a reason and there is a reason that things happen in One's life. Accept the moment for what it is, without judgement, resistance or attachment.

With an open mind and free spirit, it is possible for anyone to imagine and manifest any experience on Earth. All exists within a field of infinite possibilities in the universe. One need only close One's eyes, open One's mind and align with One's spirit. Everything is already on its way to One now. Be ready for change and allow positive experiences, people and places to be present in One's life now. Whatever needs to go – let it go. Whatever needs to come – let it come. Be the silence in the middle of life's storm and stay calm.

When One realises One's infinite potential, One will see the divine in everything now.

Walking is a great way to clear One's mind and exercise One's body. There are many benefits when One engages in such a simple activity. Create the space to mindfully walk, breathe and meditate each day. Within these actions, One can calm the mind and clear One's thoughts. In the morning reset One's internal thought clock and begin a new day with heartfelt gratitude for all the wonderful things in this world. Say to oneself, 'One is grateful for … (the sun, moon and stars, the Earth, the land, sea and sky)'.

SOL DAY 14
14 January

This is the day to acknowledge One's health and wellbeing. A day to be thankful for nature and all the natural foods that nourish One's body. The sun is warm and natural foods are nature's gift to One and all. The things which One invites into One's life and whatever One's mind–body consumes, One becomes. One's physical form and thoughts are a reflection of what One chooses to be in this world.

The Earth is a bountiful place when One takes the time to see the beauty that is all around us each and every day. Beauty is to be found in the sunrise, the songs of birds in the morning or the silent perfume and colours from flowers, plants and trees. The Earth is a sacred place for all who choose to live here now. When One cares for One's place in this world, the universe will reciprocate in kind. First Nations peoples have known this eternal wisdom of living in harmony and balance with the land, sea and sky for eons. It is now time for all humans to realise the undeniable truth about One's relationship with Earth.

In essence, this living spiritual human relationship principle can be expressed as 'One tree – many leaves', or, to put it another way, 'One ocean – many rivers'.

Everyone needs to realise that if Earth dies, so do humans. If humans die, Earth will survive. Humans will reach a tipping point from which the collapse of the planet's ecosystem will crash beyond a point of global recovery. However, this is avoidable if humans evolve within. The solution is inner transformation and changing One's external habits, practices and processes. The vision is clear for the One who seeks to change and transform from within.

Choose to honours One's spirit and nurtures One's mind and body with care, kindness and compassion. Earth needs One's love as much as One does now.

SOL DAY 15

15 January

Transcend the illusion of separateness and limitations in One's life. Use each day as a platform to continually improve One's mind–body. Make a conscious decision to fully embrace this moment in the universe and evolve into the best version of oneself. See the duality of life for what it is – light and dark, positive and negative, good and bad.

Know that One's spirit exists in non-duality within an infinite state of universal beingness. One's spirit does not feel pain or loss and is not affected by any human condition or human conditioning in One's life. Spirit exists beyond space and time. It is not bound by any human principle, rule of law or gravitational pull of any particular cosmic constellation.

The very essence of One's existence in the universe is a free spirit.

One's entire world is a projection and reflection of One's state of mind and consciousness. Whatever One believes, One perceives as One's reality in this world.

If One wants to change One's world, first change One's perception of it. A thought is just a thought and it can be changed at any time or any place in the world. The same can be said of One's beliefs and One's path in life. When One is committed to expand One's inner awareness and align to One's higher self, the universe will enable it.

Ask the universe to reveal the truth to oneself and it will be so. Allow oneself to see beyond the illusion of life and into the past, the future and, most importantly, the present moment.

Things will naturally unfold and effortlessly manifest in One's life when One is aligned from the inside out. Begin and end this day by simply staying centred in One's spirit and true to One's inner path. Let One's journey in life be One's destination 'Now'.

SOL DAY 16
16 January

Just because One is by oneself, doesn't mean that One is alone. One's silent partner on this amazing life journey is the entire universe – remember this now. When One wakes in the morning, greet the day with overflowing optimism that everything will be okay no matter what happens today. Flip the script on all negative and self-limiting thoughts to positive and limitless thinking. Imagine a future where One is consciously connected to all other sentient Beings on this planet and in the galaxy. A place where One can tap into One's intuitive intelligence at any moment of the day or night.

Know that there is no distance between oneself and One's pure presence or spirit. It resides within One in tranquil silence and eternal peace. This aspect of One's divine nature exists unconditionally wherever One is or whatever One is doing in life. One is spirit.

Anyone, anywhere on Earth, can access One's inner divine guidance, which comes from the innermost part of One's Being. Simply sit quietly and take a moment to patiently pause, breathe deeply and meditate to let go of whatever is concerning One at this particular moment in time. When One's mind is free, One can align to One's spiritual presence. Repeat the process throughout the day if One desires inner advice and a divine nudge in the right direction.

Everyone everywhere has within One the potential to change and transform One's life into something utterly amazing, wonderful and beautiful. Let today be one of those days where One enjoys living life in a way that is aligned to the best of oneself and flows effortlessly with the universe.

Imagine with mindful intention; act with spiritual intuition.

SOL DAY 17
17 January

Just be with oneself and the day as it is now. Accept what is – this is the key.

There is no need to run away from things in One's life. The better and braver option is to lean into One's fear. Embrace the unknown and challenge oneself to face the illusion that it is, then rise above it. Know that all things pass with time and that time is itself an illusion.

One's own perceived fear is not the danger. The real danger is not recognising fear as a manifestation of One's ego trying to control and manipulate One's mind into attaching itself to a certain thought in the hope that it can construct an imagined future reality.

Choose not to strive or grasp for people, things or experiences. What is coming to One will always arrive on time. Let go of the struggle to be something that One is not or force oneself to overthink and overdo things in One's life. This is a day to relax and take it easy. Do not resist the synchronous movements of the universe, simply flow in harmony with the current of life and celestial rhythms of the day.

See everything from the point of view as the 'observer' or 'witness' with a mindset of detached engagement as One moves through the day, moment by moment.

Allow people to be whomever One chooses to be in this world. When One looks at others, see a person's spirit first and honour this aspect of One's Being.

Sometimes the best thing that One can do in life is just be present with others in the moment. Not judging, not demanding and not reacting to whatever is in front of One. Just breathing and being with the other person with One's divine presence. This is enough. Trust the synchronicity of the universe to work it all out in its own way.

SOL DAY 18

18 January

In the morning, when One awakes from One's nightly sleep, take the time to pause and set an intention for this wonderful day. Say to oneself, 'It is time to awaken to One's inner spirit and live a new life on Earth now.'

When One engages in deep introspection through meditation, One realises that One's divine spiritual essence has been within One since the beginning of existence. However, an awakened consciousness cannot be realised without pain, growth and self-realisation. Everyone's path of transformation is different and yet each path has the same divine outcome of knowing One's inner truth.

Trying to escape One's awakening through fulfilling individual wants and desires will only delay the inevitable. This path can only be undertaken by oneself in the best interests of One's higher self. One will need to stand alone, as naked as a tree in the forest and be as open as the sky above. Do not depend on others to find One's way. The wellbeing of One's life journey can and will only be found in the undiscovered country of actually living a genuine and honest life. Look inward so One can see outwards into the oneness of the universe. This is the great mystery of life. It is the veil that will be lifted, like a blind man viewing the world for the first time.

Buddha says, 'I teach about suffering and how to end it.' To this end, One must graduate from being the student and become the Master of One's divine destiny. Free oneself of the intangible beliefs, thoughts and perspectives that imprison One's mind. One must open One's heart and accept personal responsibility for One's awakening on Earth. This is how to forever improve the quality of One's life now.

SOL DAY 19

19 January

Life is exactly what One imagines and co-creates it to be 'Now'.

Infinite potential already exists within One to do anything in this world. Rise up and shine a light on One's thoughts, living vibrational energy and life. Use One's gifts, talents, knowledge, wisdom, skills and abilities to recreate oneself completely. Nothing is permanent in this world. Everything is continuously changing, evolving and becoming.

One has a choice. One can either live a life according to other's expectations and rules or think for oneself and co-create a life that One imagines. Know that One is only ever a thought away from experiencing a completely new life. Take action and make a decision now. Decide to learn something new or create a new habit that serves oneself and all of humanity to live a more prosperous, abundant and awakened life. Make a positive decision today to live an inspired and spiritually centred life. Keep moving forward on this path as it unfolds naturally before One.

One's time on planet Earth is limited. Make the most of it. Stop trying to live someone else's life and be true to One's inner spirit and co-create the best version of oneself – here and now. Do not waste any time thinking about how others might perceive or judge oneself.

One will encounter 10,000 distractions or more along the way. Train One's mind to be purposefully aligned and intuitively intentional. Every simple act of kindness and compassion improves the wellbeing of all Earth citizens. Pay it forward. Together, everyone can make a positive contribution to co-create a spiritually centred Type 1 civilisation on Earth.

SOL DAY 20

20 January

Life goes on ... whatever and however One lives on Earth or elsewhere in space. The universe is continually unfolding and recreating itself. It is a perfect example of self-organising theory and the law of attraction, all within a state of altered consciousness.

Free oneself from One's pain and suffering. One can do this by choosing not to be overly sensitive and never taking anything someone says or does personally. Rise above it all and do not react out of fear, judgement or attachment – purposely function at the level of One's higher self. Remember, everyone is operating at One's own level of consciousness. Meet people where they are at now and not how One wants them to be.

Take a moment to centre oneself before One begins the day. Sit in silence and practice mindful meditation. Create the space in One's life to focus on being with One's inner eternal presence – spirit. Know now that these moments of timelessness and eternal peace are where One is truly free. This state of existence is forever unbounded and untouched by any human conditioning. In this unifying place of oneness, One is able to align with oneself and the entire universe. Living a successful life is knowing how to access this dimension within oneself at any time or any place on the planet. Life and death is simply a gateway from and to this infinite stream of pure source consciousness. Allow oneself to experience it now.

Do not try, simply be ... and know that One will be guided to this state of spiritual sanctuary and place of Earthly tranquillity. One need only believe and it will be so.

SOL DAY 21
21 January

For the One who seeks peace within oneself – then intentionally and mindfully act upon it now.

Know that One will always find answers and solutions to the things that One seeks in life. Create the space in One's life to quietly, calmly and patiently listen to the intuitive intelligence and universal wisdom of One's spirit. This is One's ultimate state of knowing, which will guide One's living knowledge and experiences on Earth and in this galaxy.

It is not peaceful people who are spiritually centred, it is the spiritually centred people who are at peace.

The universe can and will only respond to who One believes One is now. This is how the universe works. Once One decides about One's direction in life, the universe aligns to support this reality. One's vibrational reality is always being reflected by the universe.

Know that One is co-creating One's future each and every single moment of the day. One cannot escape it, because it is happening in response to how One is living on Earth. To live in the future then act in the present 'Now'. This is how One shapes One's living destiny. Too many people believe that the acquisition of matter, money and material items will make One happy and feel at peace. This is a false truth and only serves to temporarily entertain One's ego for power, control and security in One's life – it never lasts. Ego has an unquenchable thirst for more and more … it never ends. The only way to manage it is not to let it drink from the wellness stream of One's mindful existence.

Peace is not found in any of One's 10,000 things or at the top of a mountain. It is to be discovered within oneself. The way to peace is simple, look inside. It resides in all Beings now.

SOL DAY 22
22 January

Do not desire or seek the light or 'the way' – become it. End One's journey and arrive at One's destination.

One can search One's entire lifetime for something that already exists within oneself. Today is the day to realise that being 'the One' is the key to every experience on Earth. Empty One's mind of every limiting belief and unkind thought that One has collected over the years. Make an effort to continually cleanse One's mind and life. Create a gratitude journal and write in it every day. Study how to co-create the best version of oneself.

See the world for what it is – an opportunity to exist and be now in any way that One chooses. Make the most of this wonderful planet and One's experiences on it. At dawn or before, begin One's day in meditation, say 'Today, One is grateful for this living opportunity. One will co-create the best life experience today. One is spirit, One is eternal peace and One is present – now!'

Allow no individual or circumstance to disturb One's inner peace. Walk through life as if One is an enlightened alien Being visiting Earth for the very first time. Observe how humans live, talk and interact. Is it in a spirit-centred and divine-focused way, or driven principally by individual egos and within a culture of fear, separateness and scarcity thinking? Take note of the conversations between people. Are they life-affirming, giving and compassionate?

Now think about how One will choose to spend One's limited time, space and energy here on Earth. One's destiny is to be found in the way that One chooses to live life on Earth every single day. Choose wisely and act in a spirit-centred way.

SOL DAY 23
23 January

Remind oneself that it is okay not to be perfect today – no-one is on Earth. One's mind–body is a work in progress, ever-changing DNA manifested in human form.

Know that a flower does not bloom in nature all the year, nor does a wave stand still. It builds up momentum travelling across the ocean and transfers all of its energy as it crashes onto the beach or rocks.

Use One's energy discerningly and wisely each day. Know that there is a time to sleep, work, rest and play. Let today be a day where One simply flows in harmony with life and the universe. Take a moment to breathe deeply and be grateful for One's breath, health and wellness. One is alive and all that happens next is a miracle. Give thanks for the miracle of One's life and being on Earth now at this special moment in time. It is a privilege to be alive.

Greet people with a smile and say 'Thanks – enjoy this wonderful or beautiful day.' Be appreciative of others for being the person that One chooses to be now.

All that is happening in One's life is for One's higher purpose on Earth. The universe is already working to make One's aspirations, dreams and vision a reality today. Set One's intention for the day and One's life, then take the next step in that direction. Allow the universe to unfold naturally in its own way and work miracles in One's life. One's journey here and now is more important than the destination. Every little thing that One does counts in One's life. When One changes One's outlook and spiritual alignment (mind–body–spirit), One's total human vibration operates at a different and higher level of consciousness. One becomes a gateway to divine consciousness itself.

SOL DAY 24
24 January

On this day, remind oneself not to become lost in the social systems that purposely define, compartmentalise and constrain One's mind and life. Hack into this false mental matrix and co-create oneself based on One's true inner self – spirit, soul or cosmic consciousness.

One's inner path to freedom lies not outside of oneself in social and material constructs but within One's Being.

Transcend One's egoic fear-based thoughts of separateness, conditional love, anger, judgement, attachment and resistance. Do this by not dedicating One's life to, or feeding One's ego with, attention. Make a conscious decision to invest One's time, space and energy into co-creating the best version of oneself. Sometimes One must let go of the picture in One's mind of what One thought One's life would be and learn to live in peace and harmony on the journey as it unfolds naturally where One is now. Let go of the struggle to continually battle One's way through life to win at any or all costs. Simply embrace living in this moment 'Now'.

To alter the universe, One must alter One's world. To alter One's world, One must alter One's reality. To alter One's reality, One must alter One's life. To alter One's life, One must alter One's thoughts. To alter One's thought, One must alter One's awareness of oneself. Shift, change and alter One's self-perception and way in this world as many times as necessary. No single thing is fixed in this world or the universe.

Nothing stands still in nature, not even a mountain. Things are always moving, changing and adapting to a new and emerging landscape. It is time to cogni-form One's internal mindscape so One can terra-form One's external landscape.

There is no time to lose, there is no time to waste – there is only 'the way' forward now.

Embrace the journey so that it becomes One's only destination in life.

SOL DAY 25
25 January

Today is a day to transcend all the trivial things of everyday life – to let go of all the small stuff. Let's face it, most of it *is* small stuff – a look, a word or comment, a thing or object, a process, even a habit or behaviour. It is time to rise above those 10,000 insignificant things that One sees each and every day of One's life and let them pass like a gentle breeze.

When One goes outside and looks up at the night sky, One does not think that this star or that constellation is out of place or that One must fix them. One simply accepts the sky as it is. The random and somewhat imperfect placement of stars is a perfect picture of the universe itself – why would One ever want to change it? The moon glows without an agenda of self-important and the sun radiates light without ever seeking any praise or celebrity status. These celestial bodies are simply being present, as they are in the universe – and what a beautiful presence it is. Nothing need be added or taken await from these cosmic creations. One need only be in One's presence to feel the positive impact upon and within One's life on Earth.

One is truly blessed to be here now. Say this to oneself with deep reverence, and often.

The more One can see the beauty in One's life as it is, the more One will be able to create and be in a beautiful vibrational state of being. One's perception and engagement with the world around One is not dependent upon what One looks at in One's life, but how One sees, views and observes One's life. When One can see the secrets of the universe in a single flower, One will begin to know the miracle and majesty of it all.

Close One's eyes, open One's mind and align to One's spirit to access the infinite possibilities that exist now. One has a standing invitation from the universe to be One with it.

SOL DAY 26
26 January

Get excited about today, look around oneself and see just how far One has come along One's journey on planet Earth. One has reached so many milestones and surpassed all of them with flying colours. Take the time to pause and celebrate One's life and life journey in quiet silence and give oneself a hug and well-deserved acknowledgement.

It is okay to reward oneself for being where One is now. One deserves as much love and affection as anyone else in the world. Know that One's love is endless and can never run dry, no matter who drinks from it or for how long. One's divine love or inner oneness is infinite. It can never be taken away from One as it lives eternally within One's Being.

One is a spiritual warrior of light, love and oneness. To conquer and master One's ego will be the most significant achievement in One's life. This is the path of enlightenment that One must walk alone. It is also 'the way' of the universe for those who are aligned to One's inner spirit. There is nothing that One cannot do if One focuses One's mind and applies oneself to the task at hand. Little by little, One will change, grow and transform into the best version of oneself with the right intention.

Learn to take care of One's mind and body on a daily basis. Be a person who advocates for self-love, self-respect and self-worth. One does this by meditating on it, thinking about it, speaking to it and practicing it in One's life. This is how One raises this level of vibration in One's life. When others truly observe how much better One's way of life is, this feeling will begin to resonate within those who also seek it. This is how One co-creates a vibrational shift on planet Earth – one individual at a time.

SOL DAY 27
27 January

Begin this day with the positive intention to be kind, loving and compassionate to oneself. Then radiate this feel-good energy outwards to others on the planet and in the universe. When One puts both feet on the floor this morning, remind oneself to enjoy every moment of the day as possible, because it can never be experienced the same way again in One's life.

Today is going to be what it is and will be. The Earth will rotate on its axis and continue its journey around the sun. The sun will appear to rise over the horizon while the moon orbits around the Earth. The moon will influence the tides coming in and out. All these things are out of One's celestial control. However, One can imbue each lived moment with positive kind loving vibrations – so be it now.

One has the immeasurable power to be what One chooses to be in this world.

Never let the fear of anything that could potentially happen prevent or divert One's energy and direction from making something wonderful happen now. Seize the moment and go for it. It is better to try and stumble than to be a prisoner to One's fears or potential failures. Just because One falls does not mean that One fails – get up and have another go. Failure is the path to success in One's life – embrace it, learn from it and celebrate it.

One never learned to walk until One first mastered how to crawl. One never learned to run until One first mastered how to walk. First things first in One's life. Confidently take the next first step on One's journey and see how it unfolds. Be unconditionally resilient, no matter what happens. Tell oneself that the story is not over yet.

Everything changes when One changes One's way of perceiving, thinking and being in life.

SOL DAY 28
28 January

On this day, go to where One needs to be. Do what needs to be done and be thankful for the opportunity to contribute to making this world a better place. Little by little, things unfold like a flower opening for the first time in spring or like the first raindrops from a stormy sky.

Take the time to remove toxic and unkind people from One's life. Invite and spend time with people who see One's greatness and can celebrate it with One. One need not be around people all the time, so use this quiet space for self-reflection and to mindfully align with One's mind, body and spirit.

Trust the process and enjoy the journey of One's life. One cannot change others, but One can inspire people to live well, grow wisely and transform completely from within. Be patient – good things take time to emerge and manifest in One's life. Everything arrives right on time.

The universe has a way of synchronising everything at exactly the right moment in One's life. Relax and be open to things manifesting when they do and how they are presented.

Make this day and year a place where One co-creates a life of less stress, negativity and fear. Let go of how One thinks One's life should be and allow it just to be as it is. Accept everything as it is now. Transform One's life into an experience of more freedom, positivity and love. Be open and fill One's days with laughter, joy, kindness, care, love and compassion.

The desire to know oneself will rise above all other desires in One's life. This is the only true path in life that really matters in the end. To know One's Being is something that cannot be taught from chanting a scripture or reading 10,000 lines of spiritual text. These things are only guideposts along 'the way'. It can only be experienced by the One who desires to know One's divinity within oneself. This is 'the way' of the universe.

SOL DAY 29
29 January

Today may appear on the surface like any other ordinary day and, to some extent, it is. If One has lifted the veil of One's mental matrix and peered at the world from One's enlightened true self, One will know the difference and be able to clearly see the meaninglessness of humanity's egoic social programming, cultural activities and habits of greed, power, the accumulation of material objects. This also includes money and an unquenchable thirst to satisfy an endless desire to have more and more material things or personal experiences.

It is time to reject this mass global psychosis and mental illness. The sooner One realises that One can take a step towards living in the 'Now', the sooner One will move to a higher state of realised consciousness. One will notice how the struggles of One's life start to fall away and how One's suffering dissolves around One immediately. It is not possible for One to be in a state of higher spiritual awareness and also continue to manifest suffering in One's life and the lives of others. One will discover an ego switch within One's mind and consciously decide to permanently turn it off. This act of freedom will be the catalyst for changing One's life entirely.

One's natural state is One of spiritual intuitive intelligence or divine cosmic knowing.

This is achieved when One begins and can sustain living One's life from a sacred and special place of stillness, joy, peace, silence and contentment within oneself. This is One's true place of spiritual residence. It is a home without doors, windows or walls. There is no floor or ceiling either, just a feeling of eternal presence when One aligns with it. Wherever One may be or may travel on Earth or in the universe itself – this will always be One's home.

SOL DAY 30
30 January

Create space in One's life to reset, renew and refocus One's life energy. Make the effort to review One's time here on Earth and what One aims and hopes to achieve here. Will One live an honourable, simple and spiritual life of positive intent and purposeful wellness? Will One share One's living energy with others along the way or will One be lost in the chaos of meaningless desires, chasing after the next tempting thing or experience? Use mindful meditation practices to calm the mind and clear One's thoughts so One can see clearly through this fog of indecision and deception. Cut through this mental haze by realising that One's destiny is what One imagines it to be – one moment at a time.

Be the source of One's own spiritual inspiration to live an alternative divine and mindful life as part of a Type 1 spiritually based Earth civilisation.

Use the resources of this day, such as time, energy and space, to reconfigure One's thought patterns and transform One's living practices so that they align with a renewed positive wellness in One's life. Begin small, with little milestone changes first like decluttering and cleansing one area of One's life at a time – like a box, a cupboard and then a room. After that, move on to One's relationship with things, places and people. Know that it all takes time, so be gentle with oneself on this journey. Ask the universe for help and guidance because it is always on One's side.

Remember that nothing is fixed in this world, especially One's thoughts. If One's thinking is not serving One's inner peace and helping One to live a harmonious, lovingly kind and balanced life – change it. Refine One's thoughts and renew One's focus on a daily basis.

SOL DAY 31
31 January

One is an amazing and awesome Being of the universe. One's day, week and life are going to be filled with miracles, good vibes, abundance and love. It is that simple. Of course, there is work to be done, mostly on oneself. But it is all worth it in the end. Pay attention to how One perceives oneself and how One goes about living in this world. Preserving and nurturing planet Earth is everyone's responsibility. Adopt a strategy of continual quality improvement from the inside out.

Know that whatever the mind can imagine and believe, it can also manifest and make happen. Anything can form part of One's reality when One lets go of the ego's struggle to control things and One surrenders to the effortless flow of the universe.

Believe it is possible and it will be so.

Trust in the divine timing of the universe; everything is all working in divine synchronicity. Just because One cannot see it now, does not mean that the universe is not aligning this experience in One's life. One has infinite ability to co-create anything in the universe. This is One's superpower.

Be a special agent of positive change in One's own life. By doing this, One will inevitably also influence and change the vibration of the entire world.

Be open to allowing positive ideas, experiences and people to come to One in ways that One has never imagined before. Operate at a higher vibration and One will attract only good things into One's life. When the mind is empty of the past and the future, joy will be with One in the present, like a shadow that is always there.

FEBRUARY
Sol day 32-60

One believes that the time is here now. Everything is beginning to shift, alter and change significantly among awakening humans on planet Earth. The whole world is becoming aware of 'the awakening' that is happening across the world. One actively supports and positively promotes the continual improvement of being and living a mindful spiritual life as One knows it. One will use One's thoughts, words and presence to shape the future for a new Earth through mindful actions within this present moment.

During this month, One will seek out ways to align One's mind, body and spirit on a daily basis with the divine synchronicity of the universe. One will envision and project a vibrational energy of a new reality for a prosperous and abundant new way of life with other sentient Beings. One will be gracious, humble and express gratitude often for being alive and part of this awakening on Earth now.

SOL DAY 32
1 February

Tap into One's limitless potential on Earth today. Use everything available on One's personal journey to transform oneself completely into the best version of oneself. Use mindfulness practices and daily meditation sessions to align to the highest dimension of One's greatest good. It will surprise One to know that it is not possible for One to fail in this awakening quest. One can only not begin or not go far enough along the way for it not to be realised in One's life.

One has infinite free will to choose One's inner way and outer path in life. Choose wisely and with a deep sense of divine knowing. Use the intuitive wisdom of One's spirit, ancestors and the universe to guide One on One's way.

There is no greater feeling of alignment then when One is working in complete synchronicity with the universe. Conversations are easy, things flow effortlessly and obstacles simply dissolve into nothingness as if they were never there in the first place.

Life is easy, loving and kind when One perceives One's life to be so. If it works, it was meant to be; if it doesn't, simply let it go. The universe has other plans for oneself at this time.

When considering undertaking a big task or life goal that at first may seem overwhelming, break it down into manageable chunks of times and smaller tasks. Ask the universe for help and assistance, which may come in unexpected ways or signs. Be open to receiving support from any and all sources. The key is to seek and see potential solutions in everything that One perceives and in the people One may know or meet. Finally, imagine and plan for being successful in every moment of One's life. Trust the process and be unconditionally positive all the time. One co-creates One's own reality. It this reality that One perceives first. What One believes within will surely manifest itself as One's living experiences in this world.

SOL DAY 33
2 February

Embrace One's sacred inner space. Align to One's inner spirit and the universe. See One's personal material items as temporary objects and the human forms of people as they are – repurposed matter and energy or altered consciousness. Take a step back and look at life not through ego's lens of attachment but in a way that is unbiased, unfiltered and unified.

Know that the same atoms that reside in One's body were most likely also present in the rocks, trees and other animals on this planet. One's mind–body is as much a part of Earth as it is part of One's mortal form. One cannot separate the atoms that make up One's DNA or body from the atoms that make up every other living creature on this planet. There is no way of knowing if the molecules that now reside within One's mind–body were once in a frog, tree, fish, kangaroo, eagle or banana. One cannot claim original ownership of any part of One's mind–body, as it already existed for billions of years. At best, One's manifested human form is reconfigured, reconstituted and repurposed particles of stardust.

One is, in essence, spirit – spirit is 'the One' or divine Being reading this book now.

It is time to deconstruct One's old paradigms of existence and egocentric relationships with the people, places and processes in this world. New thought leaders are emerging daily who are consciously refocusing One's mindful presence to co-create a better place for all.

It is each and everyone's personal responsibility to make oneself aware of One's spirit and divine relationship that One has with all living things on Earth. From the time One wakes in the morning to the time One goes to sleep at night, One's presence is a **sacred space** from which One is host to One's mind–body. Engage the world from this sacred space and know the special role that One plays in the universe.

SOL DAY 34
3 February

Never underestimate that One single thought within One's mind can change One's whole world and existence on Earth. That is all it ever takes. One's inner mindscape can be reconfigured through enlightenment thinking, awakening awareness and evolved energy.

Know that One's mind is not fixed and can be changed at any moment or time in One's life. When One changes One's mind, One also changes the neural pathways in the brain and co-creates new connections that have never existed before within One's mind–body.

Stop grasping at distracting desires and imaginary illusions of money, fame and ego's false promises that things will be better when One has achieved a certain workplace position or acquired enough money to do something or purchased a brand new toy. Everything inside One's mind will shift when One awakens to One's divine truth and shines a light on One's inner path in life. One will never be the same again. One will be so ever grateful for this change.

There is no greater contentment in life than accepting the world as it is now. There is nothing lacking when One exists within a field of infinite possibilities. Anything is achievable when One's mind is free to imagine the future now and co-create this living reality today.

It is important to spend time alone each day – time to be with One's spirit in mindful meditation, purposefully calming and clearing One's mind to align with the universe and creating space in One's life. Allow nature's peace to permeate and flow within One's mind and body. Feel the cool waking freshness of Country (land, sea and sky) or smell the scent of the ocean sea breeze upon One's face. Bury oneself deep in this moment of oneness and connect to all that is present now.

SOL DAY 35
4 February

Today is a good day to become aware of where One is in One's life and how One is living it now. Take a moment to close One's eyes and sense all the things around One's mind-body. Identify four things that One can smell, hear, touch and taste. Now calm One's sensory inputs and quieten One's mind. Just breathe in this moment, calmly, and focus on One's rhythmic breathing. Let One's awareness increase around oneself, from One's immediate surroundings out into this world, galaxy and universe. Go beyond mind-body, beyond One's place of residence and beyond planet Earth. Allow One's awareness to expand like an endless ripple across an infinite ocean of existence in the space-time continuum. This is One's great potential as a Being of love, light, oneness and pure consciousness.

Ask these three simple questions of oneself:
What is One's intention for One's life?
What is One's intention for this day?
What is One's intention for this moment?

Sit in silence and allow the answers to reveal themselves to One – be patient, they will come. Do not pressure oneself to have everything all figured out right now or in a single moment of One's life. Good things take time to unfold and manifest.

Know that the rising sun is not a light switch and a seedling does not grow into a mighty tree in a single day. Let things flow and unfold naturally in One's life. Creating an intention is like throwing a pebble into a pond and watching the ripple move outwards until it has reached its limits. If the wave or thought is masked by other ripples, it will never be realised.

SOL DAY 36
5 February

On this day, take the time to realise that One's current 'waking life' is a construct of One's mind and collective matrix of eco-social cultural programming. One can go in any imaginable direction that One chooses in this world. One can be anywhere in the universe.

One sets One's destiny in life not by chance, but by conscious choice in every living moment that One is alive. Let today be an intentional choice to move and align with One's inner spirit and the divine wonders of the universe. Give oneself permission to just be with One's spirit. Know that everything will all work out in One's life and all will be okay in the end. This is a natural state of being for all sentient Beings on Earth.

To be or not to be? This is the ultimate question that One should concern oneself with daily. Does One choose to be virtuous? To be present? To live in the moment of One's life and co-create the best version of oneself? All of life is a continual learning experience from one moment to the next.

Learn to observe, understand and know how One co-creates One's mental perceptions and projections out of One's existing conditioning, attachments, judgements, resistance and suffering. One's life is a cosmic reflection of the state of One's consciousness in the present moment. It reflects One's vibrational energy and spiritual awareness. It is a divine relationship which cannot be broken, bent or destroyed. It is something that can only be unconsciously hidden from One's own cosmic consciousness.

The universe will only ever give One what One co-creates with One's life. This is the paradox of living life – see it clearly for oneself now.

SOL DAY 37

6 February

It does not matter when One begins One's spiritual awakening or journey of enlightenment. What is important is that One starts it now. It is about having the courage to open a new door in One's life to explore a brave new frontier that will ultimately change One's life completely by transforming One's inner mindscape and outer landscape.

What is certain is that it will change One, what is not certain is how deep this change will be within One.

Do not rob oneself of the opportunity through One's pain and suffering to be all that One can be on Earth by living in continual fear and sheltered separateness. One is powerful beyond measure when One applies oneself to becoming all that One can be 'Now'.

Be patient when making One's way in life along this inner path. Things will naturally reveal themselves to One as One frees oneself from the mental ego matrix of One's conditioned mind. As One stays true to this path, many will see One as having gone 'insane' or betrayed One's values of One's own tribe, family or social group. Others will not be able to fathom and comprehend the choices One made to leave the relative safety of One's sociocultural nest for a completely unknown alternative lifestyle. Some will see, but not believe. One will believe in One's way so passionately that others will see – eventually.

There is nothing that One can say that will convince another person to change One's perspective, especially if One's mind is operating at a lower level of consciousness or vibrational frequency. It is like trying to describe colour to a person who sees the world in black and white. Know that One's awareness will not be shifted until One makes a conscious decision to let go of One's pre-existing attachments, judgements and resistance to change.

SOL DAY 38
7 February

As One journeys from moment to moment throughout the day, take on the role as an Earthly observer of oneself and humanity. Act as a witness of One's thoughts, sensory perceptions and interactive experiences that One encounters. Remain engaged in One's life, yet detached to all that is happening around One.

It is important to focus on One's inner peace and imbue One's outer reality with this calmness, quietness and gentle way of living. Allow the timelessness of One's spirit to wash over everything that One does. It is okay to sit in stillness, think in silence and act intentionally with peace, loving kindness and compassion. Know the eternal presence that resides within One. Align with this divine state of consciousness and be free.

To be a great person does not mean that One has conquered the world, it simply means One has mastered One's own mind and aligned to One's inner spirit. Create and cultivate a practice of mindfulness in the way that One lives life. Use anything and everything as a catalyst to improve, grow, change and transform into the best version of oneself. Keep updating One's old version of oneself for the new improved mind-body model. One is not in competition with anyone on the planet, One is only on a mission to be the best version that One can be in this life.

There is nowhere to go on Earth, there is nothing that One must read or do and no single thing One should have, or person One needs to be with, for One to access and align to One's mind-body-spirit. One already has the infinite power to transform oneself. One need only the idea; the path will reveal itself when One begins on One's inner way.

SOL DAY 39

8 February

Like sunlight shining warmly and brightly to nurture a flower for the very first time, give assistance, be helpful and act with kindness where it is needed. Be open to love and greet each new morning with positive intent. One already has the potential to imagine and co-create a lifestyle of pure joy and blissful moments.

Take the time to look around oneself, pause and slow down. Stop doing and just breathe – life is now. It is happening all around One on a daily basis – breathe and take it all in. One is here to awaken to One's silent truth and see clearly now. Allow oneself to be moved by the simplest things in nature. A breeze, a tree, a leaf or even a flower. Look up and take note of the beauty and abundance of the sky above and how it serves all who see it with its vibrant palette of changing colours throughout the day.

See how everything is connected and know that nothing is ever out of place.

Allow oneself to be in a state of conscious receiving and acceptance of what has already been gifted to One now. Whatever is coming to One is already on its way as One reads this book. Just remain patient, open and grateful for everything in One's life. Let life surprise One in a good way by constantly being positive, patient and passionate. The more One lets go, the greater the space One co-creates to accept new things, people and experiences in One's life.

One is a sentient Being of the universe. An integral part of all that is now. Wherever One is, this is the right place for One to be on Earth. One's work here is important and part of a process and path that will benefit all. Stay the course and keep moving along One's inner way so One can share One's loving kindness, care and compassion with the world. Give these qualities equally to all in One's life.

SOL DAY 40
9 February

Dare oneself to dive deep within One's spirit, soul or cosmic consciousness. Go into the unknown, the inner silence of eternal bliss and unifying divine wisdom. This is where the magic and wonder lives that will illuminate One's inner way and outer path in life. It is here that One will discover One's true divine nature and mindful purpose.

It only takes one idea to grow a spiritual garden in One's life and then spend a lifetime nurturing and cultivating it with love, kindness and compassion. One is a creator of One's reality – be this creator now on this day.

A spiritual life is easy, not because One avoids suffering, but because One dares to transcend it. Let go of the life that One thought One should live, so that One can become and experience what One might be in this life. Dare to be free and so will One be.

Many people spend an entire life searching for what is already within oneself. The place where One is best served is in this present moment – 'Now'. What One seeks to change outside of oneself is better redirected within oneself. Focus One's living energy on this space and change the vibrational frequency of One's human operating system. Raise the level of One's consciousness and all things will change around One in this space at the same time. One will begin to co-create multiple gateways for One's possible living futures. Have the courage not to try, but to be, and act in One's best self-interest and higher self. One has a divine responsibility to be all that One can be in this world and on this planet.

One's destiny will not be found in some far-off distant scenario, situation or circumstance. It is created when One plants a seed of spiritual imagination to become what One is meant to be. This is the real work and destination for all living, sentient Beings on Earth.

SOL DAY 41

10 February

Today is a wonderful, exciting and amazing day to be alive. It is filled with unimaginable synchronicities. When One believes – then so shall it be. Belief is the basis upon which One builds One's foundation for the future. When One perceives, thinks and acts from a place within One's inner spirit, One will experience a river of joy flowing within. Listen to One's inner voice and let it gently guide One's purpose, direction and way of life.

Know that today is a special occasion because One is simply alive on Earth. This is the miracle of living. Use this day as an opportunity to release One's old attachments and unhealthy habits from the past through mindful meditation and discerning decision-making. Renew One's commitment to One's spirit and reset One's direction in life towards a new way of living and being. Everything changes in this world and it is up to One to continually refresh One's consciousness compass so it points true.

Remove all the barriers within One's mind so One's perception and way is clear. The first step in avoiding an obstacle, limiting belief or negative story of One's ego is being aware of it. Most people will have spent decades constructing One's own imaginary personhood or individual identity. Realise that this false truth or artificial identity has been based significantly on One's ego and fabricated ideas of separateness, insecurities and selfishness.

Work on oneself first so that One can benefit all others on Earth. Realise how wonderful and simple everything is in life. Smile often and laugh with overflowing joyfulness in One's heart. Choose to be unconditionally positive and optimistic about everything in One's life.

Be inspired by the opportunity One has been given to rise above the ordinary and co-create wonderful solutions and amazing moments in the world.

SOL DAY 42
11 February

Transform oneself without travelling, know oneself without possessing knowledge, and co-create oneself without certainty. Without looking outside One's window, One can figure out the entire world.

One will not encounter a Being of great wisdom each day that One is alive. However, the qualities that these people imbue in life is also within all sentient Beings on Earth. To be in One's company when these people appear along One's life journey is to experience an aura of positive prosperity and a wellspring of enlightened energy.

The way to happiness is along a joyful path of simple loving care, kindness and compassion. Have the courage to deeply, wholly and completely love oneself. Feel and experience the quality of loving oneness within One's Being. Love is the gateway to oneness in the universe. It is purely divine, unstained by the remorselessness of time and not eroded by the relentless waves of change or new generations of humanity.

It is everyone's gift, privilege and honour to be here now. Discover what lies behind the veil of ego and within the light of One's divine essence or spiritual presence. Take the time to focus on One's personal wellbeing and contentment. Stay true to One's divine relationship with oneself, others and the universe.

Give thanks and show gratitude for everything coming into being and manifesting in One's life at the exact moment it is needed.

To bring order to the world One lives in now, One must first bring order and discipline to One's own world. One does this through training and cultivating a mind that is mindful and by being true to oneself. Align One's mind–body–spirit daily to be virtuous by being intentionally simple, positively patient, quietly kind and caringly compassionate.

SOL DAY 43
12 February

Today is the day to realise that One is truly capable of anything. One has always held the creative power to manifest anything that One dares to imagine. It is an integral part of One's existence on Earth. Know that, within every moment that One is alive, One can change and shift One's vibrational energy to a higher level of consciousness.

There is more than enough for everyone in this world. Prosperity and abundance is more a state of mind than it is a thing or place. By aligning to One's inner spirit, One will create a gateway to One's higher self or cosmic consciousness. This is a direct path to divine source or creative source consciousness. Access it now through mindful meditation and inner inquiry.

Do not let the rules of social conditioning and tribal beliefs stop One. Be aware of the limited thought patterns that have restricted oneself while One was growing up. Know that One has the creative power to rewrite One's personal rule book and change the direction of One's life completely. Now is the moment to empower oneself to break free, into the light.

Understand that the universe will only respond to One's vibrational alignment of One's mind-body-spirit. Whatever imagined vision or beliefs One holds in One's mind for One's life is exactly what the universe is helping One to manifest now. This is how the universe works. It can only give One what One is aligned too now. Realise that One is the co-creator of One's reality.

To be an intentional creator, first free One's mind of One's ego. Then recycle, reuse and repurpose One's energy and beliefs so that they align with One's higher self. Step off the suffering trail of attachment, judgement and resistance. Walk down the awakening path of openness, acceptance and freedom. One's path lies in the present – where One's spirit exists.

SOL DAY 44
13 February

Make today a day that is free of competition and conflict. Choose not to compare oneself to any other person in the world. Everyone is a winner when One is mindful about staying spiritually on track and true to One's inner path in life. The real quest is to seek out One's own way within and live it now. One does this by acknowledging and recognising all the games and tricks that One's ego creates to lure oneself into playing its game of separation, scarcity and selfishness.

Teach oneself to read the signs when One's ego is trying to trap oneself in a contest that One knows is unwinnable. Disengage and let go. Walk away from the temptation to prove something to others or be the best at a particular thing, activity or event. Do not worry what others might say. Other people's opinions of One is none of One's business. What is important is how One conducts oneself by investing in One's own direction and destiny in life. The future is co-created today from moment to moment. This is where the action happens.

Surrender to the silent sanctuary within One's spirit. Expand One's inner love and sense of serene oneness so that One can benefit all, especially those in need. Act with intent to reconfigure this world into a better place through sharing One's care, kindness and compassion from the core of One's Being. At the centre of One's divine existence is the answer to all that One seeks. To know who One is, is to know the universe itself.

Do not try to become that which One seeks, choose only to be. Be patient, like a student who is ready, waiting, willing and able. This is when the Master will appear to guide One on One's way.

SOL DAY 45

14 February

More important than being successful is being authentic in the way One lives One's life, and in the relationships One has with other sentient Beings on Earth. Choose to be open to everything and attached to nothing. This is how to live a simple and successful life. Never let negative experiences be a blueprint for how One successfully designs a positive future. Embrace what One is – spirit, soul or spiritual consciousness. Always begin at the beginning.

There will always be people in One's life that will seek to rob One's inner beauty and poison oneself with toxic thoughts and limiting beliefs. Be objective about other's behaviours. They simply reflect One's inner relationship with the world that One chooses to co-create.

Be content with the way things are, and yet at the same time, manifest greatest in One's life through simplicity and selflessness. When One does not limit One's life with desires for this or that, One will be limitless in what One may experience at any given moment on Earth.

Allow the universe to surprise One with new people, new places and new experiences that are in One's best interests and higher self. Be mindful of co-creating the best version of oneself today. Always aim to improve One's inner practice to enable One's outer path.

The way out of where One is, is to discover a way into where One needs to be now. Allow One's spirit to shine brightly upon the world like a star in the galaxy. Be a light for others to follow, a way to experience life from One's higher self. Lean into One's fears and project a beam of unconditional light, love and compassion onto the darkness within oneself. Give oneself time to heal, change, grow and transform into something weirdly wonderful. One is like a beautiful butterfly emerging from its chrysalis. Be patient. All good things take time.

SOL DAY 46
15 February

Every day is a great day when One moves closer to One's spirit, soul or consciousness. It is time to realise who One is now. This is the purpose of living life on Earth – to awaken within.

Every path is individual and yet all paths arrive at the same outcome. When One discovers One way in life, One will truly be on One's way living life as it is meant to be. Enjoy this life and living existence on Earth. Dive deep into the wellness of One's mind–body–spirit. This is a space where all Beings can have a shared living experience and co-exist in unity. Learn to let go and discover what is already here within One's life.

Be free of doubt and the illusions of desire in this world. Explore this world with One's inner mind's eye wide open. All the experiences on Earth are here to assist One on One's way to knowing One's own divine conscious truth. Use every learning, teaching and pointing to dispel the delusions of false thoughts within One's mind. The universe is here to guide One, support One and enable One to be the best version of oneself.

Early in the morning, when One wakes, remind oneself of One's infinite presence in this world. Make a conscious decision to be in this state of existence. Align directly with presence and be with that which is untouchable. Know that no stain of human experience can ever imprint on One's Being. One is, and will always be, immortal, eternal and infinite in the universe. Be content with this and rise above all human experiences to be One with this divine consciousness within One. This is One's time to shine brightly. It is the moment to align with the source. A gateway through which One will pass and see clearly into One's life. This is One's becoming moment to be all that One can be now. A higher truth is calling to One – answer it and be free forever more.

SOL DAY 47

16 February

It is time to renew One's commitment to and alignment with One's inner way of life. Inspire and benefit humanity, not because it is easy or the right thing to do, but because it is what divine sentient Beings do in the universe. One does this by living a life in service to all others with a loving heart, together with kind virtuous thoughts, words and actions.

To the One who can master One's mind, One will be a master of anything in this world.

Enter One's daily life as if visiting a holy temple or entering a sacred space and place.

Let nothing persuade One from One's inner path of peace and divine centredness. Be a light to oneself and let One's confidence shine as brightly as it can. When One believes in One's divinity, One will be able to let go of all the pre-existing sociocultural conditioning and programming of One's past life, to enable what One may become now.

Consciously choose a path that will end One's suffering in life. Have the courage and strength to be oneself. Everything that One has gone through in life until now has prepared One for where One is at this exact moment. Now is the time to awaken to One's divine truth as spirit, soul or spiritual consciousness and embrace this eternal presence on Earth.

Listen to the silent messages within oneself – the voice of spirit. Take note of what this voice is trying to encourage within oneself. Ask oneself this simple question: Does this idea, thought or action help or serve One's higher good and purpose in life now? If the answer is yes, continue. If the answer is no, change direction immediately. Life is not a destination, but a journey towards where One needs to be.

Know that One is not a product of circumstance. One's life reflects One's awareness of oneself and One's choices to co-create One's lived experiences and observed reality.

SOL DAY 48
17 February

If One thinks that One will always get to where One is supposed to go, guess what happens? One will always arrive at this destination in life. If One never learns to change direction, One will never travel along another path towards an alternative future.

The trick is to stay grounded and centred on One's pathless path. Move in a direction that has least resistance, where there is no judgement or attachment to the situation, activity or event. Dissolve One's expectations into emptiness and be guided by the universe.

Train One's mind to stop reacting to words and negative ways from people who are suffering. Teach oneself the difference between just being alive, going through the daily motions of performing a certain role in life, and being fully present in One's life. One is the change agent of One's life. One is the master of One's destiny. One's future is defined by what One consciously chooses now for oneself in cooperation with other sentient Beings and the universe.

It is time to fully immerse oneself in this all-knowing truth of One's life. Open One's mind to the unifying oneness of all life in the universe now. One is an integral part of everything in the universe. Do not run from it. Embrace it with all of One's heart.

Just because One has had a difficult journey so far does not mean One should give up. It is time to learn, grow, change and transform oneself completely into the best version of oneself. One does this by making a commitment to oneself each day that One is alive on Earth. There is no greater mission in One's life than to awaken to One's divine reality and be fully present in every aspect of One's life. With great awakening comes an even greater awareness of who One truly is now. Be the divine Being that One seeks to be in this moment.

SOL DAY 49
18 February

Do not be afraid to embark on One's journey of self-discovery and inner personal transformation alone. This is how it has always been done since the dawn of humanity on Earth.

One cannot expect to change the outcome of One's life if One does not change the founding beliefs, thoughts, habits and practices that One has developed over time since One was born. There will be a million or more people who will dismiss One's vision to change and will try to discourage One from attempting to be better. However, there is only one person whose confidence, commitment and opinions truly count – this person is oneself.

When One is facing the right direction, all One must do is keep moving forward. One's direction is more important than One's speed. One will arrive at One's destination when One stops seeking it and becomes One with 'the way'.

One's time on Earth is extremely limited. It is too precious to waste trying to copy someone else or fit into others' expectations of how One must live One's life. The more One gives One's power away to others, the less energy One will have to invest in co-creating One's own living reality.

No other person is going to walk the path of spiritual enlightenment for One. It is a solo journey, an individual quest that must be taken in silence. A path to disassemble One's constructed identity that will enable a realised awakened state of divine consciousness within. Feel the fear, purposely lean into it and know that One is not alone on this journey. The universe is always on. It is there when One is sleeping, when One is actively involved in life, working or playing, and, of course, when One is mindfully engaged in meditation.

SOL DAY 50
19 February

Know that it will all make sense in the end. One need only trust the process of change and transformation as One makes One's way in the world. As One reconfigures One's inner mindscape by changing One's beliefs, thoughts and intentions, One will automatically begin to adjust One's outer landscape of habits, practices and experiences to be more aligned with One's higher self (mind–body–spirit).

While One may not see immediate changes today or tomorrow in One's life, the universe is proactively working in harmony to facilitate and create a new reality that directly aligns to One's existing vibrations. One will be genuinely surprised that everything will work out so well. In a couple of years, One will look back and be amazed by how far One has come. One will look at One's changes in awe and with confidence. By letting go of the outcome, One is free to allow the universe to work its magic and support One.

Focus on the people that inspire One to be great. Consciously choose to live life to the best of One's ability and wisdom. To reach One's greatest potential, One will most definitely need to explore One's greatest fears. It is in this space that One can break through and break free of One's mind's limitations and learn to dissolve the delusions within One's mindscape.

One's deepest fear is not that One is inadequate, it is that One is powerful beyond anything that One can imagine.

It is time to embrace One's infinite ability to change, adapt and completely transform One's life into something new and exciting. This is the moment to give oneself permission to ask a different question: How does One choose to live One's life? Will One shy away and cower in the darkness or will One choose to bravely shine the light of One's inner Being?

SOL DAY 51
20 February

Life is not about what One does, but how One does it. It is not about what One sees, but how One perceives it. It is not about what is in One's life, but how One lives it.

These are the important things that One needs to remember today.

When less becomes more in One's life, One will begin to experience more freedom, more time and more space for more meaningful friendships, partnerships and relationships. One's overall quality of life will incrementally improve when One truly aligns with One's inner spirit.

When enough humans believe and truly realise that One is enough, there will be a conscious global shift on planet Earth. People will begin to reorganise, reconfigure and reform One's life to support lifestyles that align with spirit and a united Earth civilisation – it is inevitable.

Consciously choose not to follow egocentric leaders whose first *priority* is maintaining inflexible, outmoded and outdated systems of governance over other people. This kind of thinking and behaviour only serves One's ego and not the people or citizens of Earth.

A new day is dawning and it brings with it a new vision that unites all citizens of Earth.

It is time to go confidently in the direction of One's vision to co-create the best version of oneself. In doing this, One will experience an improved way of living and being on Earth. With great imagination comes even greater opportunity to manifest a new future today. This day is only the beginning of One's path of change and inner transformation. As One reads this now, there are thousands of people reconfiguring One's mind, thoughts and beliefs on a daily basis. One need only imagine it clearly and the universe will respond in kind to One's aligned mind–body vibrations.

SOL DAY 52
21 February

Look at the world with an open mind. Believe that One can perceive infinite possibilities today. Ask oneself: What if? What if One's wildest vision of reality manifested itself right here, right now? What if One's aching dream, imagined desire or divine destiny appeared right before oneself in this very moment? What if One could step through a magical manifesting gateway and be teleported into a new reality of One's own conscious design and choosing?

One can assure One that it is all entirely possible. This is not a fantasy; it is an imaginable reality and One can co-create this in One's life. One simply needs to reset, renew and refocus One's mind and realign One's total Being (mind–body–spirit) in a way that believes in this new reality with unconditional love, limitless confidence and a continuity of commitment for it to be manifested now in One's life.

Openly ask oneself: What if? What if something wonderful, positive, exciting, magical, adventurous, inspiring, uplifting, heartfelt, loving, kind, compassionate, nurturing and joyful happened to One each day of One's life? This idea is utterly amazing and a possibility in life.

This type of alternative lifestyle thinking and transformative energy is the catalyst for transforming oneself beyond One's current thought reality and co-creating an alternative future today. Take the time to dive deep and discover how to alter One's way of being to align with One's imagined way of living. Allow the universe to guide One's way. Explore all the imagined possibilities and alternative dimensions. Realise what One needs to know and know what One needs to realise for this to be One's living reality now.

Invite and accept the intuitive intelligence and multi-world wisdom of all sentient Beings to guide One on One's way in the universe.

SOL DAY 53
22 February

The future is not fixed. It is always changing. It is an illusion created in the present, an imagined reality that is yet to exist. Take a deep breath and relax. Today is a day to reflect on how enlightenment can enable One to be more kind, caring and compassionate. It is the best outcome when One can cultivate a genuine spiritual life and mindful living practice.

It is time to think more positively and optimistically about life and the best way to live it now. Imbue One's living habits with intentional courage and visionary virtues. This is the gateway to aligning with One's divine nature and spiritual consciousness.

There is much that One will be able to see and experience from a higher and more intuitive intelligence when One is enlightened. One will realise that everyone on Earth is 'the One'. No matter what One does for or to another, One is actually doing it for or to oneself. Whatever One gives to someone else, One is gifting to oneself. Think about this and realise that others are simply a reflection of One, just in a different human or animal form. Nothing happens by accident and that everything is working in synchronicity with all in the universe.

Take a step back from One's life and living journey so One can create some space in which to reflect on One's spiritual life and life as a spiritual Being. Be a witness to One's thoughts and an observer of One's current way of life. See One's pain and suffering as a gift or message that must be decoded in order to evolve in the best interests of One's higher self. Know that One is a divine spirit having a human experience, not a human being having a spiritual experience. One is an integral part of the universe and essential to the natural spiritual evolution of all humanity in this solar system and galaxy.

As One awakens to One's own divinity, so too will all other sentient Beings on Earth.

SOL DAY 54
23 February

As One begins the day, pause and embrace one day at a time. Do not try and change others or the world that One lives in; instead, seek to change and transform into the best version of oneself first. This is One of the highest and noblest quests that One is capable of undertaking in One's lifetime.

The greater the challenge that One encounters in One's life, the greater the growth, awareness and awakening of oneself on this path of mindful enlightenment and spiritual awakening. One cannot expect to be safe from life's painful challenges or individual suffering by hiding in a cave or an urban regional, rural or city residence on the surface of the Earth.

To bloom, One needs to bathe in the light, like a wildflower in spring. The absence of light will do nothing to awaken One's inner enlightenment, but it may help the mind to focus on One's inner realisation and 'the way' in which all things flow in the universe.

The paradox of seeking to be 'awake' is that One must awaken within oneself first.

Eventually, One will be able to see the light in all things. One will recognise the work of altered consciousness within a single raindrop and see that all the oceans on the planet are connected. Those with the highest wisdom do not speak needlessly. One simply responds when people need assistance and becomes part of the dialogue of engaged living in this moment.

Do not lose oneself in this world of illusion or in the beliefs, opinions or perspective of those who try to convince One otherwise. Focus on being oneself. Align with One's spirit and the universe in each moment that One encounters and moves through in life. The gift of being alive on Earth is realising just how amazing and awesome One is now.

SOL DAY 55
24 February

Today is the day to have a real and authentic conversation with oneself. Communicate with One's higher self in a way that taps in, turns on and tunes into the very essence of One's divine spirit. Know that One embodies greatness within and that it is time to set it free. The only person who can express One's spiritual practice is the One who chooses to hold the light of inner conscious awareness within One's Being. No-one else can make this journey on One's behalf. It is a solitary quest along a well-worn pathless path in this present moment.

It sounds counter intuitive, but the more One is lost and loses One's mind–body attachments, the more One will gain and benefit. This is how One experiences spacious nothingness within the knowing state of One's existence. This is 'the way' One can finally and truly know oneself.

At the end of every desire One has ever had in One's life is freedom from it. One may find that One has been on a false and futile mission of acquisition for many decades with no real purpose at all. One may, upon reflection, discover that One has collected numerous artefacts of One's life achievements – people, things, money, values, attitudes, beliefs, cultures, qualifications, jobs, experiences and assets – but they matter not in the grand scheme of the universe itself. The universe has no need of these things; they are merely tools that enabled One's living experience on Earth. Know that anything that One co-creates with the universe will eventually be reformed, reused and repurposed. Everything changes, all relationships are impermanent and everyone already exists now in the universe.

It is incredibly freeing to know that One cannot accidentally destroy the universe or unintentionally extinguish One's own divine spirit, soul or spiritual consciousness. One is free.

SOL DAY 56
25 February

When One meditates mindfully and purposefully with the intention to be at one with oneself and the universe, it directly and indirectly contributes to the overall wellbeing of everyone on Earth. No positive mindful thought or action, no matter how small, ever goes to waste. It all contributes to raising the global vibration and collective spiritual consciousness of the world. A time is fast approaching when all citizens of Earth will operate from a spiritual perspective and engage in relevant spiritual discussion to benefit individual wellbeing and collective wellness. People will begin to focus on participating in a sharing culture of 'What if...' and 'Let's create a better life on Earth now'.

It is time to break free of the relentless cycle of fake new and false economies. The world needs new ways to see, new ways to live and new ways to be. Let this be the day when One begins a new conversation with oneself and others about how to embrace inner change and the mindful transformation of One's current reality. Have the courage to begin to imagine One's positive enthusiasm flowing and rippling out across the globe like a wave of awakening energy touching and uplifting all in its wake.

It is not that humans do not lack the wisdom or motivation to change, it is just that they are too attached to familiar pain and suffering to embrace a lifestyle of unknown spiritual bliss. A critical mass of awakened persons is on the increase and will expand exponentially during the coming decades. It is all part of becoming a spiritually based Type 1 civilisation and the next step in human evolution on planet Earth.

There is nowhere to hide and nothing to run to that will prevent One experiencing this spiritual evolution. It is inevitable and undeniable. Be aware – it is already here now.

SOL DAY 57

26 February

Like a drop of water in the ocean, know that all sentient Beings on Earth are One.

Being 'the One' is as great as the greatest Masters who ever lived on Earth. One is from the divine source for all things in the universe. One need only realise this truth within oneself and allow oneself to shine as brightly as One can be. Do not be afraid to work on One's mind and cultivate a practice of positive virtues and mindful living. Each day One is alive, ensure that One is as open, honest and simple as a child to every experience. Know that One will always find One's way to the truth.

The easiest way to recreate a new version of oneself is to realise that the old version of oneself is out of date and does not serve One any longer. It is time for a serious life-changing decision and an immediate upgrade. Never ever stop improving oneself or continuing to explore ways to be all that One can be now. Nature does not stand still, it is forever changing and adapting to the current living ecosystem, and One should too.

Know that everything around One comes from the divine source and so does One. Look at the land, sea and sky in awe and with great appreciation of its divine beauty. Nothing need be added or taken away for it to be perfect within its imperfection. Walk and touch the earth lightly, like a gentle breeze moving across the landscape.

There is more to life than work and rushing to the finish line of One's mind–body death. Take a moment to pause and look up at the sky and realise that One is on Starship Earth. One is already an interstellar traveller on an infinite journey across the universe. There is no time, there is no destination – there is only this moment of awakened living. Live it 'Now'.

SOL DAY 58
27 February

Today is a day to think, speak and act positively. A day to be completely positive from within One's inner Being. When One positively focuses One mind, One co-creates a ripple of positive energy that flows outwardly into the world around One. People sense it, long before they ever see it. The changing of One's thoughts changes One's mind-body vibration and how One engages with One's reality. Positive things are naturally attracted to One in many different ways. Be open to this and these experiences will come to One as easily as raindrops falling from the sky or waves crashing on the beach.

There is no better time in One's life to be overwhelmingly and unconditionally positive about everything One is experiencing. Uncouple One's thoughts from the conditions and living environment that One finds oneself in. Remove One's attachment to the circumstances and situations of One's daily life. Stand in front of a mirror and say, 'No matter what happens today, One will be UP ('Unconditionally Positive') about it.' Set a loving intention that positive things will and are going to happen today. Be confident, be bold and be brave.

The more One is willing to positively change, the more positive changes One will experience.

Too many people struggle with the belief that things need to be a certain way in order for One to feel positive or be in a positive state of mind about life and living it now. Even if One's body has a terminal disease or serious illness, One can still be optimistically positive about it. One can rise above One's personal pain and suffering, see it as a gift and put a positive lens on this living experience.

Despite everything in One's past or life – be positive, positive, positive.

SOL DAY 59
28 February

This is a wonderful day to co-create something good, amazing and wonderful on the inside and share these thoughts and feelings with oneself and all living Beings on Earth. One has a shared responsibility to raise the level of conscious awareness on the planet. One does this not by knowing 'the way' but by living it mindfully and completely in the moment.

Attaining enlightenment, Godhood or Buddhahood is a false promise or paradox. It does not exist beyond who One is now. There is no single spiritual test, godlike suffering or enlightenment challenge that One must pass to awaken to One's inner self or divine truth. One need only realise who One is – spirit, soul or spiritual consciousness – and enable One's way through life by how One chooses to be in this present moment in the world.

If One is going to look somewhere, look inside oneself to discover One's way out and into the world around One. This is where the answers to the questions that really matter about One's presence, life and journey here on Earth and in the universe will be found.

All that appears in this physical universe or altered consciousness is a very convincing and ever-present vibrating illusion. It is a co-created reality that acts as a frame of reference and point of perspective for One's ego and living experiences. It is a matrix for the mind to operate in and, at the same time, it is a reflection of all that is. Know that everything One can imagine in this world and in the universe already exists now.

Whatever One consumes mentally and physically will affect One's life. Choose wisely and select that which will nourish One's mind and body in a way that enhances and cultivates the habits of mindful meditation, virtuous living and an awakened relationship with all. Know the value of One's life and give to all as if One is giving to oneself.

SOL DAY 60
29 February

This is the day that One does not look away, hide or run from One's responsibility to be the best version of oneself. It is mandatory that One makes a commitment to oneself and takes the first step to mastering One's mind and emotions (thoughts and feelings). One is not a biological machine wandering aimlessly across the surface of the Earth, fulfilling daily functions and tasks in society with no real purpose or goal.

One purposely chose to be here on Earth during this time of great change and spiritual evolution. It is not a mistake that One is here now. It is all part of the universe's divine timing.

One is an awesome and dynamic sentient Being of the universe. Realise this and believe in the power of One's divine destiny in life. One's true path lies not in the menial tasks of work, trading One's life, energy and time for money as One slowly grows old, retires and dies.

The world needs One here and now. People need One to be a positive, inexhaustible contributor to the wellbeing of all citizens of Earth. A new life on Earth requires imagination and direct action, combined in a mindful way that is cooperative and compassionate that benefits all Beings.

Do not worry about the future or be particularly concerned with One's role within it. The universe already has a divine plan for One, so just focus on living one day at a time. It is time to change oneself so that One can share this transformation with the world and change it too.

Think not about what the world can do for oneself, but what One will do for the world by investing in oneself. This is the key to inner positive change. This is the seed that lies dormant within everyone on Earth. Water it, nurture it, love it and One will surely see it grow into a magnificent forest, able to sustain life to the furthest reaches of the universe.

MARCH
Sol day 61-91

One believes in the universe and intuitively knows that the universe believes in One too. During this month, One will confidently step into the unknown and embrace One's living journey, however it may unfold on Earth. One is confident that everything will always work out for oneself and that One will be okay in the end. One knows with absolute divine clarity that the universe is supporting One's progress along a path that is in the best interests of One's higher self, leading One to be the best version of oneself in this life. One need only face the right direction and let it all unfold as it needs to in this moment. With this belief, One will be guided along 'the way' and will effortlessly imagine and experience a new living reality filled with unending personal prosperity, amazing abundance and wonderful wakefulness.

SOL DAY 61
1 March

Today is a brand new day and new month. Regardless of what happens on this day, know that One's spirit is free. Free to be whatever and wherever One chooses to be in the universe. It has always been this way and One will continue to be free forever. There is nothing in this world that binds One's spirit to it at all, except for One's thoughts and body. As a divine sentient Being, One has infinite capacity to be present at any point or place in the universe at any given moment One chooses.

This is an amazing realisation and an incredible power that exists within all Beings.

Make a conscious decision today to not take life too seriously. Explore One's infinite freedom and allow things to be just as they are now. Step away from all conflict in One's life.

Many will view One's alternative conversations about living life, spirit and the universe with ultimate surprise and think that One has gone 'insane' or lost One's mind. This is because, for over the past 2000 years, nearly all Western human cultures have conditioned people to think about living life only in terms of a deficient model – to focus on what One doesn't have, like money, job, family, resources (land, sea and sky), time, energy, food, shelter, space, supportive relationships, personal or work-based networks and connections, a business or success.

One needs to change the script and narrative of One's life. Let oneself live a little and create some space in One's life to open One's mind. Dissolve the lessons of the past and begin to teach oneself a new way to view and embrace One's divine spirit, shared prosperity and the overflowing abundance in One's life. Learn how to be totally free now. Know that no person or thought can keep One from the truth – One is a free spirit of the universe now and always.

SOL DAY 62

2 March

What if One were able to have a conversation with oneself and discover the truth about One's existence today? What if One could change One's living perception of oneself and the world that One lives in now and forever – would One choose this path of ultimate self-awareness? What if choosing this new way of believing and seeing life meant the total loss of all pre-existing relationships? Would One still desire to know One's own inner truth? Or would One want to continue to live a lie and remain safely sheltered within One's ego matrix of illusion and deception? The choice is up to One. Only One can choose One's own path in life.

No matter what One chooses, it will be the right choice for One at this moment. Know that, whether in this lifetime or the next, One will eventually choose One's path of inner truth. It is an inevitable outcome for all Beings in the universe.

Do not underestimate the power of oneself to totally change One's daily perception and way in this world. Through One's own inner awareness, One will be able to investigate the present moment and project oneself into the future, way beyond any space or time that One has ever previously encountered in One's life. One will be able to know things before they happen and be intuitively connected in the universe like never before.

It will be a time when One will be able to shatter One's own illusion into a thousand pieces, like a broken mirror. Step through the hidden doorway within into a new world and new way of living and being now. One will feel like One has transcended time all together and reached a new and exciting threshold in One's life. Years of doubt and uncertainty will be stripped away from One's existence in a single moment. It will be like being totally cleansed of One's previous life and waking up for the very first time.

SOL DAY 63
3 March

Today is an incredible day. Give oneself time to reflect on just how awesome and amazing One is in this moment. As One rides this interstellar planetary vehicle – Starship Earth – One must realise something very special about oneself. One is a spiritual Being of the universe on a galactic voyage across the cosmos, riding a spinning celestial object that is circling a fusion reactor (the sun), which was already manifested prior to One's arrival and will eventually self-destruct and obliterate the entire current solar system as One knows it.

Death of all life on Earth is assured in the future. This is a certainty; it is going to happen whether One believes it or not. Everything alive on Earth will eventually die or dematerialise into stardust. Knowing this can either fill One with despair or hope. Be optimistic about One's life and live it well, as it is all One ever has now.

The real question is: How will One choose to live One's life today? Will One look inside oneself and see the infinite potential of One's existence on Earth? Will One rise above all the naysayers and people who will always find a thousand ways to say or tell One why something cannot be done or why it will never work? Or will One discover One's inner spirit and divine truth and realise that One is truly capable of anything that One so desires in this world? Never underestimate the power of One person to change oneself and the world.

Let the universe take care of the future. Concern oneself with living in this present moment now. Co-create a shared vision for the future but work and commit oneself to being alive and celebrating One's life today. One's positive energy will naturally attract others. One's optimistic outlook will create a gravity well of positive inspiration that people and future generations will be attracted to.

SOL DAY 64
4 March

It is time to burst the bubble of One's false identity and reveal One's true inner self. This is where One's true identity or spirit exists now. Every time One feels like the psychology of a particular identity is taking over One's mind, thoughts and actions, it is time to act. If this situation arises in One's life, it is a call to action. One must act decisively and without hesitation. The bubble of every new false identity needs to be popped as quickly and quietly as possible. Otherwise it will become a virus of virtual imprisonment, locking One's life journey into a certain way of conditioned living.

Underneath each and every individual bubble of personality or persona there is a vast cosmic consciousness waiting patiently for One to realise and align to now.

Like waves on the ocean, what One presents to others and the world as 'One's true self' is simply ripples on the surface of One's infinite Being. There is more to One than what One currently realises. While One is stuck in the labyrinth of One's mind, chasing shadows of significance, security and separateness, One will be continually distracted by One's own ego.

To break free of this illusion, One need only realise who One truly is and how One can change and transform One's inner landscape and outer life.

There is no locked door to One's path of freedom, because there is no wall. Realise this and One's house of mental conformity will also dissolve completely. But what is left? One's true identity – spirit, soul or spiritual consciousness.

Stop staring at the problem and reawaken to the solution before One. It has been there all along. One has simply been looking in the wrong place and space for the answer. Turn inward to find it within One.

SOL DAY 65
5 March

Let One begin today with the clear intention to be positive and optimistic about everything in life and on planet Earth. Clear One's mind of all distractions and settle calmly into a place and space without disturbances. Allow oneself to experience the void of no-mind in silence. Create an oasis or spiritual sanctuary where One can sit in peaceful serenity and quiet contemplation. Enter into the emptiness of nothingness within One's mindful meditation practice. Know that there is nowhere to go to and nothing to do in this world but be here now. Free oneself of all expectations and commitments. It is time to enable One's inner awareness of One's spirit, soul or spiritual consciousness while focusing on One's rhythmic breathing and breath.

For every thought that arises out of nothingness, know that it will return to it too. Observe it. Look at it with detachment, as if seeing a beautiful rainbow butterfly for the very first time in One's life. Then watch as it dissolves and disappears into the mist of infinite manifestation. Let whatever comes appear before One. Do not try to control anything. Then simply watch it go away again. With practice, One can create a calm quiet pond of gentle contemplation and relaxing reflection.

Have faith and believe in One's ability to tame the wild horse within One's mind.

Everyone has the potential to be a thought whisperer. With gentle encouragement, positive practice and persuasiveness patience, One can and will sooth the storms and silence the noise in One's head. Beyond mind is One's infinite divine spiritual consciousness.

One can directly access this presence at any moment or place on Earth in One's life. One need only to be aware of it and make it so.

Believe in co-creating One's reality, and so too will the universe will align with it now.

SOL DAY 66
6 March

Today is a day to be calm, caring and compassionate. A day to reflect on creating a balance between One's active and passive states in life. As a sovereign spiritual entity in the universe, it is One's responsibility to look at One's mind beyond the symptoms of One's fears or uncomfortable energies and follow One's unique path on Earth. Learn to train One's mind and respond in a positive and mindful way to whatever arises in One's life.

Teach oneself to break down One's fears and go behind them to reveal the root cause of this distorted, destructive and dysfunctional energy. One will eventually see that every fear is just an illusion created in One's mind. It is important to remove the emotional charge when looking at One's fear, and then decommission it permanently. One's job is to clear and cleanse every aspect of fear by taking the thought offline forever and making it obsolete as One co-creates the best version of oneself now.

Know that all is well in the universe and One's wellness is always within One now.

Be aware of One's higher self and give to oneself – this is the first principle of creating wellness within. One will be amazed how this simple approach will have an incredible ripple effect on all aspects of One's life. Take the time to access One's infinite energy and intuitive intelligence. Listen to One's inner voice or spirit, as it comes directly from the source.

Let One's giving be free and unconditional to One and all on Earth. Know that One's energy signature is in everything that One thinks, says and does in life. Tap into One's positive energy, thoughts and vision to co-create a more positive path and living experience.

The universe will open a gateway of infinite possibilities where One had only previously perceived closed doors. It is always making way for One's path and higher self.

SOL DAY 67

7 March

What if One was told the truth about oneself? What if One secretly knew at the deepest part of One's inner Being this truth all along – and One was not surprised at all? What if thinking and speaking this divine actuality out in the open changed the very nature of One's relationship with oneself, One's loved Ones and One's reality on Earth? What if this truth is inevitable and undeniable in One's life and One simply needs to come to terms with it?

Would One have the courage and capacity to respond to this intuitive knowing in a mature and mindful way? Or would One crumble into a heap and allow oneself to be blinded by ego's false promises of plausible deniability?

The day is fast approaching when the 'language of spirit' will be taught in every corner of the world. Through this platform, One will begin to believe in a new way of being and living on Earth. It will become the way forward to create a harmonious spirit Type 1 civilisation on Earth. It will be the genesis of inner transformation, outer change and spiritual evolution for all peoples as united and diverse citizens of Earth.

If One can learn this language early enough, One will be able to transcend time and space. One will naturally have the capacity to move beyond the mindscape of physical realities and into another dimension of cosmic experience.

Life will take on a new and higher meaning of expression and existence. What is viewed now as 'contemporary modern thinking' will be seen as obsolete thought patterns of an age when society purposely devalued and denigrated self-awareness and spiritual enlightenment as a mystical form of 'hippie healing'.

This new age of awakened awareness is already here. Choose to align with it now.

SOL DAY 68
8 March

Reset, refocus and renew One's day by reformatting One's mental scaffolding and current operating system. Switch off One's established programming and social conditioning that directs how One would normally start the day. Choose a new starting place and new thought point to initialise this day. Begin with the most basic and fundamental belief, such as: 'One is spirit, soul or cosmic consciousness'.

Follow this thought up with: 'Today is an amazing and exciting day. One will experience being awesome ... and be positive in everything that One thinks, says and does today. One is blessed to be alive on Earth at this time. This is a wonderful and beautiful day in One's life.'

It is particularly important to remind oneself that One is 'powerful beyond anything that One can imagine' and able to manifest any reality in One's life on Earth here and now.

When One changes the way the One starts the day, everything that follows will most likely align to this intention and energy.

Instead of thinking, 'One needs, wants or desires a particular good thing to happen so that One can be happy', change this thought to, 'One is joyful therefore good things will naturally and effortlessly happen today'. It is that simple when One is shown the way to recreate One's daily life, one thought at a time.

The key to changing the cognitive systems or integrated thought patterns within One's mind is to create a 'flip filter' that can translate 'old thoughts' into 'new thoughts' from a perspective of spiritual awareness and centred beingness.

One is still the co-creator of One's reality and responsible for all thoughts within One's mind. What One thinks, One becomes, and this then manifests as One's reality.

SOL DAY 69
9 March

Set One's intention for today to be a wonderful, great and magical day in line with One's highest vibrational energy and vision for life. Now let go completely of how One will arrive at these moments, while still being purposely and proactively engaged on the path in front of One. There is no single route that will deliver One to where One needs to be in this moment. It is all unfolding as per the operating principles and cosmic consciousness of the universe.

One's journey in life is meant to be an unknown adventure on Earth that could unfold in an infinite number of inconceivable ways. A life influenced by a range of harmonic variables and entangled spiritual possibilities. It sounds complicated, but it is actually very simple.

Look not to chisel out a defined path of certainty for oneself. Instead, explore One's life with renewed enthusiasm as it unfolds from moment to moment each and every day. Be the path that One's seek in life and know that One has arrived.

One has been taught from an early age that One must try and try again to succeed in life if One is to be the best at something. To some extent this is true. However, what most social and formal educational structures do not teach is how to question or inquire about the process of actually thinking or learning things for oneself. Self-awareness is key. Ask oneself: 'What is success?' Success is the ability to be aware of the path of least resistance and surrender to it.

The universe is a vast expansive space and Earth is only a very tiny part of it.

While humans have the capacity to destroy the Earth many times over, One needs to realise that One is already powerful beyond measure with the capacity to co-create a spiritually based Type 1 civilisation on Earth, where a unifying way of living and being becomes infinitely greater than the sum of individuals who live here now.

SOL DAY 70
10 March

Embrace One's inner truth today as spirit, soul or cosmic consciousness. It is time to open One's mind unconditionally, without judgement, resistance or attachment to anything or anyone. Let go of One's selfish and separatist defences, dissolve the walls of fear and wash away the mountain of expectation that One has built up over time.

One is an eternal and immortal Being, existing within a field of infinite possibilities and living out One's existence in an ocean of divine consciousness in the universe.

To know this is to have access to the master key, which can transcend all constructed identities, self-limiting beliefs, unhealthy habits, negative thought patterns, dysfunctional relationships and polarised perceptions. The cycle of One's personal suffering is no more than a movie that One is choosing to watch repeatedly and play out in real life. Remember to give oneself this message: One is in charge of the remote-control switch within One's mind and life – if life is not working for One, get up, take action and change the channel.

Turn off the noise and unhelpful self-talk in One's mind. Stop listening to those internal contagious viral messages that say One needs to live life a certain way or that if One seeks to be successful One must play by ego's rules of social conformity, individual competition and economic cabalism. Free oneself from the global corporate mission to consume as much of oneself and everything else as One can in this life before dying of exhaustion.

Learn to cultivate a daily practice of peaceful meditation, spiritual awareness and mindful living. Give oneself space to grow, change and transform completely, like a flower opening to greet the sun for the very first time. One is an evolving work in progress and everyone is part of the garden of humanity on Earth.

SOL DAY 71
11 March

There are a million or more ways that One's mind can start and end the day. It is best not to think about any of them right now. Simply face in the right direction and keep moving forward in a positive way. With every step, walk in peace; with every breath, breathe with loving kindness, compassion and contentment. Live One's life like this now and know peace within.

There is nothing so great that it cannot be accomplished with love, kindness and the cooperation of other sentient Beings on planet Earth. Give up trying to conquer everything in One's life and embrace being alive in this moment now. See the joy in all that is. Stay in the moment for as long as One can, until it moves to the next moment – then so on and so forth.

It is okay to have personal aspirations, dreams and goals as long as One is not a slave to One's ego, driven by a ruthless desire to make it happen at all costs. Life was not meant for the accumulation of assets or accolades. Life is a place for One to awaken to the divinity within One's Being. The moment One begins to question the intention of the culture in which One was born into, One will have planted a seed of doubt about the conditioning of One's role, function and purpose in this life. This is a good thing – embrace it.

Each day, move a little close to aligning to One's spirit, soul or cosmic consciousness. This is where One's true identity and freedom exists. Do not dwell on the years spent unconsciously going through the motions of fulfilling some arbitrary function or role in life.

Believe in One's innate ability to change and transform oneself and the world that One lives in now. Sit in silent meditation and reach into the unknown of One's inner presence. It is there One will find what One has been seeking all along. This is the untouchable, unstainable and immutable divinity of One's Being. Believe and One will experience it now.

SOL DAY 72
12 March

It is time to stop apologising for being the loveable, kind and compassionate person that One is. One is not here to entertain people or make them feel comfortable about the uncomfortableness in One's life. Other people need to work on being the best version of oneself. This is One's complete and total job description.

The best way to improve One's life is to start by improving oneself. The way forward to a better life begins by looking inward to being completely focused in the present. This is where One's spirit exists – not in the past or the future. These perspectives are merely illusions created in One's mind to distract oneself from One's true existence in the universe.

This is the day to start loving the awkward, weird and idiosyncratic ways that One expresses the joy of being alive on this wonderful and amazing planet. One's unique sense of humour, style and approach to life is all part of One's irresistible charm and likeable qualities.

Know that not everyone will like or fall in love with One – this is okay. It is a reflection of One's conscious vibrational energy and spiritual alignment on Earth. It is One's job to love and honour oneself first above all else. Then One can go out into the world and share this light with others so that it can light a path for all to enable One's way in the world.

Everyone is on the same path in life, just different journeys. Some will take the quick route and pass through the lessons of suffering to spiritual enlightenment very quickly. Others will need more time to figure out why One is repeating the same lessons over and over again. It is not until One lets go of One's attachments, resistance and judgements that One's path will become clear in life. The ending of suffering is possible and spiritual enlightenment is merely a return to a state of divine clarity of One's spiritual Being.

SOL DAY 73
13 March

Every day is a good day to celebrate One's awakening. Know that enlightenment is just a process of realisation and awakening to One's own divine truth in the universe. Everything is connected – all is One. Everything that ever was or will be created in the universe arises from nothingness, which is manifested from altered consciousness. The point of origin for all things and experiences is source or source consciousness. One is and always will be a holographic refraction of the divine in this present moment.

It does not matter how far One travels or what One does on Earth, One will always be in an ocean of conscious existence in the universe. This is the paradox of being a spiritual entity.

The more One can release oneself from trying to live life to a certain social or cultural standard, the more One will be able to enjoy living a simple life. Never underestimate One's ability to rise above the challenges of everyday life by surrendering to it.

All paths contain challenges to assist One in the process of awakening. One is not able to escape these challenges through ignorance, or hide from them by denying One's inner way in this world. Eventually all Beings on Earth will come to a point of self-reflection and self-realisation. This could happen as One encounters challenges like illness or injury, or perhaps on One's deathbed. The important thing is to use all of One's life experiences to awaken in this moment now.

The best journey ahead lies not in knowing the future or remembering the past, but in living mindfully from moment to moment each day of One's life. Within each living Being on Earth is an intuitive inner spiritual guidance system that can assist One in making the best decision in every moment – use it.

SOL DAY 74
14 March

Today is a day to marvel at all the wonders and miracles around One and in One's life. Notice how life is bursting with energy, how the sun is effortlessly beaming and unconditionally giving life to all of nature on Earth. There is prosperity and abundance in nature without One ever having to lift a single finger to make it happen. This is the true miracle of life on Earth.

Every human being is blessed to be here on Earth now. One lives in awe of nature.

Be grateful for the simple things in One's life. A bird song in the morning, a flower opening to greet the sun, bees collecting nectar to make honey. It is amazing how all of nature works without One initiating anything or intervening to assist it. Nature is perfect in its simplicity and majestic magnificence. From a single drop of rain through to the creeks, rivers, lakes and oceans – everything flows effortlessly in the right direction.

Seasons come and go and the cycle of life on Earth keeps rolling on like waves crashing onto a deserted or remote beach. Of course, there are extreme natural weather events like droughts, floods, cyclones or bushfires, but these are all part of nature rebalancing itself and bringing things back into alignment. For every significant weather event or lighting storm that has come and gone, with the destruction and devastation that they bring, they also bring benefits to nature, and humans as well. There are countless opportunities in nature and the built environment for renewal, redesign and redevelopment.

Without the sun, none of this life on Earth would be possible. Without source consciousness or One's soul or spirit, One would never be here. Acknowledge the simple things in One's life. They are a guide to the divine chaos of the entire universe.

SOL DAY 75
15 March

Today is a day to slow down and activate One's healing energy and positive health. A time to really get in touch with One's inner health and wellbeing on planet Earth. Begin this day with the intention to improve One's personal mind–body space. One's mental and physical health is as important as it ever was in One's life. Make space to meditate and make time for nurturing and pro-love experiences. Create opportunities to align with One's inner spirit, soul or cosmic consciousness. Everyone on Earth deserves love, affection and compassion – be an advocate for One's self-love and oneself today.

Learn to love all of oneself openly, honestly and genuinely from a place of acceptance.

Look at how One can do simple things to improve One's health and wellbeing, like mindful conversations (positive self-talk) with oneself and others, clarifying One's positive wellbeing intentions for the day, walking or gentle exercise, drinking plenty of water, eating healthy green foods, sipping on tea, being with loved Ones or partners and enjoying the company of positive people in One's life. The list is endless. Think of three simple things that One can do today and make it so. Manifest a better life and living experiences by envisioning a better vibrational wellness energy signature and then taking simple actions to enable this lifestyle.

One's positive personal wellbeing is not something that One needs to achieve as a life goal. It is way of life to stay centred in the moment, living life while aligning to One's feel-good awareness within mind, body and spirit. There is no right or wrong way to do this. There is only just 'the way' of being aligned to One's mind–body–spirit in this forever moment.

Know that in silence, spirit speaks – this is when the answers that One seeks will come to One. Be patient.

SOL DAY 76
16 March

Use One's time today to see the impermanence of things in One's life. Be grateful for everyone and everything that comes into and leaves One's life. Rejoice in the moments that One has regardless of what it is. The universe flows. Everything is energy or altered consciousness.

Know that everyone's parents die and so too does every daughter or son. This is just life. It is a cycle of occurrences, like the moon orbiting the Earth or the Earth circling the sun.

Nothing that One calls reality is stable. It is all a wonderful, amazing illusion. So convincing is this illusion that it continues to blind billions of humans to the truth of One's spiritual existence on Earth. However, people are waking up to One's own inner truth and seeing One's new flexible reality. One is realising that One's reality is not the fixed construct of the past, but a living, flowing, manifesting field of infinite possibilities in the present.

All Beings on Earth are synergised within a field of **spiritual entanglement** in one way or another. Everyone's mind–body is a vibrational source of energy influencing the space and people around it. One has the capacity to change this aura of energy by merely shifting One's thoughts from low to high. Know that One's individual vibrations change every aspect of One's reality in the 'Now'. The more positive One is about One's life and living direction, the higher One's vibration will be in life. This higher vibration will resonate with other people at the same vibrational frequency and naturally attract these people into One's life along with whatever One's intentional manifesting vision is at the same time.

See One's life journey as an infinite river flowing back to its source. Let go of the struggle to try and tame it, simply flow with this divine current of the universe.

SOL DAY 77
17 March

It is time to welcome wellness, abundance, prosperity and positive experiences into One's life now. This is the moment to create the reality that aligns with One's best version of oneself, One's higher purpose and divine existence on Earth. Know that the universe is always on One's side as One aligns with One's new vision of oneself.

Know that One is under no obligation to be the same person One was five minutes ago. It is okay to completely change One's perspectives, beliefs and thoughts so that One can renew One's life and lifestyle to become the best version of oneself. In addition, it is perfectly natural to transform oneself to enable a new life, new lifestyle and new living experiences in life.

Allow oneself to flow effortlessly in the direction of these inner realisations and internal changes. Good things and positive experiences will always appear at the right moment. Look through the pain and suffering of One's life and a path of enlightenment will be revealed to One in this moment. Let go of resistance to change, attachment and judgement within One's mind.

'The way' forward will appear out of nowhere, as if by magic. In fact, it was always there –waiting patiently for One to rediscover it. One merely needed to remove the cloud of ego from One's mind to openly see the path, like a clear blue sky on a winter's day.

The trick to seeing this path is to realise how One sees and processes One's perspective in the world that One creates daily. One will notice that people who speak of love, abundance, prosperity and wellness naturally possess or radiate these vibrational qualities by being oneself. When One feels these things completely, One will unsurprisingly attract more of the same into One's life. The universe is giving One a gift for simply being as One is now.

SOL DAY 78
18 March

Realise that One's social conditioning over the years from One's family, tribe, kin, schooling and peer groups or friendship networks have effectively brainwashed One into thinking that One needs to meet certain standards to be successful, worthy of love, accepted and valued in the family or society. This common global value system is totally false and a product of intergenerational ego grooming. It is a way of keeping One's mind-body in a cycle of perpetual busyness, continually doing something to justify One's existence in society and on Earth.

It is time to break free of this way of thinking and be the best version of oneself today.

The old pattern of thinking goes something like this: One must be doing something approved by others in order to be a valued member of society. Meanwhile, the culture of modernity has been to remove menial labour functions, dangerous and repetitive tasks from human life. Creating work-life efficiencies to improve the overall wellbeing of human life.

A new way of thinking is more like this: One is valued as spirit, soul or cosmic consciousness, a divine Being of the universe. One is immortal, eternal and infinite. One is here to awaken to the light of One's own divine consciousness and be virtuous in all aspects of One's life. One exists here and now; One is whole and accepted as is. One is a creator of One's reality. One's place in this new world is to be all that One can be now.

It is important to realise that One has infinite potential and untold value simply because One exists at this point in time on Earth. One does not need to prove oneself to anyone for anything, One simply needs to see One's own light and truth from within.

Now is the time to align with One's divine oneness on Earth. Step out of the shadows and celebrate One's greatness and awesomeness as a Being of love, light and oneness.

SOL DAY 79
19 March

Create a vibrational blueprint for One's day and life. Start each day with a grateful, lovingly kind and compassionate mindset. Do this by focusing One's attention and thoughts on the positive aspects of One's life. Identify three things that One is grateful for each day of One's life and write it down in One's gratitude journal. Keep this journal beside One's bed. Undertake this task every morning for 30 days and review at the end of the month. One will be amazed how many things One will find. Eventually this will become an automatic habit. Know that One's life and reality is mostly a reflection of One's habitual thought patterns and feelings.

If One seeks to change One's living experiences in life, begin by changing One's thoughts, feelings and behaviours. Review, renew and reset One's intentions at the start of each morning just after One has woken. At the top of the page in the same gratitude journal, complete this simple statement: 'One's intention for today is to be ….'

Note down the intention for today. For example, 'One's intention for today is to be mindful, grateful or present in all aspects of One's life today.' One could simply choose to be positive and welcome good things into One's life. The possibilities are infinite.

Free One's mind and allow One's spirit to guide One. Focus on creating the right conditions to enable solutions in One's life. Too often, people start the day from a negative mindset. It is time to flip the script on this dysfunctional narrative and create a new positive mindset or new language of being and living in the present, one that is encouraging and optimistic about One's life on planet Earth. It all begins with One's gratitude. Practicing this virtue will open a spiritual gateway and alignment to One's inner states of Being.

With One's thoughts, One co-creates One's reality now.

SOL DAY 80
20 March

As One begins to dissolve the blockages of mental attachments and clear away the distorted filters of judgement within One's mind, One will notice a greater clarity coming into One's life. Resistance to change will not bother One as much as One embraces an adaptive and flexible attitude to living life. Things will unfold with a certain effortlessness and tasks once thought of as difficult or challenging will be easy or disappear altogether.

This new understanding of life will bring forth an opportunity to be a receiver of positive prosperity and loving abundance.

The more One feels blessed with One's life as well as the things and people in it, the more One will feel a sense of contentment and freedom. This newfound freedom will act as a catalyst for things to become better and better. It will also ignite and inspire One to create the best version of oneself. Nothing will dampen One's positive energy or diminish One's spirit. An air of lightness will be present in One's life and it will become evident to One that everything is always working out for the best.

One will begin to enjoy the journey of life as it unfolds along 'the way'.

The dawning of this realisation will deliver a new awareness that One is here on Earth as a purposeful and deliberate co-creator of One's living's reality. When One understands the potential that One has to manifest the life of One's choosing, One will simply change and realign One's vibrational energy with this vision. One now realises that anything is possible.

One will feel extremely excited about shifting One's energy and aligning oneself to One's new vision to be the best version of oneself in this world. One will wake each morning with renewed enthusiasm for the day and One's life on Earth. One will give thanks to the universe.

SOL DAY 81
21 March

Make this day be about attracting unconditional love, abundance, high vibrational experiences and sacred spiritual connections into One's life.

The way to do this is to clearly set this intention for today then let it go to allow the universe to work its magic. In support of this manifestation, create space for oneself to meditate, be virtuous, read and write affirmations that align with this intention, eat healthy foods, drink water, move One's body, spend time outdoors in nature and allow oneself to rest, relax and renew. It is time to invest in oneself. Know that One is worthy of these things as part of a normal and healthy lifestyle.

Create a belief within oneself that says: One is absolutely worthy of unconditional love, abundance, high vibrational experiences and sacred spiritual connections in One's life now. Write it on a sticky note and put it on the fridge or bathroom mirror to continually remind and reinforce oneself of this positive belief. Say it to oneself each and every day until One instinctively believes it to be true.

With this thought in mind, also meditate on it for a minimum of twenty minutes at the beginning of the day and just before One goes to sleep. Do this for twenty-one days and notice how One's living energy and life experiences begin to shift and change to align with this belief.

The universe will only respond to One's innermost beliefs, aligned thoughts and feelings. If One says something that does not align with One's underling belief, the universe will not enable this manifestation in One's life due to this internal conflict or misaligned vibrational energy pattern. It is so simple and yet so many people miss this point completely.

Because One exists here now, know that One is a worthy divine Being of the universe.

SOL DAY 82
22 March

The moment One decides to be the best version of oneself or align to One's inner soul, spirit or cosmic consciousness is the same moment that the entire universe shifts and begins to align to support One to realise this reality. As spirit and host of a human form, know that the most dominate mind–body thought is the One that vibrationally speaks to the universe. This is what the universe is listening to and will respond to in kind as One lives One's life.

No amount of praying, worshipping or wishing for good luck will change One's path in life if One's mind is preoccupied with a dysfunctional, self-limiting and negative narrative. Take a closer look at the self-talk that is going on in One's mind and reboot One's mindset.

It is time to live a new life by being well, rather than trying to do well and expect wellbeing just to show up and appear in One's life. Wellness is about creating and enjoying a wonderful, inspiring and productive day. Align One's mind, body and spirit so that One is in tune with the universe and living One's life from a place of peace and harmony with all things.

One is oneness. One is loved and appreciated for the Being that One is. Let One's creativity flow freely like a gently river to the ocean. When One does this, notice how quickly the universe will manifest One's new visions, desires and reality. Develop the habit of existing and experiencing One's life from within a perspective, spiritual bubble or aura of love, kindness and compassion.

Never be fearful of radiating One's positivity and optimism into the world. Celebrate each day that One is alive on Earth. Be a person who only attracts people that will contribute to One's living success, positive energy and healthy wellness.

The universe will always match One's highest version, vision and vibration of oneself.

SOL DAY 83
23 March

Learn to say 'Yes' to the universe and surrender to being and living in the moment.

Create space in One's life to align with the natural flow and rhythm of cosmic energy that surrounds oneself now. Notice the ebb and flow of the tides at the beach over the course of the day. Be mindful of the ongoing transition of day to night and night to day as the Earth spins effortlessly in orbit around the sun. See the cycle of life within nature through the changing times of the year, from spring to summer then autumn to winter in succession or from the dry season to wet season as in Australia. Give oneself permission to be immersed in these life moments. Learn to read the signs of synchronicity in the universe and One's life.

Motivate and inspire oneself to develop a positive, uplifting and empowering attitude. Activate an enabling mindset and new way of saying 'Yes' to all the good things that One chooses to manifest in One's life.

Rather than saying 'No, thank you' to things One does not like, reframe it and say 'Thank you for the offer, however I'd prefer to say yes to ...' This way, One is creating a visual image of the thing that One desires most in that moment. It may sound like a simple play on words, but it has a deeper and more profound intention to realign the current environment and experience so that it aligns to One's vibrational vision. This is how One changes One's reality simply by changing One's thoughts, words, speech and actions. Whatever happens next, accept it as part of the process and move on with One's life.

It is important to mindfully change One's thoughts or mental operating system so that it is purposely welcoming and proactively intentional. Consciously only invite good experiences, good people, good activities, events and occurrences into One's life.

SOL DAY 84
24 March

Great sages and Masters of enlightenment have only ever pointed the way. One must undertake the journey of inner realisation and awakening by oneself. As One moves further along this path of spiritual awareness, the deeper One's alignment to One's inner Being becomes. Even though the path may seem difficult, confusing and lonely at times, know that One is never alone in the universe. As spirit, soul or cosmic consciousness One is spiritually entangled to all and all to One. When One can brush away the dust of doubt from the mirror of self-reflection within One's mind, what One will find is clarity, certainty and a sense of complete contentment.

Learn to love the unknown and make it One's friend. It is in this space of silence that One's spirit will speak the loudest to One and guide One on One's way in life. Do not be particularly concerned with the voices of others who echo doubt, fear and uncertainty on One's path.

The right people will come to One at the right moment and in the right way. Look for the gift in every situation. These opportunities are a blessing when they manifest in One's life.

One's path in life is not to be rushed, hurried or undertaken at light speed so that One can get on with the next big thing in One's life. This is not how it works. Slow down, take a deep breath and be completely present where One is now. This is the time; this is the moment where One's life is happening. The best way to conduct oneself is like the movement of water – flow with flexibility as One is drawn effortlessly along by the gravity of interstellar oneness.

Things may appear not to make sense initially, but that is okay – go with the flow and let One's spirit and universe guide One on One's way. No matter where One is now, everything will be okay in the end.

SOL DAY 85
25 March

The way One's sees oneself, life and the universe becomes the lens through which One perceives the world that One co-creates and lives in today. The looking glass through which One has been viewing the world has been manipulated, moulded and made as a distraction from aligning with the truth of One's soul, spirit or cosmic consciousness.

When One finally wakes from this state of unconscious living, One will see that nothing really exists at all. All that appears is an elaborate, albeit very clever, illusion. It provides the perfect matrix and playground for the perceived realities of One's ego and life as One knows it.

To see things as they really are is to see the world as altered consciousness manifesting in infinite forms of vibrational energy. There is no true name for a thing and things only vary One's vibrational energy and how it is manifested in this moment. Quantum physics tells us that, at some point in time, waves begin to behave like particles and particles begin to behave as waves. The standard laws of physics no longer apply within this quantum realm.

Spirituality and science are fast reaching a point of singularity in explaining the world One lives in, where everything is as real as One believes it to be. It is also notable that when One changes the way that One looks at things, the things that One looks at also change.

In an awakened state, One will see no difference from One person to another, only a variance in the manifesting form of One's current time-bound energy. The same principle can also be applied to trees, plants and animals. While the external difference between rock and water is very apparent, on another level, they are the same, just manifesting in a different form or structure. All is One and One is all part of the same altered consciousness in the universe. Appreciate the beauty of diversity in all things, as it all originates from source.

SOL DAY 86
26 March

Do not look in churches, mosques or temples to finds One's divinity; it does not live there. Seek it not in a specific book, text or scripture either, as these may only hint at its existence. Be not tempted to blindly follow a specific spiritual guru, Master or messiah, as the path that enlightened Beings walk is alone and only unto oneself.

The truth of what One seeks lies not in any external source but within One now.

Choose 'the way' within oneself above all other paths in life. This is a journey into the unknown, where One will need to drown One's ego in a sea of spiritual light and cleanse One's mind of the dirt of deception and delusion that has been built up over time.

It is a process of great transformation and comes with unimaginable benefits of wisdom, insight and intuition.

One will reach a point and ask oneself if it is all worth it. The answer is an unequivocal 'Yes'. Just keep moving forward along the path in a positive direction. However slow One's progress is in life, it is still progress. Direction is always more important than speed.

One's egoic mind will do everything it can to convince oneself of the fruitlessness of this path and demand evidence, proof and results as to why One should still be on this journey. Know that there is nothing that will convince an egoic mind to surrender its power and control. It seeks to be in charge, even in the midst of absolute and certain failure. Whatever One thinks within One's egocentric mind it will try and prove – this way, it is in charge of the agenda. When an egoic mind has no seat at the table of divine guidance and spiritual intuition, it is without purpose. This is when One will feel most lost, yet this is the exact moment of One's greatest freedom.

SOL DAY 87
27 March

The light of cosmic consciousness shines brightly within all Beings on planet Earth. It is not in some special, enlightened few, it is within all. It has been here since One's arrival and will continue long after One's departure from this place. However, some have chosen to hide from it, others ignore it and some have decided to embrace it in One's life.

There are many paths along 'the way' and One must decide for oneself which is the best path for One at the time of its choosing. As long as One is facing the right direction, One simply needs to take the next step forward. The universe is always present and on One's side. Use this all-knowing divine intelligence and One's spirit to assist One on One's way in the world.

The practice of being deeply in the 'Now' through mindfulness meditation and mindful living will allow One to align with and access One's soul, spirit or cosmic consciousness. This will enable One to heal One's mind–body and life. It will also be an opportunity to increase One's intuitive awareness and spiritual sense-making skills.

It is this simple, yet often overlooked, practice that will assist One to co-create new ways of thinking, living and being in this present moment. Learn to undertake the practice of being a witness to all things. Observe but do not absorb. Be engaged with life and detached from it at the same time. These might sound incompatible or directly opposite each other, but they are not. One is just not reacting to anyone or anything that is before One in One's life. This does not mean One is walking the streets like a zombie devoid of any emotion. It simply means that One allows all people and all things to be as they present themselves in this moment.

In short, One is neither reactive nor judgemental. One is simply deeply present in this moment 'Now'.

SOL DAY 88
28 March

On this day, know that One is exactly where One needs to be now. All is where it is, doing exactly what it is meant to do. Sun is warm and grass is green. This is the 'is-ness' of life. Everything is in its place and there is a place for everything in this world. The universe does not create fear, human beings do this all by themselves. Danger is ever-present where it is, but this is not the fear that is created in One's mind. As a co-creator of One's reality, it is up to oneself to choose to manifest love or fear.

Let go of the linear timelines and designer plans that One has for One's life. Now is the time to trust the universe and know that it has a greater plan through One's self-realisation and awakening on Earth. Allow all things to naturally unfold and move like a wave moving effortlessly across the ocean. Everything that is meant for One will come to One. One will have not missed out on anything than is not meant for One. The universe uses divine synchronicity to ensure that everything happens exactly on time. Be patient. There is nothing to worry about and even less to fear.

Learn to be immune to the dysfunction and negative opinions of friends and family. Create an aura of impenetrable positivity, loving kindness and compassion as One focuses on being the best version of oneself that One can be in this life. What people say to and about One is a projection of other's current perceptions and reality.

Be the hero of One's own life story. Take the time to rewrite the tales of One's adventures and self-exploration as many times as One needs to get them right. Allow oneself to make mistakes and forgive oneself as easily as the sun rises on a brand new day. Do not dwell in the past or linger aimlessly in the future. Master being present and learn to live in this way daily.

SOL DAY 89
29 March

As soon as One lets go, One's spiritual path and way in life will be revealed to One.

One's mind may try and seek it, but it is One's spirit that will know 'the way'. Many paths – One way. Nothing is hidden in the darkness when One's light shines from within.

Do not be discouraged if One has spent decades or even One's entire life accumulating possessions and fine-tuning One's identity as a slave to One's own ego, only to awaken and realise that these things are merely props in the universe's play called life. One could be forgiven for thinking that One's life has been a great waste of time, but it has not. It is all part of the divine process of realising and awakening to One's true place in this world and universe. One has not loss any time at all. Everything One has done in One's life has been to bring One to this point of spiritual awareness. Without personal challenges there can be no change, transformation or awakening. Just as the metamorphosis of a colourful butterfly requires it to be a grub before it transforms into a beautiful new form and flies away, human beings need a similar mind–body transfiguration process for spiritual enlightenment before One is free to experience a new way of being and living life.

There is nowhere to go and nothing to hide from when One's way is clear.

Let go of chasing rainbows in the sky. Look inside the paradox of truth and beauty all around One now. Find contentment in the simplest of things in One's life. There is as much inner peace and serenity in a single breath as there is in all the air in the sky. Let go and just breathe …

Be like an eagle drifting on the current of the wind. See how it glides effortlessly in life, not clinging to a single thing. Learn how to fly free and live life without fear.

SOL DAY 90
30 March

Accept oneself as One is today. Stop oneself from looking at One's mind–body or where One is in this life and judging it. A seedling does not grow under the weight of the forest's expectation and neither should One. It merely seeks out the light and strives to be all it can be. At no stage of its growing does a tree doubt itself – it is an expression of its inner essence.

One is a wonderful work in progress. Continually in motion, learning, growing and changing to be the best version of oneself. Create an inner wellspring overflowing with positive self-talk, self-love and self-encouragement within oneself. Drink this water for life.

Break free from the poisonous patterns of self-generated images of fear, failing or judgement. Move One's mind into a loving landscape of self-exploration, self-inquiry and self-praise. Be thankful and grateful for all that One is and where One is now.

One has not come this far by pure chance or luck alone. Know that every step that One has taken along the path of spiritual enlightenment and life, other people and the universe have been with One too – step by step. Everyone on Earth is interconnected in this world. Every sentient Being in the universe is spiritually entangled with One another too.

Sometimes it hard to see the connection when One's life is filled with pain, fear and delusion – but it is there. At times, the stress of living and life itself can seem overwhelming, but have faith. Learn to train One's mind to rise above the ordinary and see the glorious radiant light of One's spirit, soul or cosmic consciousness within oneself now. No person, place or thing can ever hide One's true identity from oneself.

As spirit, One is not bound by the normal rules of humanity or physics. One exists within a state of infinite beingness, a divine presence of timelessness and host to One's human form.

SOL DAY 91
31 March

Wake up every morning with a sense of clarity knowing exactly who One is now. One is an immortal, eternal and infinite Being of the universe. One's primary purpose on Earth is to first awaken to One's divine self as a reflection of cosmic consciousness or source. Each day that One is alive is an opportunity to move closer or further away from One's inner Being. One's spirit, soul or cosmic consciousness is One's spiritual identity that is 'One'. There is no higher realm of existence in the universe for One to align to and experience One's divinity.

It feels good to know that One is part of something greater than oneself in the universe. Living on Earth is an utterly amazing experience. There is nothing else like it that One is aware of in this part of the galaxy. Earth is a special place that everyone has a shared responsibility to pass on to the next generation in the best state that it can be now.

One is powerful beyond measure in being able to co-create One's living reality. The question is not about what reality One chooses, but how One chooses to live within the reality that One co-creates on Earth. Will One choose to extinguish the selfish flames of greed, fear and control of One's own ego in favour of developing healthy habits of being spiritually centred, virtuous and mindful? Every chosen path creates a ripple of energy in the world.

One need only step outside and look up at the night sky to remind oneself of the magnificence and majesty of the universe. One may be a very small part of a noticeably big universe, but One is an important part of it, nonetheless. One is and will continue to exist long after the current generation of humans are merely ashes blowing in the wind. The more One can see the divinity of One's Being, the greater One's clarity will be seen in One's life now.

APRIL
Sol day 92-121

One believes that everyone has an individual and collective responsibility for both One's positive wellbeing together with the perpetual prosperity and living abundance of planet Earth. This global goal may seem like an insurmountable task, but be assured it is totally achievable in this lifetime.

Wellness does not fall like rain from the clouds, it is something that lives within One's inner mindscape and is projected out into the world in which One lives. It crosses all social boundaries and exists across the spectrum of all living cultures. Human beings have infinite potential to co-create the reality that One seeks in this world. Everything One desires in life requires the cooperation of other sentient Beings on this planet.

Never underestimate the ability of one dedicated person with one small idea to inspire and co-create an everlasting big change in the world. Ideas change lives and lives are changed by a single person's simple idea. One's life, energy and presence today are far more valuable than One realises. Now is the time for One to stand up in spiritual unity, speak out in aligned harmony and shine brightly as a sentient Being of the universe. Imagine intentionally, think mindfully and act virtuously to positively change the future trajectory of this world.

This is how One benefits everyone and all future generations on Earth.

SOL DAY 92
1 April

Divine cosmic consciousness is always present for everyone, wherever One is in the world. It exists in all moments of One's life and in every aspect of what One chooses to do or not do. All who align with it, will know it 'Now'. When One becomes aware of this universal presence, One will know that it is also a gateway to eternal peace.

As One begins to quieten One's mind and remove the egoic agendas from One's life through mindful meditation and conscious choice, One will be able to experience great unity with the purity of source consciousness. Things will flow as effortless as a summer breeze gliding gently across the land, sea and sky. One will begin to experience delightful and pleasing moments on a daily basis, as if these occurrences had been perfectly scripted into One's life on purpose. One will begin to imagine things and they will manifest in One's life like magic.

One will start to realise that this is how One's life can be now. Without trying to organise or orchestrate anything, One simply allows people and things to exist as they appear to be. One remains centred within One's soul, spirit or cosmic consciousness like a great Master, moving from one moment to the next like a gentle river flowing calmly and quietly to the ocean.

To master One's mind is to experience One's spirit fully present in One's life.

The more One tries to take control of One's mind, the more One is likely to fail at being in control. The way to do it is to reset One's living mental operating system and become spirit-centred. Know that One's mind is not the Master of oneself; its real purpose is to be a servant of One's divine expressions and virtuous intentions.

SOL DAY 93
2 April

It is time to put One's hand on One's heart and take three long, deep, slow breaths. Now is the moment to connect within and align with One's Great Divine Spirit. As One does this, it will allow oneself to be with One's inner soul, spirit or cosmic consciousness. Give oneself permission to relax, trust completely and simply let go. Shift into this space of self-awareness. Use this time to bring oneself into this free space so One can feel centred within One's divine presence. Allow oneself in this waking moment to just be ... and enjoy being.

The most important relationship One will ever have is with oneself. One needs to honour One's spirit and the relationship with oneself before One can honour others in this world. Sometimes One lets the world direct One's thoughts and life patterns in a negative way before One can refocus on One's inner wellness and spiritual Being.

Many people will walk with and away from oneself over the course of One's natural life. There will also be people who will significantly challenge One's values, beliefs and way of life. All these moments are lessons that One can use to grow and transform into a better person. This is not the time to play the blame game with anyone else or have a pity party for any loss, fear, guilt or shame in One's life. It is time to seek out and vibrate with prosperity and abundance in One's life. Let these difficult happenings be an opportunity to review, reset and refocus One's living experiences so One is being mindful, and more mindfully being.

One needs to become the centre of each and every relationship in One's life.

Give oneself the time and space to reflect on One's life lessons. Look for the gift and how it will benefit One to move forward in One's life. Breathe in everything that is for One's higher purpose and greater good. The universe is always working in One's best self-interest.

SOL DAY 94
3 April

Rest assured that One's current situation is not One's final destination in life while on this cosmic spiritual journey across the universe. One is only a visitor to planet Earth – a temporary traveller on the intergalactic highway of infinite possibilities within an ocean of conscious existence. As a guest hosting a specific human form along the space–time continuum, One's time and moments are limited here in this world. Every chance that One gets to experience and express One's divinity on Earth – go for it. Allow One's energy to be a river overflowing with joy and physical presence to be a tree of inner contentment.

Many have come before One and many more will come after One. Every child's parents die and eventually every parent's child will also pass away. Humans are short-term shadows on a transitioning landscape of life, living for only a brief time – approximately 100 Earth cycles around the sun. Make the most of living and being part of this magnificent expression of life as One knows it. Look at life through a child's eye and see the wonder and beauty every day. Celebrate simply being alive and be grateful for this opportunity to be here now on Earth.

Shared living moments with loved Ones are a unique and special gift.

Know that everything that One's experiences in One's human form has no permanence in this life. The creation of every thought or experience of every emotion or feeling will all fade over time. At the time of One's eventual passing, One will align completely with One's pure spiritual identity. Know that no human being, ancient elder, spiritual guru or enlightened Master has ever escaped One's own death. It is simply a natural inevitability of One's human form.

One's life in many respects is a living reflection of the reality that One co-creates 'Now'.

SOL DAY 95
4 April

One begins One's life with nothing and will end it with nothing. At the end of everyone's life on Earth, as spirit, One will take nothing upon returning to source or the realm of divine consciousness. All that One has accomplished and achieved over the course of One's life will be left behind for others to observe, notice and make reference to through One's current cultural lens or personal perspective. Every experience that One will have manifested in life, be it pain or pleasure, will have been out of nothing. One's real-time and worldly reality will be entirely compose of energy and matter or altered consciousness. The greatest asset that One will realise is the emptiness of space or infinite potential of nothingness in One's life.

For some people, this all-encompassing and overarching summary of One's life will be too difficult to come to terms with now. One's ego will seek to justify its actions and validate its existence. If the mind is only an instrument to be exercised in the moment, then ego, which resides in the mind, must face the fact that it is merely a humble servant and not the Master of One's life or destiny.

Make a conscious decision today to free oneself from all that does not serve One, One's higher self or One's divine purpose in life. Do this by creating space in One's life.

Little by little, day by day, no matter what One has done before in One's life, One can turn it around to become the best version of oneself. Do not replay One's mistakes repeatedly in One's mind like a broken record. Learn how to create a new and improved version of oneself. Ask the universe for assistance and it will come to One. Seek out helpful mentors, life coaches and respected persons that can guide One on One's path of reflection and renewal. Make it One's mission to change to a new way of living and being in life.

SOL DAY 96
5 April

Successful people believe in One's ability to be the Master of One's destiny.

People of this magnitude do not try and control things, but act in alignment with the way of the universe as it unfolds in front of One. One is flexible, adaptable and adjusts One's plans and actions in response to daily changes and continuing challenges. Doubt is not something that One entertains at all within One's mindscape. There are good days and not-so-good days in One's life. However, One is grateful for all the setbacks, learnings and progress that One makes as part of this special life journey. One is also very appreciative of all the people that One has met and relationships that One has had along the way trying to live a 'normal life'.

Being a successful leader means blazing a new trail into the unknown of One's own life.

One soon realises that all One desires in life requires the cooperation of other sentient Beings and the universe working in harmony to manifest these successes, so it aligns to One's new vision of reality. One can achieve anything in this world when One works in alignment with oneself, others and the universe.

When One is completely committed to honouring One's mind, body and spirit, as well as the way of the universe, amazing things begin to magically happen. Unexpected connections form with others and a flow of positive energy moves effortlessly into One's life. One projects a vision of success in all that One aspires to think, say and do. One knows that One's reality is shaped and influenced by One's visual imagery in the 'Now'. One operates with a high level of confidence, radiating prosperity and abundance in One's life.

The space between moments in One's life is honoured as much as the moments of living and being successful. Big things are created when little things work and flow in harmony.

SOL DAY 97
6 April

Waiting for no-one and wanting for nothing is a beautiful way to live One's life. When One does this, One is free to live mindfully in the present moment without distractions or disturbances. Learn to flow effortlessly in the stream of One's own timelessness. Comfort oneself in the blanket of One's own inner beingness – know that One is never alone. This way, One can weather all moments, any events or personal challenges in One's life. Immerse oneself within this silence. It is a blessing to know One's true spiritual self.

Give oneself ample time to be more intuitively aligned to One's mind, body and spirit. This is an opportunity to experience oneself more deeply by simply enjoying just being in the universe. A chance to get to know the 'real Being', the One who is always present now. One can confidently remove the social masks and familiar roles that One dutifully plays and be truly open. As the noise and busyness of life fades away, One can align with the innermost sense of One's spiritual Being. This is where One can be aligned in pure harmony with oneself and experience a level of divine intimacy like no other moment in One's life on Earth.

One is whole in this space; One needs nothing or no person to complete One. Simply affirm the great divinity that exists within One now. One is not of this world, but One's human form is.

The rhythmic patterns of the universe flow in and through all things. Everything exists in oneness and yet, at the same moment, in an infinite field of pure potentiality.

One need not wait in anticipation for some great happening or special time to come in One's life. One need only flow with life as it is now, like the sun arcing across the sky during the day or the full moon rising at night.

SOL DAY 98
7 April

Dedicate today solely to healing and nurturing One's mind and body. Turn off all electronic devices, put One's friends on pause and realise that it is okay to be gentle, lovingly kind and compassionate to oneself. As a spiritual Being and host of One's mind–body, it is important to take care of it daily, not just when One is feeling stressed. This human avatar of experiences is a temple for One's life on Earth. It needs proper maintenance, love and attention – the kind of caring that is deep and penetrating to One's very core of positive wellness and inner wellbeing.

Whatever mind–body stress has accumulated over One's work–life, be it daily or weekly activities, it is time to release it. Make 'release' a key word in One's healing vocabulary. One's healing pathway is clear when One's mind is still and free from the chatter of everyday life. Create a loving, kind space to drown out the noise of busyness in One's mind–body with silence – the silence to just be and enjoy being 'Now', being with One's mind and body. Notice how it feels in this moment. Be aware of the space that it occupies on Earth.

Say to oneself, 'It is time to release mind, it is time to release body. Release all that is painful, stressful and does not serve One's inner peace, tranquillity and harmony. This is One's mind and body (take a deep breath) – relax and release, relax and release, relax and release.'

Cultivate a path of wellness and practice positive wellbeing in One's life. Focus on resting, relaxing, releasing and renewing One's mind–body in this world. To be kind, caring and compassionate to oneself is One of the greatest gifts that One can give to support One's life and living experiences. Being healthy is about being in touch with One's inner mind–body life energy and ensuring it is at optimal levels of wellness at any age.

SOL DAY 99
8 April

The path of positive prosperity in One's life is a journey of fearless optimism into the unknown. Let One be clear here. There is enough air, food, water and shelter for all people on Earth to live in dignity and harmony with each another. Many individuals within established governance structures still choose to cling to ego matrix ideas of separateness, fear and control. This is a symptom of living life in a conditioned or unawaken state of existence.

However, vast shifts and major awakenings are occurring in One's cosmic consciousness at this time with people in different parts of the world. Individual transformations are quietly happening daily, which is adding to the critical mass of awake people living 'Now'.

More and more people are coming to realise that 'everyone is One' and part of the great oneness of life in this divine universe. One is releasing oneself from the illusions and constructs of previous generations and opening One's mind eye for the very first time and asking, 'Why is it so? What does this all mean now?' This a great time of inner reflection, deep healing and even greater awakening to what is 'Now'.

There is much to be learn from looking at One's mistakes, mishaps and modern achievements. But the greatest wisdom comes in personally knowing One's spirit, soul or cosmic consciousness. This learning can only be done alone; this knowing of oneself is best taught by oneself. A teacher or Master can only show One 'the way'. One must travel this path by oneself. This is a journey undertaken in silence. Only then will 'the way' be revealed to One.

Time matters not, when One is on an inner path of self-realisation and personal transformation. Nothing that One has achieved thus far in this world will compare to the riches that await One in this divine space of nothingness.

SOL DAY 100
9 April

In time, One will see that everything is as it should be. Some people will come into One's life and make great promises of love and light but leave as quickly as the morning dew on the grass. There are other people that will return to One's life like a passing storm or seasonal cyclone, bringing all the drama, like the downpour of damaging, flooding rains, only to run away and never been seen until next time. Then there are a few people that will journey with One, like the sun travelling across the sky, until One's death. These are the Ones who make no promises, bring no drama, only being present as One lives One's life.

One does not need experiences or people to validate One's divine existence. No external reality will ever validate One's inner truth – now or ever.

Do not waste One's life energy trying to fix people on Earth or the world. Align with the way and flow naturally along with it. Promote a dialogue of prosperity and path to peace.

The way out of individual suffering is to realise the illusion that is life. When One can see this, One will tilt One's head up at the sky and laugh uncontrollably. One will look at the world in disbelief and bemusement at all the silliness of human beings so desperately trying to control One's own life, the lives of others and nature too. When One can recognise that all the social conditioning, economic transactions and cultural programming means nothing in the universe, One will break into fits of hysterical laughter.

As One becomes less serious about life, One will be more open to appreciating the absurdity of the way most humans currently function on planet Earth, blinded by comparison, competition and addicted to greed. It is a sickening psychosis of human mindlessness and mental illness that originates from One's ego. It is a form of living intergenerational stupidity.

SOL DAY 101
10 April

One does not need to move mountains or invent the next best thing to be of value in this world. One is intrinsically imbued with great spiritual value, divine purpose and infinite potential. The universe is inherently aware of this and so should One be too. One is an awesome spirit, soul or cosmic consciousness. One is divine by design and integral to the universe itself.

One need only remind oneself that One is powerful beyond measure and gifted with unlimited spiritual intuition. One is host to a mind-body that can acquire any skill set given the right enabling conditions, motivation and encouragement. One can surpass contemporary standards or living expectations for any functional task in life and share One's learnings, knowledge and wisdom with all who live on Earth. One is most likely to succeed in life when One learns to align with One's spirit and be truly present in One's life.

It is not One's fear that scares One the most, it is One's inner light, love and oneness.

When One can align with One's spirit, know One's inner truth and speak with this voice, One will have the courage to move forward in any direction in life. One will be freely independent of the negative opinions and toxic perspectives of others as One makes One's way in this world. One will make mistakes – this is unavoidable and a necessary aspect of One's personal growth and spiritual enlightenment – but One will know 'the way'.

There are many paths that One may choose to go down and all flow one way back to source. Focus on co-creating One's own path of inner awareness and positive progress. Forget about comparing oneself to others. When the student is ready, One's Master, teacher or lesson will naturally appear.

SOL DAY 102
11 April

Be patient today. Everything in One's life is coming together at the right time, in the right space, by the right way and with the right person. Allow the synchronicity of the universe to work its magic. Give oneself space and time to heal, rest, sleep, work, learn, earn, love and play or simply be 'Now'. All good things take time to manifest. Let go and trust the process.

Create a balance of doing and being throughout One's life. Whatever One is waiting for to be manifested in One's life is already on its way to One now – give the universe a chance to unfold naturally. Stay open and committed to the vision and continually align to the vibration that One seeks. Be grateful for all the signs that indicate One is on the right path in One's life.

The universe has its own way of getting everything done, right on time.

In the meantime, work on oneself. Work on One's personal wellbeing, positive attitude and optimistic mindset. See the world as it is and not how One wants it to be. Look for the gift in every situation, circumstance and conversation in One's life. All is a blessing or learning if One chooses to see it as such. Set an intention for One's day with clarity – perhaps write it down in a life journal. Say to oneself, 'One is grateful to be alive. One feels great, awesome and fantastic today ... being this way One joyfully welcomes all positive things, people and experiences to flow effortlessly into One's life 'Now'.' Write this down on a sticky note and post it in key locations in One's home and watch how quickly the universe responses.

The more One can be patient and adjust One's doing into being in the moment, the more One will see life flowing like a continual river of moments into a great lake of One's life experiences on Earth.

SOL DAY 103
12 April

Just because One cannot see something in the world doesn't mean that it does not currently exist now. If One was asked to prove that love exists in the here and now, One would have a very difficult time holding it in One's hand, tasting it, touching it or showing it to another person like a tangible material object. Although One would say that love is a real thing, there is no hard evidence or physical proof of its existence in the world at all. One might even put One's hand on One's chest where One's heart or heart chakra is and say One's love comes from within oneself. This is an oversimplification of where One might find the source of love within a human being, but it is a great starting point for an interesting conversation.

One could also apply the same reasoning to One's spirit, soul or cosmic consciousness.

By practicing the virtue of openness, One will experience a gateway for love to flow to One, through One and in One's life. Mindful practice will allow One's mind-body to align with the divine state of oneness that exists in all sentient Beings. When One's mind-body is open and free, One is capable of loving any and all things in the universe. There is no distinction, only the beauty of oneness in its infinite diversity of all forms or altered consciousness.

Love is said to be one of the most powerful emotions that a human being can possess and demonstrate for another person or animal in One's life. It is an amazing human emotion that is a catalyst for creating some incredible human bonds and relationships between people. One will do incredible things in the name of love. This is how One experiences One's spiritual oneness for another Being on Earth. Love is all-consuming and has the potential to cause a kind of temporary blindness in the way One perceives things and relates to other people. Honour all other spiritual Beings and approach love from a place of oneness.

SOL DAY 104

13 April

One deserves to light up this world, One truly does. As One reads these words on this page, realise that One is a powerful, beautiful and amazing sentient Being of the universe. Know that what One does makes a difference in this world. Believe it 'Now'. One is good enough, One is worthy enough, One is special and divine enough. As One lives and acts in alignment, One will become a '**Bright**' or divine light warrior or spiritual worker.

One must not be swayed or influenced by others along One's healing journey or path of enlightenment. Sometimes this may mean One is going against the opinions, advice and suggestions of loved Ones, family or friends. In most cases, when One decides to live a more spiritual life, One will be going against the crowd of commonly held beliefs, group think and collective social norms. However, it will bring great joy and freedom to One's heart and mind. In the end, One will thank oneself for taking this leap of faith into the unknown.

It is okay to stand alone as a free Being, rather than drown in a tide of social fear, constrictive control and corrupt conditioning. Egoic freedom may feel lonely at first.

Good people who have One's best interests at heart will naturally welcome and support One's spiritual way of life. One will harmonise with these people's living vibrations. As for the others, One will have become a 'new age' oddity, black sheep of the family with a mental health issue or someone who has betrayed everything that One was ever taught and raised.

Take comfort in knowing that all great spiritual leaders of the past have been viewed as people who lived life on the edge or fringe of acceptable, rational and social thoughts until what One was saying shifted the common understanding into a higher vibrational pattern of conscious living. The world is a truly a better place when One shares One's light and life.

SOL DAY 105
14 April

Where oneness exits there is no 'I'. One, as spirit is oneness or cosmic consciousness and, therefore, there can be no 'I'. The self, known as 'I' is a false construct within One's personhood of identity. It has been created within One's mind to reinforce ego's separateness and to create a false sense of control and certainty. It is how ego explains and justifies variances and differences in the world to suit itself. Ego wants to be in charge of everything.

The 'I' that One so desperately clings to as a child and through One's developmental years is nothing more than a conceptual ripple of artificial intelligence on the surface of One's cosmic consciousness. One is the all-knowing awareness behind all human forms on Earth. One's form is merely a manifestation of altered consciousness, presenting itself within a space–time continuum for a momentary period of relativity. In time, One's form will disappear completely to rejoin the essence of Earth's elements – earth, air, fire and water. All of One's individual atoms and molecules will be repurposed and reused as part of the universe's field of pure potentiality.

One's true identity lies not in One's human form, language group, First Nation, gender, community, society or nation state on Earth, but in One's egoless nature as a divine, immortal, eternal and infinite Being of the universe. 'All is One – everything is connected.'

Just realising this profound spiritual wisdom will co-create a paradigm shift in One's current reality. It will open an enlightenment gateway to a dimension of infinite existence in the universe. One will not look at the world the same way again. One will see a unifying field of oneness in all things. The differences One will see in One's life will simply be expressions of the divine manifesting as variances of oneness or altered consciousness.

SOL DAY 106
15 April

An awake Being responds in the moment and not in some other time. One acts mindfully and in a way that is detached from any perceived drama, stress or negativity in One's life. One simply accepts the moment as it is and seeks to be virtuous in it.

Spirit asks, 'How can One help?' Ego asks, 'What is in it for me?'

There is nothing to be gained by taking advantage of another person in distress, discomfort or acting out as part of One's dysfunctional life patterns. Money, time and even life are all great cosmic illusions. Do not buy into it. Avoid being caught in the vortex of devaluing One's spiritual integrity for the sake of One's ego or temporary happiness. Learn to see the patterns of people who purposely and continually chase after money, power and control. Teach oneself not to play this game and instead stay centred within One's peace, tranquillity and mindful living space. Always bring oneself gently back to the present through mindful awareness.

Know that One's way in life is not a straight line. It is perfectly natural for One to occasionally divert from the path to explore or smell the wildflowers in bloom. Life is an opportunity to experience living mindfully and being present 'Now'. Know that whatever One chooses to do today, the sun will rise over the horizon tomorrow. When the morning does eventually come, stay with this moment as long as possible and appreciate the beauty of it.

Be inspired to be on Earth. Create joyful excitement within One's mind and body.

Help oneself to start the day in gratitude and appreciation for all that is in One's life. Rise with grace, humility, gentleness, loving kindness and compassion for oneself and all other sentient Beings around the world. Each new day is a chance to renew, reset and restart.

SOL DAY 107
16 April

One's intrinsic nature exists beyond space and time in a continuum of infinite beingness. It is not something that can ever be located in physical space–time or that has definable points of definition. One's spirit, soul or cosmic consciousness is everlasting and indomitable.

To try and be a 'somebody' in this world is to be a slave to false promises of admiration and importance. It is an illusion constructed by society that holds no real or ongoing value. Its only purpose is to validate the worth and special qualities of a human being by a collective, club, cohort of individuals or another person in recognition of One's living achievements and accomplishments or for exceeding a particular standard.

The divine essence of One's Being is a timeless, faceless, endless 'nobody' – a nobody of everlasting spiritual light, unconditional love and unifying oneness.

The paradox of being a 'nobody' in a 'somebody' world is that One is intuitively aligned to One's spirit and the universe. To be a 'somebody' in a 'nobody' world is to be connected only to the physical realm of One's life on Earth.

To be the best version of oneself in this world is a quest of noble and honourable undertaking. Just because One falls and stumbles along the way does not mean that One has lost One's way in life. It simply means that One is engaged in a learning and growing process – this is perfectly natural. Continually praise and encourage oneself. Give oneself unconditional loving care, kindness and compassion as One makes One's way in this world.

Being a 'nobody' in a 'somebody' world is an extremely important divine decision. This is where One will realise that One's greatest achievement is not outside oneself but within. It is where the magic happens. This is where the real work of self-transformation is done.

SOL DAY 108
17 April

Nurture, nourish and be naturally kind and compassionate to oneself today. It takes very little time to set One's intention for this day. Make today naturally nourishing and nurturing for One's mind, body and spirit. Being mindfully nice to oneself should come easy and effortlessly. Continually reward and praise oneself for completing any task or simply being kind.

The more One replenishes and fills the wellspring of One's own positive wellbeing, the more it will overflow into One's life. Do not wait for One's inner wellness to run dry before One refills it. Incorporate a wellness attitude, mindset and philosophy as a healthy habit in One's life. Take action to support this new wellbeing outlook in One's life.

Say to oneself, 'It is perfectly natural and naturally perfect to nurture and nourish One's mind, body and spirit.' Repeat often and remind oneself on a daily basis if need be.

Find a wellbeing buddy to support One's daily healthy habits. Join a group whose focus is mindful living and living mindfully. Change or expand One's friendship circle to include people who care about healthy habits, quality choices and creating positive changes in One's life.

Make a conscious decision to focus on feeling great and healthy. Be positive and optimistic about changing One's life for the better and improving One's overall wellness and wellbeing. Take this a step at a time. Keep a journal of One's progress and set realistic and achievable goals for One's inner health and wellbeing. Start with something simple, like swapping fried food for fresh food. Commit to a plan but, if it is not working, keep changing things until it aligns with One's mind, body and spirit.

Co-create a new vision, vibration and version for how One chooses to be in this world. Be guided by One's spirit and the universe to make it happen now.

SOL DAY 109

18 April

Today is a day to live life with a more focused state of inner awareness. It is a day to sit in silent reflection and quiet contemplation of oneself, One's spirit and the universe.

Create a space in One's life for meditation in the 'Now'. Learn to focus on One's breathing to surrender to the stillness of the universe and dive deep into the abyss of spacious nothingness that is 'no-mind'.

When One aligns with One's spiritual awareness, One will notice an automatic shift in suffering as One surrenders to it. A silent stream of solutions will begin flowing from within. Learn to trust One's spirit, inner voice and intuition. Practice recognising and reading One's inner spiritual compass. Notice how it gently prompts and guides oneself towards better decisions, better actions and better outcomes. Over time, One will be able to sense this more and more intuitively as One expands One's awareness when operating in real time and in life.

One will be able to intuitively sense and know things before they happen. One will be able to 'see' into the future as if it is happening 'Now'. One's ability to manifest experiences will become more and more powerful as One aligns to One's inner spirit. One will find that One can vibrate at a much higher level of consciousness than previously before and things in One's life will begin to positively shift in ways that One could have never imagined.

One's awareness is likely to expand exponentially and in every direction.

Know that One's normal divine state is inner joy and peaceful contentment. When One is operating from a conscious state of spiritual awareness, One is unable to co-create ongoing suffering in One's life or the lives of others in this world. One becomes an advocate for peace, harmony and oneness on Earth and in the universe.

SOL DAY 110
19 April

Today is a day to slow down. A day to simplify One's life and lifestyle by going slow, being mindful and moving purposely. Give oneself permission to make today a 'go slow day'. Know that the world will not end if One chooses to set this intention for oneself. Announce it to loved Ones, colleagues or the world on social media. Affirm it in a text message or video call or simply say it out loud when someone asks 'How are you going today?' It is perfectly okay not to hurry or rush through One's day or life today. Learn to practice self-care and create a sense of goodwill for oneself and others.

It is okay to move slowly and not travel at hyperspeed. Replace One's immediate tasks and life goals with a higher life priority. Give up guilt and embrace the freedom that comes from letting go and aligning to a softer, quieter and gentler inner rhythm. Go with grace and gratitude in One's life. This is the pace and tempo of the natural patterns of nature and the universe. When birds greet each other in song at the dawning of the morning sun, it is not hurried or rushed through in order to meet a schedule or deadline. It simply flows beautifully, in harmony with nature as part of being on Country (land, sea and sky).

Learn to train One's mind–body to shift into a lower gear and still get done all the good things that One was intending to do. Some tasks may need to be rescheduled, delegated or dropped completely off One's agenda. That's okay – the world is not going to end and One is not going to disappear or self-destruct into a million pieces. One is entitled to a life of peace, harmony and work–life balance as much as anyone else on Earth.

It is time to restructure One's life and reorganise One's lifestyle into 'go slow' mode. The universe is on One's side and so too is all of nature.

SOL DAY 111
20 April

The best kind people who come into One's life are those who ask for nothing but are able to inspire everything in One. One feels an automatic shift in One's presence to be positive and optimistic where One may have previously been negativity and pessimistic. These are the people that believe in One so much that One also begins to believe. These people have a brilliant glowing divine aura that radiates an extremely high vibration of love (oneness). One cannot explain it, but One is immediately attracted to these Beings even before One has met them in real life. They resonate within One. They spark and activate One's inner joy and motivate One to be all that One can be in this life.

A person of this nature loves unconditionally and loves One for being the human being that One is now. One knows that a person of this magnitude speaks and acts with the intention of encouraging One to be One's best version of oneself in this lifetime. No question is too silly and no request is too minor or trivial. One is drawn to emulate the great calm, great wisdom and great presence that emanates from this type of sentient Being on Earth.

One knows that One is in the presence of greatness because One also realises this greatness within oneself. One is inspired to transform and spiritually evolve.

Without realising it, One's old paradigm of beliefs and thoughts patterns are challenged and instantly dissolves. One is invited to co-create and manifest a new reality that is aligned to One's true nature, higher self and the universe. This person sees One's true purpose, place and potential in life, even if One does not. This person is powerful beyond measure and a positive influencer in One's life, whether One is in close proximity or on the other side of the planet.

SOL DAY 112
21 April

Today is the day to fall in love with oneself. To love One's mind and body unconditionally now.

Whatever One's human shape, colour, size, gender, complexion, DNA or culture, it does not matter. What is important is that One undertakes a self-diagnostic assessment of oneself – a truthful reflection of where One has been and where One is now.

Sit in quiet meditation and allow One's body to speak to One. Let it reveal where it hurts or where One senses feelings of resting comfort. Let One's mind–body communicate with oneself about what requires: attention, love and support. All of One's previous thoughts and actions have been a stepping stone to this moment. Listen and act with love.

The universe only gives One what One is capable of handling. Even if One perceives One's life as being in chaos, pain and suffering, it is a gift to rise above it and transcend One's current thinking, beliefs and behaviours. Look at life's challenges as gifts and opportunities.

One is the landlord of One's mind and body. One is also the housekeeper – in charge of what One puts into One's mind and body. One cannot absolve One's responsibilities for One's mind and body in life for the sake of convenience or in the pursuit of an immediate work goal or temporary pleasure. One will always need to return to being the Master of One's house.

To love oneself as oneself is a mature and highly intelligent life-giving thing to do. Do not be discouraged by the doubters for taking time out to be gentle, loving, caring and kind to oneself. It is time to co-create a personal wellbeing plan of action for One's life. A way of being mindful about One's mind and body in all that One does. Turn One's life upside down if One needs to, shift things around or simply stop doing things that are no longer in One's best self-interest or higher purpose in life. If One loses friends along the way, so be it – have no fear.

SOL DAY 113
22 April

Know that One can completely recreate oneself if One chooses to do so today. It is not how many times life knocks One down that matters, but what One does when One gets back up. Understand that nothing is fixed or permanent in this world. Just because One may have had a particular thought about oneself, does not mean that it is true or false. One is not under any obligation to continue thinking anything about oneself from One moment to the next. One does not have a thought or life contract with the universe to only think, believe or behave in a certain way. One can change how One chooses to live at any moment in time, or 'Now'.

All is vibrating in a relationship of pure synchronicity with everything else in the universe, as determined by its self-organising operating frequency. Just because One has journeyed along a difficult, challenging and winding road so far, does not mean that One is locked into travelling the same way into the future. In fact, it is best if One stops completely, breathes slowly, deeply and reflects on co-creating the best version of oneself. Reset One's intention, personal priorities and living agenda for life.

It is important to understand that One is not stuck. One has infinite capacity to change One's beliefs, thoughts and behaviours at any given moment in One's life. When One does this, One will be able to manifest a different reality and co-create new and alternative positive life experiences. Shifting One's vibration to a higher operating frequency transforms oneself.

Realise that, if One desires, One has the capacity to change oneself and One's life experiences. Now is the moment to alter oneself to reconfigure and co-create the best version of oneself. Think new thoughts, create new habits and make new choices in the best interests of One's higher self. All that matters is that One begins today and never looks back.

SOL DAY 114
23 April

It is time to reject the familiar identifying term of 'I am' and replace it with 'One is' when referring to oneself. Give oneself permission to shift One's life perspective from a mortal-based view of the world to an immortal vision of oneself in the universe.

Learn to train One's mind to serve One's divine spirit and not be a slave to One's ego.

Create an affirmation statement and say to oneself each morning, 'One is immortal, eternal and infinite. One is a divine sentient Being of the universe. One is powerful beyond measure. One is (One's mind–body is ...) creative, intelligent, positive, awesome, supported, amazing, loved, prosperous and abundant, enlightened, spiritual, excited, motivated, joyful, vibrant, resilient, kind and caring, excited, healthy, optimistic, virtuous and aligned to One's spirit and the universe.'

The more One believes in oneself, the more the universe will support One in this belief. The universe is always on One's side. It simply responds to the reality that One chooses to believe in. Whatever One can imagine or accept as being true – so it will be.

Truth is beauty and beauty is in the eye of the beholder. One may look with One's eyes, but sees with One's mind. It is this foresight within One's mind that is most powerful in shifting, changing and transforming One's perspective and place on Earth. Never underestimate One's power to affirm and co-create a new reality now.

Make a conscious decision to change One's way of thinking, perspective and life today. Even though time is an illusion and every human form is bound by it on Earth, do not make the mistake of thinking that One will always be here to access it in One's lifetime. Take a leap of faith into the unknown and know that the universe will always catch One.

SOL DAY 115
24 April

One is a free spirit, soul or cosmic consciousness. With this freedom comes One's ability to imagine and co-create anything that One desires in this life. Be consciously purposeful when setting the intention for today and One's life.

Believe in oneself and One's spiritual path on Earth. One's mind-body is pure vibration. The more One can let go of attachments, judgements and resistance to change, the more One will vibrate at a higher frequency. Everything that was every manifested into form or experience was first imagined in someone's mind. Allow oneself to align with One's wisdom and be guided by the universe in all that One seeks to be or manifest in this world.

Allow One's life to be full of serendipity as One flows effortlessly along 'the way'. The universe has an uncanny way of surprising One when One least expects it. When One stops looking or seeking something in One's life, it will naturally appear in One's path as if was meant to be.

Know that One has nothing to prove in this world to anyone. One's only responsibility is to awaken oneself and be the best possible version that on can be now. Accept people as they are and waste no energy on trying to change someone into something other than what One chooses to be. It is better to use One's time and energy investing in oneself in order to create the change that One seeks in this world.

Be a role model to all. An enlightened Being living a simple, mindful, lovingly kind and virtuous life. One's time on Earth will pass like a cloud moving across an empty sky.

Focus One's life on being free now and go with the flow of the universe. Greet each new day or change of season with excitement and a sense of wonder, joy and gratitude.

SOL DAY 116
25 April

Today is a day to acknowledge that not everyone who comes into One's life is meant to stay. Some people are meant to be guides; others bring with them specific life challenges and opportunities. Some will become One's lifelong true friend. It is time to stop holding on to people who clearly do not want to be with One. This can be a painful and bitter lesson that One may need to relearn time and time again until One clearly understands.

Be oneself in all circumstances with everyone. One's own vibration will naturally attract people who will align with One's inner peace, love and harmony. Others will fade away from One's friendship circle, like a sunset.

Remember that people do not have to like One today, tomorrow or ever. Conversely, One is under no obligation to care either. Other people's opinions and perspectives of One have nothing to do with One's own reality or self-worth. This is not about being arrogant or dismissive of others, but simply being centred on One's own individual personal life story and journey of awakening.

One needs to be the hero of One's own life – this is an absolute must if One is committed to truly succeeding and being the best version of oneself. One must write oneself into the script of living life on One's own terms as the protagonist and recognise that One's ego is the antagonist.

Set the intention of this story to awaken to One's inner truth and divine beauty, because this will be the greatest quest that One will ever undertake on Earth. Know that the divine door between oneself and One's spirit does not exist, because the wall itself is an illusion.

SOL DAY 117
26 April

Make today a day when One grants oneself three wishes. The first wish is to take much better care of One's mind, body and spirit daily. The second wish is to love and accept oneself unconditionally for who One is at this moment in time in One's life. The third wish is to make continuous positive changes to One's life to realise and awaken to One's true identity as spirit, soul or cosmic consciousness – a sentient Being of the universe.

Do everything in One's power to grant these three wishes to oneself and, in doing so, manifest a new life now. Believe in One's divine destiny, oneself and make it so. The universe is here for One – just begin now. One is the dream-maker, the risk-taker and the life-creator.

One cannot hide from One's responsibility to co-create a new version of oneself. One needs to genuinely and honestly look oneself in the mirror and say, 'Who is this person in the mirror? How can One become all that One can be now? One's new life begins now!'

It does not matter how often One stumbles, falls or fails along this path of positive quality improvement. What matters is that One gets back up, learns the lessons from One's mistakes and continues moving in a positive direction. The universe gives One what is in the best interests of One's higher self. In addition, the universe has no vocabulary for failure – its only language is that of vibrational alignment.

For One to succeed, One must first believe in One's own success. It is that simple.

One is capable of anything in this life if One believes in oneself and One's divine destiny on Earth. The more One vibrates with this inner belief at the core of One's mind–body, the more the universe will naturally and intuitively respond to One in life. Doorways to new opportunities will magically manifest before One and life will flow with ease and contentment.

SOL DAY 118
27 April

The only person who can realise and transform One's life is oneself. No-one else can and no-one else will awaken oneself. The time to begin is today, yes right now, in this very moment. Make a commitment to oneself to be open to receiving wisdom and guidance from One's spirit and the universe to make the necessary changes in One's life to enable One's higher self and divine light to shine from within.

Every day, make incremental shifts in being the best that One can be. Start small, with a mindful thought, a healthy habit or a meditation practice, and envision where One seeks to be in the future so One can make it a reality in the 'Now'. The shaping of One's destiny begins in the present. It is always achieved in the present moment and lived in the present.

There are many ways to co-create the best version of oneself in this life. Begin where One is now. Take a deep breath, relax and allow things to flow from there. Put no internal pressure on oneself that something must be done by a certain time. Figure out what works with One's work–life balance and continue to adjust One's daily routine as One moves forward today.

Use a life journal to assist with One's goals and help One stay on track throughout the week and year. Make notes on One's progress and remember to write uplifting statements of congratulations when One has achieved something or completed a certain mind–body healthy habit or positive practice.

It is also important to schedule free time into One's life, where One can do nothing. One simply allows everything to be as it is, so One can just be oneself. Many people make the mistake of over-planning, over-thinking and over-doing. Give oneself permission to 'just be' in this world. Simply sit quietly, breathe deeply and be content just being now.

SOL DAY 119
28 April

One's natural state of being is pure joy. Begin One's day from within oneself and allow things to flow outwardly from here. Be joyful in thoughts, words and actions for the entire day. Bring this feeling of lightness and delightful enjoyment to all that One meets and converses with today. Carry a joyful sense of just being in One's outlook and all that One does on this day. Notice how One's joyful energy influences and assists other people to raise One's vibration.

In fact, be joyful for no particular reason at all.

Know that the universe is not serious at all – how could it ever be like this? It was not designed to be a place for serious scrutiny, stern silences or sarcastic synergy.

In all of One's travels around the planet, One will never come across serious land, sea or sky. Serious water does not fall from serious clouds and serious trees do not grow from serious land, dirt or soil. Do not think that living life is very serious business and that One must be a serious person in order to achieve greatness or live 'the right way'.

One suggests to be the complete opposite. To get the most out of life, One needs to align with One's inner joy and radiate this joyfulness to the world. It is not the apparent external conditions or circumstances which brings most pain and suffering to One's life, it is the absence of joy within oneself. One's inner joy is unconditional.

To create more joy in One's life, One must become joy itself. Practice a joyful and grateful attitude each and every day. Look for things that bring a sense of joy to One's life. Joy is free and ever-present wherever One is on Earth. One need not pay for it, get a loan or even put it on One's credit card. Joy is available to all and at any moment. One can access joy directly from within One's inner consciousness. Align with joy and be joyful 'Now'.

SOL DAY 120
29 April

The belief that One's spiritual enlightenment and awakening only comes through a series of wonderful and profoundly beautiful experiences is sadly mistaken. There are people on Earth who experience unstructured realisations and spontaneous awakenings as part of One's natural process of living life, but this is rare and is not the case for the majority of enlightenment seekers.

Allow One to be real and honest for a moment. The path for most people is found through the experience of very personal challenges, life events or a series of activities. This usually involves going through an individual growth moment of realisation after experiencing pain and suffering. This experience or critical life incident is the catalyst that breaks One's mind free of past patterns of thoughts, behaviours and beliefs.

It is important that One acknowledges this reality and is not distracted by thinking that One should only choose to walk down a path of feel-good and life-safe selections. This does not mean that One should be risk-adverse – just mindful of the choices that One is making.

Most people who seek the path of enlightenment do not agree to sign up to a process of personal pain and significant suffering. These people simply want enlightenment on One's own terms and according to One's particular vision of awakening, so One can reach nirvana in comfort. It comes as an incredible shock to have these firmly held thoughts shattered.

However, the experience of self-realisation and awakening is a wonderful and, in most part, a divinely profound life event. It is a moment that brings with it untold amounts of inner peace, tranquil joy and an indescribable lightness to One's life. The way is to be found when One stops seeking it and allows oneself to simply be it 'Now'.

SOL DAY 121
30 April

No matter how lovingly kind, compassionate and genuinely open One is, people can only meet One as deeply as One has been able to meet oneself. Find ecstasy within oneself and be joyful that it is the only place that One will ever know it to be true. The One whom One seeks the most in One's life is already within One now. Every person that One meets in life is simply a reflection of oneself from a different point of view or divine fractal perspective.

Do not run from oneself. One has been running One's whole life from the truth within oneself. One has been escaping to the past and trying to hide in the future to avoid being present with oneself now. Stop wasting time. It serves no purpose other than to distract One's mind from where One really needs to be, and that place is here now.

One does not need to go anywhere to discover that the cosmic consciousness of the universe resides within One. It lives within all sentient Beings on Earth, not just in those who have awoken or are on a spiritual quest for One's divine cosmic truth.

To know oneself truly and deeply is to know the entire universe itself.

One's divine enlightenment exists beyond the illusion of life and death. It is in this timeless dimensionless realm that One will realise that all which is present now is merely a manifestation of altered consciousness. Part of the oneness of the entire universe. Wherever One goes on Earth, the same oneness is expressed as shifted or altered consciousness. Everything vibrating at different frequencies, arranged in various ways and endless combinations along a spectrum of altered consciousness in various forms. Face any of the four directions and see only unifying sameness in an infinite number of ways on Earth. Everything arises out of nothingness. All things come full circle in the end.

MAY
Sol day 122-152

One believes that it is possible for all people to live an awakened, prosperous and abundant life on Earth. Everyone has the responsibly to choose to be joyful for no particular reason at all. It is within the realm of each and every Earth citizen to see oneself as belonging to part of a global family with shared custodial responsibilities for this world and planet. Every act of kindness and compassion has a positive ripple effect in One's life and on the lives of others around the globe.

Being more mindful, lovingly kind, caring and compassionate to oneself is an act of creative consciousness. This simple decision has the ability to shift the paradigm of living life to better align with One's mind, body and spirit. The more One believes in One's immeasurable power as a sentient Being of the universe, the more One will see that One can co-create and shape the destiny of One's life in this world. The future is not fixed and it is One's divine responsibility to share One's positive vision for a new, unified, spiritually based Type 1 civilisation with the world.

SOL DAY 122
1 May

Today is a great day to simply let life flow. Let whatever comes, come. Let whatever goes, go. Now is the time to stop trying to drive One's life in a particular direction towards a certain outcome. Let life simply drive itself as it has always done. One is not in control of the universe. One never was or will ever be... this is important to keep in mind over the course of One's life. The universe is already in motion and exists to serve as a point of infinite reflection of source consciousness. One is simply part of the synchronicity of this celestial unifying rhythm.

Life will become so much easier when One stops pretending to be in charge and allow the universe to do what it does best. When One lets go, it enables One to experience a field of infinite possibilities in One's human form on Earth at this present moment.

One did not come here to Earth to live life just so that One can experience ongoing pain and suffering. One's aim is not to be in continual conflict or to participate in dysfunctional relationships with other humans. One chose One's parents and the beginning point of One's life for a reason. One is here to awaken to One's divine spirit and experience life as an awake, sentient Being of the universe. One is on a mission to be the best version of oneself on Earth. One is in the right place and this is the right time to fulfil One's mission so One can benefit all.

The more One becomes aware of One's divine place in the universe, the more One will be indomitable in speaking and acting with One's own inner truth. One is capable of so much more in this life than One realises. One's way is not to drive life but to be driven by it. Look around oneself now and notice how the elements of life have no particular agenda but to be a natural part of nature itself. Water flows, wind blows, fire burns and land holds.

SOL DAY 123
2 May

Today is the perfect day to start thinking positively about being free. One is already a free spirit, soul or cosmic consciousness. It is time to free oneself from One's own ego. In doing this, One will also remove greed, fear, separateness and the feeling that One is never good enough. One is free to experience anything if One chooses to manifest it in One's life. The key is to simply let go of One's attachments, judgements and resistance to change on Earth now. Know that the universe is always with One. Believe this with absolute truth and certainty.

One needs to recognise that as part of One's states of spiritual consciousness, One is free will itself. One is already imbued with this divine essence and One has the capacity to choose to be whatever One imagines oneself to be. One can also be anywhere One seeks to be too.

Know that One is free will and with this free will comes One's freedom in the here and now.

One's free spirit will never be recognised or validated by One's friends, family, kin, community, First Nation or nation state. It is up to One to seize the moment and the day. It is important to honour One's spirit and declare to the world that One is a free spirit. One is here on Earth to affirm this free will as a beautiful, sentient Being of the universe.

With One's free will, One creates One's freedom in this world and in the universe.

No human law or principle can ever take away One's inherent spiritual freedom, which exists within One's divine cosmic consciousness. One is and has always been a free spirit. Even if One's human form is bound by space and time, One's spirit is eternal and exists in infinite beingness. This is why One is always free … free to think, free to do and free to simply exist and just be on Earth as One is now.

SOL DAY 124
3 May

Use One's energy to imagine everything that is going to go well and that is going to be right in One's life today. See things flowing effortlessly in a positive direction, wherever One is. Problems are illusions created in One's mind. Rise above the noise and let go now.

Create the intention to invest One's positive mental energy in imagining the best-case scenario for oneself. Visualise being the best version of oneself on this day, during this week and throughout the year. Be open to receiving awesome and amazing opportunities from the universe. Allow great things, people and experiences to come into One's life. Now will always be the best time to accept gifts. Grant oneself permission to change for the better. Transform One's mind–body so that it aligns to One's higher self and the divine oneness of the universe.

Release One's old limiting thoughts, habits and beliefs. Co-create space to enable a new version of oneself by first imaging a new reality. Affirm it through healthy habits, mindful meditation and aligned virtuous living. One's life will naturally reconfigure to represent this new residual image that One has of oneself. Step by step, little by little, like a bird building its nest, so too can One become all that One can be in this life.

Do not look upon the journey as how far One must go. Stay focused in the present moment and on taking the next step along 'the way'. For the One who is confident in being where One is now, One will experience a sense of clarity and contentment in this space that will guide One to the next moment … and so on.

Living One's life is a path of self-realisation and inner awakening to One's spirit and divine light within oneself. Be a 'Bright', a warrior of the light, so that others may see in the dark.

SOL DAY 125
4 May

May the force be with One on this wonderful, glorious and marvellous day. Be open and invite good things to arise spontaneously and creatively within One's mind and in One's life. Today is a brand new day with new opportunities to experience life on Earth. Take a breath … quietly, calmly and with loving stillness.

Align with One's inner spirit and be patient in this moment. Do not hurry oneself to set the agenda for the day. Do not rush the process of living life itself. Remind oneself to be gentle, peaceful and kind to oneself on this day. Flow with 'the way' and natural rhythm of life.

Dissolve all expectations that One has to be a certain sort of person to be of worth or value to oneself and others in this world. One is a work in progress and all that One needs is to be the best for the moment that One is in now. Be consciously loving, kind and compassionate to oneself throughout the day. When One needs to rest, rest. When One needs to pause, stop and reflect. When One needs to engage with others, focus One's attention on the conversation or task at hand. Be fully present in this moment.

The more One can train One's mind to not react to the world that One lives in, the more One will be able to access the silent serenity and eternal tranquillity in being present in this moment. It takes effort, but One's first response to any situation or circumstance is not to react to it, but to be present with it. This might appear non-caring, but it is not. Just because something happens or someone says something does not meant that One needs to respond.

Being fully present in the moment with another person is One of the best gifts that One can give another human being on planet Earth. One's life force energy is incredibly significant and has the power to positively influence One and others' living outcomes.

SOL DAY 126
5 May

One maybe ahead or behind the wave of enlightened consciousness currently moving across the planet. This kind of inner light of change has come and gone over the centuries, ever since human beings first began to think and became spiritually self-aware.

This global pattern of shared realisation and awakening is happening faster this time, due to the connectivity of all humans on Earth. Through the internet, like-minded individuals can connect faster and align more quickly to One's inner truth and shared divinity. It is part of the natural process of a continual stream of awakening for each new generation. Sometimes it happens in pockets of communities or cultures, at other times it is more far reaching. It is safe to assume that spiritual evolutions for high order sentient beings in humanoid form occur in pretty much the same way, no matter where One is in the universe. The important part is not to destroy oneself in the process, as the whole planet undertakes a paradigm shift in becoming awake and moving towards a unified, spiritually based Type 1 civilisation with a shared realisation of One's divine consciousness.

Countless generations of humans over the centuries have allowed One's ego to be the primary basis upon which decisions were made. One's spirit has been ignored and put in the mental box of things that One does not speak about or acknowledge in One's life. There has been an unspoken cone of silence about One's eternal spirit on Earth. Spirit, soul or cosmic consciousness has been purposely suppressed and continually devalued by those egoic minded people in power who purposely choose power, greed, separation, fear and control.

However, things are changing. The best thing that One can do is awaken 'Now' and be a divine light of inspiration to all on Earth. Trust in One's spirit to know One's way in life.

SOL DAY 127
6 May

Taking care of One's mental health is an absolute necessity. It is time One makes One's mental health and wellbeing a personal priority in One's life. Scheduling in regular mental health days is not only good for oneself, it is also good for One's friends, family, community and the entire world. If everyone elevated One's mental health to a higher level of importance and gave it the same level of attention as One places on money in the modern economy, One would begin to see noticeable and significant changes in One's life, workplace and community.

Mental wellness days are extremely important to One's health and wellbeing. Never underestimate the value of investing in One's mental wellness. The mind is the tool and bio-vehicle that drives One's life. Where One's mind goes, One's energy flows. It is as simple as that. What One believes, One becomes in life. This is why One's mental health, wellness and wellbeing is so important. Do what must be done and rest One's mind now.

It is perfectly okay to take time off to rebalance, refresh and renew One's mental health. One's mind is an incredible and powerful instrument that, if used correctly, can transcend One's current level of thinking to a much higher frequency and radiate this vibrational energy into the world in which One's lives.

Peace is an inside job. The peace within One's mind directly aligns to One's state of consciousness. When One is at peace, One is capable of solving anything, co-creating awe-inspiring ideas and manifesting amazing new realities in One's life.

Remove oneself from the fabricated false truths of modern life and centre on co-creating a place of peaceful sanctuary and quiet tranquillity for One's mind, body and spirit. Always create space for One's wellness and wellbeing on Earth.

SOL DAY 128
7 May

The first step in knowing a better way of living is realising the existence of it now. Know that whatever One has been or done, that this does not matter when One seeks a higher level of consciousness and is fully present. Let today be the first day of the rest of One's new life.

Make a conscious decision to become all that One can be. In this moment of honesty and openness, invite all genuine loving people, spirits and the universe to help One on One's way in life. Say to oneself, 'One is open to receiving guidance and help from all sources in the universe to improve and be the best that One can be now. One invites prosperity and the abundance of wealth, wellness, love, kindness, compassion, patience, simplicity and divine wisdom into One's life now. One lets go of all barriers and dissolves all conditioning so as to enable a space to manifest this new reality in One's life. So be it now.'

Accept all of One's mistakes, mishaps and misadventures as life lessons. Be gentle and kind with oneself about the experiences One has had along the way. This is not a time to beat oneself up about what could have been. It is a time to focus on living in this present moment with a view of being the best version that One can be now.

All One can do is acknowledge the past and stay focused in this present moment – 'Now'.

Accept that whatever is meant for One will be present in One's life.

Now is the time for new beliefs, new thoughts, new actions and new habits. This is how One begins to reimagine and co-create a new reality and new way of life by envisioning it now. Remember that One is always only ever a single thought away from changing One's life completely. One's divine power as a sentient Being of the universe is and will always be immeasurable, beyond any human condition, law or principle.

SOL DAY 129
8 May

To make a difference in the world, One must first make a difference in One's own life. One does not need to create something incredible or start a global movement to change the world. One does not need to find a miracle cure for cancer or end world poverty. One simply needs to align with One's higher self to enable One's transformation and transcendence to One's divine essence or inner truth.

The answer to any global issue is not to inoculate or condition humans against the adverse impacts of these sufferings but for everyone to awaken within. It is time to look at oneself and the world through a more spiritually aligned lens and reject the intergenerational ego template for living life and social transactions in society. One must burn One's ego in the divine fire of truth and cleanse oneself in the flames of pure openness and honesty to be free. One needs a personal paradigm shift of One's inner perception of self and life. It is truly profound and inspiring being the co-creator of One's new way of life and destiny on Earth.

Let go of what was, accept what is and embrace One's power to change oneself.

Everything One has endured, encountered and survived has led One to this moment. One has not lost anything because One is right on time. Never doubt One's ability to change oneself, lead by example and influence the world that One lives in. One has infinite potential.

Like a raindrop falling from the sky, every act of kindness and compassion contributes to an ocean of positive wellness on the planet. One is capable of making a huge difference in this world simply by being spiritually aligned and acting virtuously to help others every day.

One is capable of great things in One's life and this world. Set One's intention to be all that One can be now. Serve One's higher self and One will also be of service to the world.

SOL DAY 130
9 May

Today is a good day to remind oneself to trust the process and timing of all things in One's life and the universe. Allow people, places and things to be exactly as they appear to be now. Let things come into One's life as easily as a leaf falling from a tree or a majestic river flowing gently to the ocean. This is the synchronicity of the universe at work in each and every moment. Learn to let go and set One's intention to flow freely with the day.

Accept that what is meant for One is here now or already on its way.

In time, all things will be revealed and manifested in One's life. This is 'the way'.

A sunrise or sunset cannot be rushed, nor can a tree grow in a single day. One cannot make the tide come in any faster than it does. Nature operates according to its own timetable and so does life on planet Earth. Whenever One is in a hurry for something to happen, be patient and remember this natural rhythm of the world in which One lives. Everything arises in One's life in synchronicity with all other things. It is important to be centred, non-attached and open to 'the way' of the universe in this present moment 'Now'.

Live life as it is, where One is. Look not outside oneself; look inside to see the light, love and grace of One's infinite spirit, soul or cosmic consciousness.

The sooner One slows down, the quicker things will appear and manifest in One's life. It is time to stop over-planning, over-thinking and over-doing things in One's life. It is time to simply be with One's inner light and allow One's spirit, soul or cosmic consciousness to guide One on One's way in life. Trust the process and that everything will work out.

Being 'the One' is the key to experiencing life in a more profound and deeper way. Simply be aware of the natural rhythm of nature and how One's mind–body needs to flow with it.

SOL DAY 131
10 May

Today is a day to release oneself from One's past. There is nothing that One has to return to in One's past life to relive, fix or feel any kind of regret or negativity about now. Everyone has made mistakes or said or done things that One could have done better. No-one gets things right the first time all the time – this is what it means to be human. There are probably a thousand things One should or could have said or done differently, but that moment has gone forever. Wishing for a different outcome will not make it so.

One is unable to fix the past by playing it over and over in One's head. One can only accept oneself, forgive oneself and be aware that One is a work in progress as One learns, grows and transforms oneself from the inside out.

Use One's lucid dreams to accept and respond to issues that One's subconscious mind is struggling to come to terms with. One is the key to inner change. Before going to sleep, create a calming ritual by cleansing One's body and mind. Light a candle or incense, use lavender oil or meditate for One's mind, body and spirit. Say to oneself, 'Whatever arises within oneself as One sleeps, One has the intuitive knowledge, wisdom and intelligence to peacefully and lovingly resolve it. One releases any and all fears, regrets and negativity that One may hold. One's spirit is free. One aligns with One's natural state of infinite pure divine light, love and oneness. One embraces One's inner child and aligns to One's higher self.'

Sleep is a gateway to the hidden world of One's subconscious mind. It can reveal things that One keeps suppressed on a daily basis. Know that no matter what arises, One will be okay. Learn to accept and love One's inner child, let it show One 'the way' to be at peace with all that is a part of One's life.

SOL DAY 132
11 May

This is the day to realise with absolute certainty that One is changing the fabric of the entire universe by simply being present where One is now. One is essential to the spiritual evolution of all human beings on Earth. Know that One is a unique sentient Being of the universe.

Keep planting seeds of positivity, inspiration and optimism in One's garden of life.

Wherever One goes, go with confidence. One is a powerhouse of positive energy and is able to shine a great light of significance on this planet. Burn as brightly as One can now. Bring One's inner joy, divine peace and life force or chi into everything that One does, thinks or says. Do not be afraid of what others might think or how the world might react to One. Stay true to oneself and learn how to be One's true genuine self. Speak from One's heart and with a great love for all people on Earth and Country (land, sea and sky).

There are different acronyms for the word 'FEAR': False Experiences Appearing Real, F—k Everyone And Run, and finally, Feel Everything And Rise.

It is time to choose to be the leader that One desires to be in this world. Will One feel more like a leader if One is leading people by running away from One's fears, or will One feel more like a leader if One is helping others to rise to the challenge to conquer One's own fears?

Many paths exist along the road of enlightenment and most of them have to do with shinning a light on One's own fear, pain and suffering. It is not until One has come to terms with One's own egoic ways of thinking, believing and living that One will truly be able to rise above this delusion and destroy it within oneself. Face One's fear with love, kindness and compassion, then One will become 'the way' that One is seeking to be.

SOL DAY 133
12 May

It is a great day to be hopeful and helpful. Make a conscious decision to connect with the divine light within oneself today. Create a safe space for One to be at peace and awaken to the divine radiance within One's spirit. Let One's light shine brightly from within, as well as upon the world in which One lives. Help oneself to be truly awake and divinely conscious on this day. Help oneself to let go of the noise of One's egoic desires and society's demands that One must think, act and behave in a certain way to be significant or special in this life.

Know that One is already a divine sentient Being of the universe and integral to the composition of the cosmos. One is not alone in life. One is part of something great. It is time to stop staring at the ground and asking 'Why?' One needs to look up to the sky and the vastness of the universe and ask, 'Why not now?'

Be a channel and champion of love, light and positive energy on planet Earth.

Know that the divine already exists within One's cosmic consciousness now. One need not look outside oneself to be enlightened, One need only look within to see One's own divine light. This is 'the way' and the path. One is not One's pain or suffering. One's experiences are merely a doorway leading oneself back to One's spiritual sovereignty.

Be aware that One has the power to set oneself free of the collective negativity and social violence simply by raising the level of One's frequency and aligning to One's higher self. Stay centred within One's own pure spiritual space of peace, love and harmony. Just because One is invited to join collective, low-level energy perspectives, activities or events of others, does not mean that One must participate in this shared experience. Stand apart without fear and be free. Declare to oneself and the world that One is here for a higher purpose.

SOL DAY 134
13 May

It is perfectly okay to remove toxic people and relationships from One's life, even if it is One's long-term friends, partner, kin or birth family. This can be a very scary decision to make, especially if this is all One has ever known. But One owes it to oneself to muster courage, be brave and act with kindness and compassion in the best interests of oneself. Know that toxic people do not serve One's higher self or higher purpose in life. It is time to let them go and cleanse the way for a new beginning.

Do not be fearful of change and the unknown; the universe is on One's side. Bring a higher level of awareness to One's place, purpose and path in life. Investing in oneself for the benefit of One's Being is a sacred, spiritual act that reflects One's divinity, not One's selfishness.

Be open to change to become more open. This is how One co-creates new opportunities and positive possibilities in One's life. If One can imagine an alternative reality for One's life, One can manifest it too. It is as simple as that. Be clear and concise with One's vision and vibrations so the universe can respond now.

All that has transpired in One's life has led One to this moment and decision point. At these crossroads of uncertainty, it is time to choose a different path, which is much more closely aligned to One's spirit and 'the way' of the universe. Give oneself permission to embrace change and be the best version of oneself today. The way is and has always been within One, no matter what the external reality was or is at this moment.

Be thankful and grateful for all the lessons of the past and use them to reconfigure a new reality in which One is operating at One's best. Be the best version of oneself for oneself and watch how the universe naturally flows in supporting One's higher self, vision and vibrations.

SOL DAY 135
14 May

Forget the rules of social conformity and collective conditioning in One's life. It is time to break free of the 'should', 'need to' and 'must do' messaging that One has been bombarded with for One's entire life. Take a moment to think and look outside the box of One's own mental matrix.

Make a conscious decision to be a Being of love and light that lives life based on a spiritual existence first. Free oneself from One's ego and egoic rules of the world in which One lives.

There are certain rules that are meant to keep One safe, maintain social order and be aware of danger, which are important for One's survival. However, not all rules are meant for One nor will they help One to spiritually evolve and be an enlightened Being on Earth. Most of the rules and messaging currently in society and across the world are extremely egocentric. These rules are there to support human social systems that reinforce separation, scarcity, fear and control. They act as a distraction from One's spirit and inner way of life. They have been purposely designed to trick and create an illusion of global fear so that One will purposely not look closely within oneself towards One's spirit.

One needs basic rules for humanity to operate and navigate the intricacies of living in a modern society. However, most of the so-called 'social rules' of society have now been distorted into perpetuating an egoic social operating system.

The way to rise above it all is to transform oneself and transcend to a higher level of consciousness. Solutions will only be created at a higher level of consciousness than that which created the problem in the first place.

A global solution will arise when most humans on Earth awaken.

SOL DAY 136
15 May

Know that One is an indomitable spirit. A divine, beautiful, loveable child of the universe. No-one can destroy One's spirit because One is unbreakable. When One truly realises this, One will begin to come to terms with the true nature of One's divinity and spiritual sovereignty.

It is a great privilege to be a divine Being on Earth at this moment. One did not come here to operate at a lower level of vibration, cause conflict, engage in futile arguments and fights with other people or contribute to the spectrum of fear in workplaces, friendship circles, on media platforms or in family, community or society itself.

One is here to awaken to One's own divine truth and be a 'Bright' – an awake Being of enlightened oneness and light warrior of the highest consciousness possible in the universe. One is here to shine a light for others to see 'the way' and be a lantern on the hill for living a mindful life filled with prosperity, abundance and awakened enlightenment.

Whatever work function One has in this world, know that it is only a role through which One can shine One's light and bring One's spirit, soul or cosmic consciousness into play. One has an immeasurable gift to bring to the world now. It is up to each spiritual Being on Earth to awaken to the divine light within oneself. It is time to shine and radiate One's love, light and positive energy across this world.

Know that wherever One goes, One is capable of utterly amazing and awesome things because One is already a wonderful, amazing and awesome spiritual Being. Never let anyone tell One otherwise. It does not matter if One falls, what matters is what One does when One gets back up and continues One's path of enlightenment to be truly awake now.

SOL DAY 137
16 May

Know that consciously kind people are kind to other people in this world and the same goes for unconsciously hurt people. Patterns of kindness, love and compassion are easily learned and can be passed from one person to another and from One generation to the next. Notice the patterns of behaviours that One has adopted as One's own living operating system. Are they kind or hurtful to oneself or other people in One's life? Take responsibility for One's thoughts, behaviours and actions. But be forgiving if One does not get it right. Life is a series of unfolding moments, not a formula to be fast-tracked on the way to success.

Know that everyone in the world is a perfectly imperfect person (both awakened and consciously unenlightened) – this is what makes it perfect. One cannot fix people; only One can heal and enlighten oneself. It is a process and journey that must be completed alone.

The best way to respond to unkindness and a lack of emotional intelligence is to be compassionate and operate at the highest vibrational frequency that One can in this moment. No matter the circumstance or situation, remember to remove oneself or One's personhood from the equation of life to allow the best version of oneself to be present now.

Meet and greet all egregious acts with compassion, a sense of quiet interest and helpful inquiry. Like wounded animals, most people in pain will act out in direct proportion to the perception of pain and suffering that One is feeling and experiencing at the time. Because that is all that One can see. Sometimes One needs to give another person space and time to settle, like muddy water in a glass, to see things clearly. In the meantime, be patient and allow the person to calm down and the situation to cool off. Ask, 'Help me to understand … why is One feeling this way? How may One help?' Then allow the situation to unfold naturally, as it will.

SOL DAY 138

17 May

Know that the universe is not in a hurry, because it has nowhere that it needs to be and no place to go. Its only purpose is to exist now. This is what it does best and so should One. This is important to remember in One's life, life choices and living practices.

Being anxious, worried or concerned that something has or has not happened or may or may not occur in the future does not serve oneself, others, the world or the universe. Stay focused in this present moment. Let go and trust the universe – go with the flow of life.

Know that life simply goes on … at its own pace. Everyone comes; everyone goes.

The sun and moon spin and rotate to their own celestial rhythms. The changing seasons on Earth continually merge into each another in an unending cycle of transformation without ever being managed by any human or external intervention. This is the true underlying beauty of nature. Everything gets done without One ever having to do anything. It is a divine miracle and a blessing all in One. What a marvellous planet that One lives on, where this occurs naturally and effortlessly. One need only be here now to enjoy and experience all these events as they unfold in the world. Everyone on Earth is very lucky to be part of these shared happenings and experiences.

Before One goes to bed, try this meditation practice. Say to oneself, 'Calm One's mind and clear One's thoughts, everything is okay, One is safe here and now. Whatever is meant for One will come to One, and whatever is not will not. One releases all negative thoughts, patterns and energy from One's Being. One is open to receiving positive energy, divine wisdom, unconditional love, prosperity and abundance in One's life. So be it now.'

Proceed with quiet patience and radiate One's positive energy into the world.

SOL DAY 139
18 May

One awakens simply by realising who and what One is now – spirit, soul or cosmic consciousness. When One has the courage to lift the veil of ego from One's mind, One will be able to see clearly for the first time in One's life. It will feel as if One has been previously living in a self-constructed false and fabricated reality. A kind of artificial unconscious living or illusionary dream state on Earth.

During this transition period, One will be able to observe notable changes within oneself. Where once, One may have thought some things to be critically important, like the accumulation of money, material items and social status, this will no longer be the case. They will hold much less appeal and attraction. Other things, like social bonds based on ego and attachments to inauthentic persona's and fake people, judgement of others, resistance to change and fear of the unknown, will be easily dissolved in One's mind.

This is the moment when others may turn away from oneself, because One's vibrating frequency has shifted to a higher level of consciousness. Friends and family may even disown oneself or think that One has gone completely 'insane'. One might even be looked upon as having betrayed the values and culture that One was raised in. There will be some people that, no matter how hard they try, will not be able to appreciate or 'get' One. These people will be blind to this awakened way of perceiving, being and experiencing life in the world.

One will have entered a time when all may turn against One and seek to discredit and disown One. One may feel great moments of aloneness on this unknown path of personal transformation and enlightened realisation.

The universe is on One's side now and always. It is One's silent partner in all of One's life.

SOL DAY 140
19 May

It is okay if the only thing One does today is simply breathe. This is a perfect way to be with oneself on this day. Breathe and be present with One's spirit, soul or cosmic consciousness. Learn to silence the mind so that the body may heal, and One may align to the universe now. Let go of all negative, dysfunctional and harmful thought patterns within One's mind. Remind oneself not to be particularly concerned about what is happening elsewhere in the world. Know that it will all take care of itself in a way that is consistent with self-organising theory and the law of attraction.

It is important to be truly present within oneself now and be an advocate for One's overall holistic wellness and positive wellbeing. Simply focus on One's breathing in this moment.

Whatever One has endured in One's life, One can, has and will always overcome it. Use mindful meditation, self-care, self-love, kindness, personal support and compassion to be a better version of oneself today. Create the space, time and habits to adopt a virtuous practice of being compassionate, helpful, accepting, generous, simple, patient and open to oneself. Learn how to invoke and practice being virtuous in all that One aspires to be in this life. Realise that everything One aspires to or desires in this world requires the cooperation of other sentient Beings on Earth.

Everyone exists within the same spiritual realm or divine dimension. Everything began and arose out of the same infinite source or unified consciousness. Therefore, All is One – Everything is connected.

Breathe out negativity, fear and separateness and breathe in positivity, love and unity. See the miracle of life in a single flower, rain drop or moment happening now and smile to oneself.

SOL DAY 141
20 May

At the beginning of each day, believe in oneself first. Believe in One's inner spirit and the universe. Believe that One's way will be revealed to One. Believe that One will be or is an awakened Being of enlightened oneness. Believe that One is a Being with great courage, passion and presence in this world. Believe that One is a sentient Being of divine love and light, and that nothing or no-one can hurt, damage or destroy One's spirit. Believe that One is a spiritual warrior of the universe. One has come here on an important mission and purpose to inspire all of humanity to rise above the ordinary to co-create a new Earth of divine consciousness. Believe in oneself completely and unconditionally. Believe without a doubt that One is and will always be powerful beyond measure.

It is time to believe in oneself first and foremost as an influencer of inner truth and a positive change agent in the world. Earth is the place and this is the time for One to be all that One aspires to be now.

Stop waiting for some special day to come along before One sets One's mind free. Focus on what matters most in One's life. Believe in what One is, what One does and where One is going now.

Many people have become lost in the customer consumption cycle of fear, temporary purchase, pleasure and loss. The only way to win this modern game is not to play it at all. One is already whole. There is no need for One to fear anything when all is an illusion.

When One believes in oneself, One knows that anything is possible. A better life begins the moment One decides to believe in oneself. Believing in oneself is like turning on the brightness of a billion suns of self-love, self-confidence and self-worth within oneself.

SOL DAY 142
21 May

Create a powerful intention today to transform, evolve and be the best version of oneself. Be present with this intention and let it reside within every cell within One's body.

It is time to be truly present and here for oneself now. Trust oneself, One's spirit and the universe. Act in the best interests of One's higher self and give gratitude for One's loving, kind heart and One's beautiful journey on Earth. Even if One has experienced a significant amount of pain and suffering during One's lifetime, it is time to clear and cleanse any and all blockages in One's life. Just because One has held something within One's mind–body in the past doesn't mean that it belongs here now or in the future.

Step into One's new divine essence so One can experience everything that One deserves and desires. Allow magic to come into One's life. Be open to new opportunities arriving and manifesting in One's life. One is here to experience speaking One's truth and true essence.

Know that One is truly worthy of love, kindness, affection, compassion and feeling whole in this life. One is an awesome sentient Being and child of the universe. Celebrate this belief within One's mind–body–spirit. Say to oneself, 'One is enough, One is worthy, One is deserving and whole.'

Accept the clearing of all that is not serving oneself and invite the guidance of Elders, Masters, divine angels and ancestral spirits. Align with One's inner Being, spirit and source consciousness. Be open to the flow of positive energy through One, dimensions and space.

It is okay to transform oneself by being clear about One's intention. Remove and cleanse all negative, limiting thought patterns and co-create a new space for a new reality in One's life. Before One knows it, One's vibrations will be raised to reflect One's new intention.

SOL DAY 143
22 May

Have faith that everything will be okay and will work out for oneself. One of the most powerful things that One can do in One's life is reassure oneself that everything will be okay. Take the time to meditate on this thought and let the truth of this belief permeate to the depth of One's inner Being. The universe was here when One was born and it will be here long after One has left this small, blue-green planet and returned to One's state of pure consciousness.

There is nothing that One needs to particularly do while here on Earth, except become fully awake and present now. This is One's primary spiritual job, role or divine life goal. What comes next will be revealed to One along 'the way'.

Know that all the answers will come to One. Silence One's mind and allow One's spirit to speak to One in this space. The universe will only give One what One can handle.

As a sentient Being of the universe, One is host to One's human form while here on Earth. It does not matter if One is host to a female, male or transgender form. All forms are a vehicle for experience and a temple of divine expression. It is a place from which to know One's truth, act with One's truth and speak One's truth in this world.

The sovereignty of One's spirit is the only true measure that One can speak with totally authority about. All other boundaries are merely artificial social constructs existing within a temporary space–time continuum. Every relationship that One will have on Earth is and will be impermanent, except for the relationship that One has with One's own divine spirit.

To have faith in something greater than oneself is to believe in the universe. Trust that no matter how dark things may appear to get in One's life, there will always be an eternal light within oneself which can never be extinguished. A continuum of infinite beingness within.

SOL DAY 144
23 May

Make space in One's life for the things that matter most to oneself. Create a short list of things, people, places and processes that value add to One's life. Now look at the list and see if One can simplify it even more. It is time to live less out of old egoic habits and act with a more loving, kind and compassionate intention towards One's mind–body first.

Before One does anything today, take a moment to say or write down three things that One is thankful or grateful for in One's life. At the most basic level, One can be grateful to be alive, to be host to a mind and body, and to breathe and be alive on Earth today.

Create a morning and evening ritual or process that allows oneself and One's partner or family to identify three things that One is grateful for prior to starting the day or beginning One's meal together. Choose something different each day. Notice that, when One is being virtuous and thinking about gratitude in One's life, it changes the energy and vibrational alignment of One's own mind–body. Now go even further and put a daily reminder in One's phone or diary that expresses One's gratitude about living life and being in this world.

One will be surprised just how much this simple task can have a big effect and positive radiating influence on One's own vibrational energy. Notice how One's life begins to shift and change. The universe will always give One what One is energetically and vibrationally aligned to the most in life. Vibrational harmony is at the core of the operating system for the universe.

Through daily mindfulness and gratitude practices, One will be able to reduce the noise of everyday living and life challenges. Every atom within every cell of One's body has the potential to align to One's greater good and support One's intentions for life. One simply needs to set the intention of gratitude and communicate it within One's entire mind–body.

SOL DAY 145
24 May

Know that One's life is bound within a continual cosmic cycle of forming and reforming. Things, people, places and processes come together and move apart from each other. Everyone and everything is vibrating at self-determined and specific frequencies. One (mind–body–spirit) and Country (land, sea and sky) radiate and resonate with a certain vibration. This is why being at the beach, in the outback or up in the mountains feels so different. Salt water and fresh water also have different resting vibrational energies. It is in this motion of everyone and everything that One experiences either holding on to something or letting it go.

The sooner One realises that all relationships in One's life are impermanent, the sooner One can come to terms with the constant change and way of the universe. No person or thing is permanent in this world. This is how the divine illusion of life works.

Developing a universal awareness and appreciation for the transitory moments of One's life will go a long way towards serving oneself on Earth. No matter where One is or what One sees, things are always changing. Just look at the evolution of Earth itself.

No-one lives forever. It is important to make the most of each day that One is alive now.

Although One may not be able to predict the expiration date of One's human form (mind–body), One can ensure One lives life well by enjoying and celebrating each and every moment with a sense of graciousness and gratitude. Stay centred within the timelessness of One's infinite Being and be thankful for the little things in One's life. Be an observer for all that is 'Now'.

Be in the moment, enjoy the moment and move on to the next moment as it unfolds in One's life. Approach life with a sense of non-judgement, non-attachment and non-resistance.

SOL DAY 146
25 May

Be patient today, especially if things are not going the way that One thought they should or need to. Everything has its time and there is a time for everything. Accept that what is coming to One will come to One in the right way and at the right moment. Take three deep, slow, calming breaths and relax ... relax ... relax. No matter the emotion or situation, say to oneself, 'All things pass and so shall this too. It is time to let go, accept the present moment as it is and relax ... breathe ... relax.' Be socially detached and spiritually present with whatever is happing in One's life now.

Do not underestimate One's abilities, gifts and skills, including One's divine alignment with One's own spirit and the universe to alter, change and influence One's life, presence and way in this world. One has infinite potential within oneself, much more than One realises. One is an incredible co-creator of One's life, lifestyle and living destiny on Earth.

One is a beautiful sentient Being of the universe and is spiritually entangled with all of source consciousness and the divine itself. Realise that this existence is eternal and timeless.

Let the fearlessness of One's spirit guide oneself into the bright light of reality. Allow oneself to shine as brightly as One chooses to be. Let no person dim, dampen or diminish One's inner joy. Express the love and joy within oneself through service to oneself and others.

One's life is meant to be lived in harmony and balance with all things, especially Country (land, sea and sky) and all that lives on and within it. Do not try and rush through the process of One's growth and development. Learn to lean into the pain so One can cultivate a new way of thinking, living and being on Earth. Live in a way that honours One's spirit and the divinity of all sentient Beings. Act without egoic expectation and live with spiritual intention.

SOL DAY 147
26 May

Be mindful that living life is a process and it all takes time. One needs time, too – time to change and transform to be the best version of oneself on Earth now. One's path of inner enlightenment is never a straight line and most often comes when One is experiencing great personal suffering and significant challenges in One's life. This is perfectly natural and a naturally perfect way to experience a change with One's cosmic consciousness. However, it is not the only path and there are many examples of human beings where One has become awake through mere meditation and mindful contemplation. Do not be deterred if One is thinking that suffering is the only path to enlightenment, because it is not.

Know that every human born on Earth is already enlightened. What happens next is that most children in the world are educated to believe in One's ego-identity, which is reinforced by social values, norms and morals for approximately the next thirty years. At the same time, One is trained to deny, suppress and mask One's intuitive intelligence and spiritual presence in this world. This all contributes to people experiencing a crisis of confidence and misaligned consciousness. It also fuels feelings of personal worthlessness, not being good enough and an inability to take self-correcting, healing and positive virtuous action.

The best version of oneself will only be revealed when One's egoic thoughts and negative streaming patterns within One's mind are dissolved, decommissioned or deleted.

For every egoic thought and attachment that One lets go of within One's mind and stored energy within One's body, there will be an unimaginable positive effect on One's life, wellness and living experiences on Earth. Be gentle, kind and patient with oneself as One's path unfolds before One. One's inner way to an awakened mindful life begins today.

SOL DAY 148
27 May

It is time to completely reject and totally dissolve the idea that One must continually work harder and harder and push oneself towards One's breaking point to be a successful human being living on Earth. One needs to wholeheartedly let go of these unkind thoughts and way of thinking. These intergenerational thought patterns falsely suggest that this type of modern human existence is necessary for a good life. Nothing could be further from the truth.

One needs to realise that society is an artificial construct, organised for the benefit of the people living within it and the survival of the population. All human systems arise out of human thoughts within One's mind. If One has a thought, it can be changed at any time.

A better way of living life is to embrace the concept that rest, renewal and reflection are essential elements of a joyful, successful and beautiful life.

The world has the technology and resources to free all of humanity. There is enough food, water and renewable energy in the world to feed everyone, so there should be no hunger anywhere on the planet. The Earth is a prosperous and abundant place for all peoples, so why is this not the case everywhere? Prosperity and abundance are not at the forefront of people's mind because some 'key elite humans' in society have chosen to adopt and upload poverty, scarcity and separatist thinking. These individuals are more interested in maintaining control and power than creating or facilitating change for a better world.

This old way of doing business originates from an egoic framework and is largely based in fear of the unknown. What most people do not realise is that there is only one human race who are all sharing the same planet. There is only one people with one collective consciousness who are all part of the same oneness of this divine universe.

SOL DAY 149
28 May

Know that on this day, One is being presented with two choices: to grow, change and transform; or to repeat the lessons of One's past. One's path of realisation and enlightenment will always be found on the road that One tries to avoid.

To quiet One's mind and be still is One of the best ways to align with One's spirit and the unbounded timelessness of One's divine essence or true nature. One does not need to do anything special to find inner peace. Wherever One is now, One is able to access One's cosmic consciousness within. Sit and practice being still with One's mind, body and spirit. Learn how to focus on One's breathing, wherever One is in the world. With each slow breath in and out, focus on relaxing into a deeper and calmer state of infinite peace within oneself.

It is time to stop making excuses, hiding or running away from oneself. Destination addiction only serves One's ego and the fear in One's mind that says, 'Any other place is better than where One is now.' Accept One's spirit, soul or cosmic consciousness in this moment.

Create the right atmosphere to promote, pamper and be positive about doing something different, so One can co-create a new way of living and being in the world today. One does not have to get everything right the first time. In fact, it is probably a good thing that One learns, grows and develops at an incremental pace that will be reflective of One's current outlook (thoughts and beliefs) and conscious awareness.

Take responsibility for teaching oneself how to align with One's spirit. Stay in those initial feelings of uncomfortableness, as they will soon pass. Ride out the wave of frustration and trust that One is on the right path. Everything will become clearer as soon as One drops the camouflage and illusions of One's false identity, persona and personhood.

SOL DAY 150
29 May

Today is a day to breathe, relax and be kind to oneself. Smile at oneself in the mirror and be thankful for being alive on this wonderful, glorious day. Wherever One is in the world is the right place for One now. Whatever One is doing today, ensure that One is present.

The world is a much better place when One is mindful of how One chooses to live and be on Earth. Act without expectation and live with love. One's future and destiny is shaped and influenced by One's vibrational energy and the level of consciousness One embraces and radiates today. Think well of oneself and recognise the distance that One has already come in One's life. Acknowledge One's scars, progress and success – One is doing great!

Let this day be filled with the enjoyment of a few of life's simple pleasures, like a cup of tea, coffee or water. Pay attention to the beauty of a single flower or the warmth and light of the sun on One's cheek. Look up at the sky and notice the openness of it all. Imagine soaring free like an eagle. Hold this thought of freedom and effortlessness in One's mind and heart. Allow oneself to experience this feeling and sensation throughout One's day and life.

Create an impenetrable shield or bubble of protective blue light around oneself in order to not let any negativity into One's space or One's mind. Keep One's vibrating frequency high. Do not sink to the low level of negative thoughts of others around One. Always look for the gift in every situation. Be 100 per cent positive and optimistic about life and living it now.

Choose to move on with One's life. Stop pondering and mulling over past mistakes and bad decisions. As hard as it is to leave these alone, One must nudge oneself continually into the present moment by asking these simple questions: 'How is One being present now? What is best for One now?' Listen in silence – the answer will always come to One.

SOL DAY 151
30 May

It is okay if One is alone today. Everyone comes into this world alone and will leave this way when One has passed One's human (mind–body) end-of-life date. Being alone does not mean that One is naturally lonely. Loneliness is a thought and feeling of being separate from someone or something. If One is aligned to One's inner spirit, soul or cosmic consciousness, One can never be alone. This inner alignment is a direct path to source consciousness itself. Within One is the oneness of One's infinite, immortal and eternal Being. This oneness is the same as all other divine sentient Beings in the universe.

Take comfort in knowing that One has never and will never be alone in the universe. One is a beloved Being of the cosmos and a divine child of the universe. One's body is made of stardust and One's inner essence is love, light and oneness. One is purposely manifested into this world and truly worthy. One deserves being here now. Be joyful and celebrate life.

Realise that One's own outlook in life can break One's mind and send One into a negative and depressive spiral of low vibrational energy, limited self-worth and diminished wellness. It is important that One rises above any limiting beliefs or thoughts that may start One off on this unkind and unhealthy mind–body path.

It is time to discover or reconnect with One's passion in life and pursue it with all the positive intention and radiant energy One can summon in this moment. Create space in One's life to rest, heal and transform One's mind–body. Upload the brightest life-giving ideas, highest positive thoughts and purest love energy. Seek out people who encourage One to be One's best version of oneself in this world, people who will challenge and support One's enlightenment path of self-realisation, inner transformation and spiritual awakening.

SOL DAY 152
31 May

One's day, life and lifetime on Earth are bound and limited within a manifested space-time reality and field of infinite possibilities. This is how the universe was and is now. Be aware of it and become awake now. A time to face the false truths of One's past, the perceived imperfections with One's mind-body so One can improve and upgrade One's life. Know that this world is always changing, no matter how solid it may appear on the surface.

Today is a day to flip the script on One's previous way of thinking and learn to say 'Yes' to new ways of living and being in this world. One has infinite power to transform every aspect of One's life into something truly wild and unimaginable. It is time to reshape and reconfigure the thoughts within One's mind and the actions that One seeks to take so One can move closer to manifesting and experiencing One's new future reality and lifestyle today.

It is important to be unconditionally upbeat, positive and optimistic about manifesting a new life. Do not listen to anyone who is trying to distract or disempower One by saying that it cannot be done or realised. Great achievements have always been accomplished by people with great visions and an unequivocal belief in oneself.

When One's vision is clear and concise, there is no ambiguity in One's vibrational alignment or the message that One is radiating into the universe.

Although One is unable to precisely predict the future and how everything will exactly unfold, with faith in oneself and the cooperation of other sentient Beings and the universe, anything is possible. Use every aspect of One's life force and cosmic energy to co-create a living legacy for all future generations. One owes it to oneself and everyone else to be the best that One can be and to manifest One's greatest vision in this world.

JUNE
Sol day 153-182

One believes that One needs to embrace the unknown and dance joyfully to the rhythm of uncertainty in One's life. Just because One cannot see something doesn't mean that it does not exist. Many things will appear and manifest in One's life, especially when One least expects them. This is particularly true at times when One is guided by One's intuitive intelligence to be somewhere and somehow it all just falls into place.

This is the magic of synchronicity – the universe's default operating system for life and everything. When One's inner beliefs are clear and concise, the universe will align to One's vibrational energies and co-create this reality in the world. Believe and it will be so ...

SOL DAY 153
1 June

There comes a point in One's life when One needs to embrace and accept oneself completely (mind–body–spirit). At the very core of this process is the acceptance of One's divine spirit, soul or cosmic consciousness. If One chooses to not hold this space, One will continue to suffer in ignorance and denial of that which is One's true essence in the universe. There will always be people who will inspire One to be better and more aligned with One's inner way and divine consciousness. Invite these people into One's life, make friends with One or use One's learnings, teachings and pointing's to guide One's life and living now.

Be fearless in confronting One's own self in a positive, gentle and lovingly kind way. It is time to get real with oneself. Artificial pleasures will never satisfy imaginary desires. Know that One is whole. There is no external validation that can compare with the divine joy, peace and oneness within One. One needs to own One's mistakes and let them go now. Release any trapped negative thoughts or harmful energy into the universe. Open a space within oneself for positive change and inner transformation. Just begin today.

As the sun rises each and every day, create an outlook within One's mind that begins the day by acknowledging to oneself that today is a lovely, beautiful day to be on Earth. Make a point of operating from One's spirit centre, and be virtuous to oneself and everyone else in the world. Allow oneself to be open to receiving gifts of wisdom and guidance from One and all. Be mindful and move through the day as if One is a spiritual Being visiting here for the first time.

Help others in this world by helping oneself first. This does not mean that One is selfish, rather One is selfless in serving oneself, others and the universe. One must first cultivate peace, love and harmony within oneself. Then One can co-create this change in the world.

SOL DAY 154
2 June

Not everyone on Earth will understand or like One's human form, personal energy field and projected personhood today or tomorrow. This is okay, be patient with oneself and others. Hold space in One's heart for shining and sharing the best of oneself with the world. It is not other people's job to 'get One' or love One unconditionally. Being lovingly kind, caring and compassionate to oneself is One's own responsibility. As long as One is speaking One's truth and acting in a way that aligns with One's virtues, values and vision, everything is sure to work itself out in the end. Like-minded people will naturally be drawn to One throughout One's entire life. Look for the signs and be open to the ways that people can connect with One now.

No matter who or what One encounters in life, do not let anything disturb One's inner peace. Trust in the natural process of life that the universe will resolve any and all things.

Create the space and time to simplify One's day and One's life by only focusing on that which is right in front of One at this present moment. Let the sun shine, the wind blow and the rain or snow fall. Allow things and people to manifest in One's life as they choose to. The more One can let go, the more One will be able to experience less complexity and chaos. This will create space for greater serenity, tranquillity and peace to manifest in One's life.

There will always be human issues of disharmony and dysfunction in the world.

Know that every lake, river and ocean on Earth has been filled and replenished by single raindrops. Small things make a big difference. For the world to become a conscious Type 1 civilisation, One needs to bring a higher level of consciousness to all of humanity by being this now. When everyone is awake, it will light the way for every future generation.

SOL DAY 155
3 June

The only person who is going to make a significant impact and difference in One's life and on One's lifestyle is the One who is reading this sentence now. This is the truth. One may have grown up in a nurturing family unit and had the best teachers, coaches, mentors and Master to guide, support and advise One in life, but at the end of the day, it is still One's responsibility to co-create the change within oneself. It is okay if One fails, everyone does. It is a natural part of the process of living, growing and changing.

There is no easy way to say this. One has to take intentional action or it will not happen. Just do it ... now! The love, light and oneness within One needs to be shared with the world in One's own unique way. The world invites and welcomes One now. Lean into this moment and set oneself free from One's ego so that One can share One's gifts, imagination, ideas and beautiful light with other citizens on Earth. Do not hide in the shadows of self-doubt, self-loathing and internalised fear. It is time to be truly present in One's life. This is how One makes a positive difference in the world. The world and planet Earth needs One now.

Surrender all attachments to people, places and things so that One can be free and truly be oneself. Be One's true and authentic self. People crave real, genuine and authentic conversations, connections and relationships with each other.

Millions of people are suffering from being overloaded by information and are unable to switch off the continuous flow, bits and bytes of data. It is time to draw an invisible circle of proactive and personal protection around oneself to keep One safe. One needs a light warrior attitude and aura to defend oneself against all the destructive, divisive and damaging memes on social media platforms and outlets around the globe.

SOL DAY 156
4 June

One is a magnificent spirit, soul or cosmic consciousness at One's core. Recognise that within One's true divine essence is a bright light of conscious oneness and love that can never be extinguished in the universe. Sit, stand and walk with pride, knowing that nothing needs to be added or subtracted from the beauty of One's inner Being. Joyfully celebrate that One is a kind, compassionate and loving person. A beautiful Being of the universe. Never regret choosing to be a kind person in this world. This is what the world needs now.

There is no shame in being gentle in One's manner and attitude, or easygoing about living life in a spirit-centred way. It is appropriate to be considerate of others who are in pain and suffering along One's own personal journey of enlightenment – these attributes are a genuine strength, show great character and are part of One's superpowers. When others step back, it is time to stand up and be truly present in One's life.

How One projects oneself to the world is a direct reflection of One's inner beliefs, residual self-image and vibrational energy signature. Whoever One has encountered and had a relationship with in One's life was meant to experience One's divine light and personal energy at that time. What was meant to be has already happened. What happens next is unknown and will be revealed to One within an infinite field of possibilities.

The ups and downs of life will always be there until One learns to ride the waves of change and smooth out One's life so that it feels easy and flows gently, like a soothing river.

The more One becomes comfortable in the knowledge that One is a force for positive change in the world by being the source of One's own positivity and optimism, the more One will be able to influence and shift the world around One, simply by being oneself.

SOL DAY 157
5 June

How others filter, reframe and receive One's words, thoughts and personal energy is completely out of One's control in life. One can no more stop the rain from falling from the clouds or the sun shining in the sky than regulate the thoughts of another human being on Earth. This is the wonder and mystery of independent thinking and spiritual free will. People can and do continually choose One's own weird, wonderful and wacky thoughts all day long.

Anything that One does or says in the world will always be filtered through another person's lens. There is nothing that One can or need do about it. Accept that how One chooses to perceive One's reality is a very personal and intimate choice. Everyone's lens or looking glass will be influenced by whatever One is carrying around in One's head at the time. Never try to guess what is in someone's mind, simply ask and invite One to share One's thoughts, ideas and perspective. Be present and listen without an agenda.

One will always have a better chance of establishing free-flowing and open conversations with another person if One can create a shared and safe space for dialogue – a space without judgement, resistance, opinions, criticisms, disapproval or blame.

Good communication is a great enabler that can inspire and motivate people to think more positively or differently about One's self-perception. One can always rise to the challenge to be the best version of oneself. It is extremely important to stop any negative self-talk and replace it with a narrative that is nurturing, encouraging and inspiring. Positive self-talk is the key to building a new narrative about oneself. Even if One does not feel it at the time, talk lovingly to oneself with words of kind-heartedness, compassion and loving care.

SOL DAY 158
6 June

What One's thinks and believes, One becomes. One's life journey is a reflection of this living and universal principle. If One believes that One has the power to intuitively heal oneself, so it will be. Learning to heal One's mind–body with natural and modern medicine, without creating a change in the relationship with One's mind–body and spirit, may only be a temporary fix. One must look beyond the initial treatment and more deeply into the presenting cause to cure One's limited wellness, condition or illness completely. Otherwise, One will find oneself in a never-ending cycle of pain and ongoing suffering.

Long-lasting healing requires One to change the thoughts in One's mind, lovingly heal the collective living wellness of One's body and shift in alignment with One's inner spirit.

Know that One's mind–body is a gateway for One's human form to experience being alive and living on Earth. One may have thought that One was invincible when One was young, but One soon learns that One's mind–body is a physical and mental record of all the impacts, accidents and adventures of living life.

To lead oneself out of the experience of illness or suffering, One needs to turn One's attention to finding and walking the path to positive wellness. Any pain in One's mind–body is a lesson that One needs to understand in order to be healthy. The major sickness of modern society is a denial of One's living wellness and a result of subjecting oneself to too much stress and pressure to achieve, accomplish and attain a particular outcome.

The outcome for all needs to be an overall sense of living wellness and a high level of personal wellbeing. Never doubt that One has the ability to change One's life, living experiences and positive presence in the world.

SOL DAY 159
7 June

Today is a good day to undertake an audit of One's relationships in life. Some will be based around a loving, spiritual connection, some will be based on a shared living trauma and others will be based on mutual convenience, interests or opportunity. There will also be relationships that do not easily fit into a box or category. Not everything needs to fit neatly into a square for it to be valuable or of quality in One's life.

One will intuitively know if One is in a toxic relationship and what One needs to do to extract oneself from this situation. Learn to listen to One's inner voice and be guided by One's spiritual intuitive intelligence. Rest assured that One's perfect companion, partner or lover is seeking One at this very moment. It is just a matter being mentally, physically and spiritual aligned so that this experience will manifest in One's life.

One owes it to oneself to remove all the negative thoughts patterns in One's mind that have kept One locked into an unwholesome situation and mindless repetitive cycle. One needs to free One's life of poisonous partners, harmful unhealthy habits and toxic living today.

It is time to break free of the fear in One's mind and find a new way of living and being in the world. Sometimes it is helpful to find a motivated friend to help One with these personal challenges. Invite and seek out help from all sources to be a better person. Know that One has the power to begin living a better and healthier lifestyle. It is okay to ask for help – everyone needs help at some point in One's life. Ask the universe for immediate assistance and then be proactive in manifesting One's new vision, new reality and new life. Take the first step today. Feel the fear and do it anyway. The universe is on One's side.

Know that One has infinite potential to change and be the best version of oneself.

SOL DAY 160
8 June

As difficult as it may be, trust that where One is at this moment of One's life is exactly where One needs to be now. Wonderful, amazing things are unfolding in One's life. Stay calm, be positive and always remain open. One never knows what might wash ashore into One's life when One allows the universe to do what it does best. Be patient with the tide of time and let things flow easily and effortlessly in One's life.

There is nothing as beautiful as watching a flower bloom where it grows. With nurturing, loving kindness and compassion, everything reaches its full potential in life. This is how nature works and how One must be with oneself.

Stop wishing that One were somewhere else in One's life. Learn to let go of the things One cannot control or manipulate. Live life where One is now – this is the trick to making the most out of life and living in the moment.

Gently and softly bring oneself back to the present whenever One feels One is being pulled away by the currents of the past or the future. Being present is the only place where life happens.

Fear not what the future may hold or bring to One, for One's time is now in this present moment. As the rain falls from the sky and across the land, seas and water on planet Earth, everything in nature is replenished. There is a time to be born, a time to grow and experience living life on Earth and a time to return to the source. One is an integral part of the circle of life in the cosmos.

End One's search to fulfil ego's empty void in One's mind. Be aligned to One's spiritual sanctuary and eternal place of tranquillity in the world.

SOL DAY 161
9 June

One has a choice each and every single day that One is alive on Earth. One can move closer to One's spirit, soul or cosmic consciousness or further away from it. One has the power to choose to be excited, inspired, motivated, light, graceful or joyful. One can also choose to feel blessed, humble or grateful. It is up to One to choose how One sees oneself and the way that One desires to live and be in this world.

Never let the thoughts and feelings of others influence One's ability to change One's sense of spiritual identity. Sometimes external events may trigger One's emotions, but this is only a sign that One needs to do more work in this area. Begin from One's spiritual heart first.

Be an influencer of peace, love and prosperity in this world. Change One's mind-body to raise One's harmonic vibrations of inner joy and carefree happiness, then radiate this feeling and energy out into the world. The higher One's vibrational energy is, the less chance there is that One will be affected by people at lower unconscious levels of existence in the world.

One owes it to oneself to be the best version of oneself in this life. Never regret or be ashamed of continually evolving and recreating oneself. One's external identity is only an illusion for another's point of reference. Keep believing in oneself with unconditional love and an unending commitment. Never give up and never surrender to the mass of unconscious human beings on Earth. One is not lost, One is simply finding One's way in this world.

The more One frees One's mind, the more One will align to light, love and oneness in life.

There is something special about knowing that One has the power to choose to be a different person today. Be aware that One is not attached to One's past. At any moment, One can change direction to be an improved version of the person that One was a moment ago.

SOL DAY 162

10 June

Difficult moments and relationships come into One's life to teach One lessons. They are blessings in disguise and One should look upon them as gifts and seek out the learning within these experiences. Often these situations or people challenge One's preconditioned beliefs and thought patterns about the world – how things should be, must be and can only be for One in this life. Know that all relationships are impermanent. Even the Earth that One is living on now will eventually be obliterated into stardust with the collapse of the sun.

If One allows oneself to be open, One can learn from all of One's life experiences. Difficult endings will often disguise new beginnings. If something is falling apart in One's life, this probably means that something else is coming together at the same time. When the universe closes one door, several other doors or pathways are bound to be presented to One. Choose wisely from a place of positivity, love and optimism – not fear.

The primary lesson in all relationships is letting go – letting go of all attachments, judgements and resistance to change in One's life. Often lessons in One's life will become louder and more significant if One fails to heed the message the first time. The universe will at first silently 'spiritually tap' One on the shoulder to nudge One towards a better way of living life. When lessons are repeatedly and continually ignored, it will put a brick wall in One's path, in the interests of One's higher self.

Learn how to read the signs in One's life, in One's mind–body and along One's way in this world. Everyone and everything is available to help One. Simply silence the voices of self-doubt, endless chatter and noise in One's mind. It is in silence that One's spirit and the universe speaks to One.

SOL DAY 163
11 June

Know that what One believes, thinks, says and does co-creates One's reality on Earth. One cannot control the people, places and happenings in One's life. However, One does have control over how One responds to things, circumstances or activities that occur. Just because something happens at a particular point in One's life or on the planet does not mean that One should immediately react to it. What One gives One's attention to, also flows One's energy towards it. Be mindful that One has limited energy each and every day that must be renewed and replenished. Invest wisely, consciously and mindfully.

Between action and reaction, there is space. It is in this space that One's freedom exists. Freedom to choose how One would like to live One's life on Earth in this present moment.

Do not be pulled into the vibrational vortex of other people's agenda in order to please them or have these people value One. Learn to stand with dignity and confidence in One's spiritual sovereignty. Acknowledge the situation as it is and honour the spirit in all Beings. Be helpful in the way that One approaches others and ask without reservation: 'How may One be of assistance?' Allow whatever comes next to unfold naturally and effortlessly.

Be mindful of One's capacity to be helpful and seek out others more qualified or with more knowledge of what is being asked of One. Have no agenda other than being present in spirit and virtuous in mind and action. Things will naturally take care of themselves. The universe has got this ... One is referring to all of life, of course.

The way One feels about oneself and others will be filtered through One's internal beliefs.

Know that One's form (male, female or transgender) is not good or bad. What One does with it is up to One's intention and how One chooses to co-create One's reality in this world.

SOL DAY 164
12 June

Have the courage to rise above One's imaginary fears and walk One's unknown path. This is the path that One has always been attracted to and is inevitably drawn towards. Just because One cannot see the path clearly does not mean it doesn't exist. Muster One's bravery and inner nerve and take that next step along One's path to inner realisation and awakening on Earth. Be bold and have a go … if nothing else, at least One will have learned something about oneself. If One falls, get back up. Keep moving forward with positivity and optimism.

Sometimes One can feel alone when One is struggling to meet life's daily challenges. In these moments, surviving may seem very overwhelming. Press the pause button, take a long, deep breath and have a break. This is exactly what One needs now. Know that within One is an unshakable faith in One's spirit and that the universe is always on One's side. Do not give up. This world needs One's presence, gifts and magic today. Pause and hit the reset button as many times as One needs in One's day and in One's life.

Never ever feel guilty about looking after One's mind and body. One is host to One's human form on Earth and One needs to take good care of it. Use whatever time, support, resources and advice One needs to pamper, nurture and nourish One's mind–body. What One does for One's mind also affects One's body. The two are interlinked. Never apologise for creating space in One's life for relaxing, refreshing and renewing One's positive wellbeing.

It is okay if others do not understand One's attitude to being a healer for One's own life. In time, people will see the value of being mindful and having a positive attitude to One's personal wellbeing and overall living wellness on Earth.

SOL DAY 165
13 June

Always start the day by accepting the beauty of One's divine spirit, being grateful and having a lovingly kind, joyful and super-positive intention for this new day. Look in the mirror and say to oneself, 'One is a beautiful divine Being of the universe and today is going to be a wonderful, magical and truly positive day on Earth.'

Allow the experience of prosperity and abundance to easily and effortlessly flow to One in One's life. Look upon the simple act of breathing as a brilliant blessing and being alive now as a truly divine glorious gift. Smile joyfully and celebrate One's living adventure on this amazing, unique, blue-green planet.

Know that every moment throughout the day can never be relived or returned to in this life. Like water passing through a fishing net, moments can never be caught, only captured through video and photographic images as a record of what happened and was experienced. That is why it is so important to live each and every moment to the fullest. One never knows how many moments One has on Earth. One's human form and experiences are bound by time.

Whatever One admires in others, use to inspire oneself in this moment.

One must respect, treasure and support oneself to be the best version of oneself in this world. If One only knew how important One's spiritual presence here on Earth actually is, One would be truly astounded. Know that everything in the universe is also within One. Ever since One was a little child, One has been aware of One's divinity and cosmic connection to source, the universe and everything. Over time, One's teachers, friends, family, kin, society and social networks have denied One's spiritual place and sacredness in the universe. However, One is and will always be an enlightened Being.

SOL DAY 166
14 June

Today is a day to know that gratitude keeps One focused on the good things in One's life and not the lack of something or someone. Be aware of what is already part of One's life and appreciate this occurrence and manifestation. Thank the universe for being able to experience it in this moment. Every atom on Earth is exactly where it needs to be; nothing needs to be added or subtracted from Earth's alluring natural beauty.

Being gracious and showing gratitude, no matter how small, will always be a blessing in One's life. Know that the universe is always listening and responding to One's harmonic vibrations. Building a virtuous life based on One's gratitude is a good recipe for ensuring future experiences of simple prosperity, abundance and divine alignment with the universe.

See every greeting with another human being as an opportunity to honour One's spirit and give thanks. There will come a time when these people will no longer be in One's life. Let One's gratitude cleanse the way for all who come to One and all who leave.

The easiest way to give thanks is with a genuine, loving, kind smile from the divine essence of One's inner Being. A smile costs nothing and has the power to light up someone's day. Give freely of oneself and expect nothing in return. Be joyful for the opportunity to give and give well. Do not let external circumstances or situations stop One from sharing this joy with others. Be a rainbow of love, light and oneness in this world.

The more One is grateful for the simple things in life, the more the universe will align with this vibration and give One more of the same.

Be grateful for One's overall health and positive wellbeing. Also be grateful when One is healing and nurturing oneself out of unwellness and restoring One mind–body to balance.

SOL DAY 167
15 June

When One is more aware of One's own vibration, One is better able to focus on co-creating One's new version of oneself and reality. One will always attract things, people and experiences into One's life that align with this vibration. One is already a cosmic magnet for all the things that flow to One now. To change One's living destiny, all One has to do is alter and adjust One's core vibrating beliefs, thought patterns and healthy habits. Change One's inner self at One's human core. Sometimes this requires small changes, other times it requires a complete dismantling of One's preconditioned sociocultural beliefs and assumptions about oneself.

Know that One can make a course correction to the direction of One's life at any moment in time. One merely needs the motivation and positive intention to do so. Remember that One's life is not fixed, it never has been and never will be. Change is a constant in the universe.

To work on healing oneself, One needs to create an intentional healing thought stream filled with gentleness, love and lots of positive energy. Be open to being guided by One's spirit and the universe. In order to co-create peace in One's life, One must first create peace within oneself. Conflict in the world only arises when there is conflict within oneself. When One is free of mental conflict, One will be able to radiate at a high level of vibration and bring this harmonic energy to where One is on Earth. Be mindful about One's inner landscape and bring calmness, a quiet sense of serenity and eternal peace to all. The first step in living a lovingly kind, compassionate and peaceful life is knowing of its existence now.

Know that One's outer life is a reflection of One's inner way of believing, thinking and being. One's job is to do the inner work – let the universe take care of the rest of the world.

SOL DAY 168
16 June

When each new day comes into existence, choose to not be overly concerned with the negativity and unkindness in the world. Learn to stay calm in this present moment, then shift One's focus and energy to co-creating a better life for oneself.

It is okay to have clear boundaries for One's protection, safety, health and positive wellbeing. Learning to say 'No' to unhealthy activities and 'Yes' to healthy habits. This is a clear sign that One is on the path to being a better version of oneself. Never feel guilty when One is making a choice to act in One's own best interest and higher self. In order to break a bad habit, One needs to create a new habit for One's life.

Sometimes it takes time to get things working just right, so be patient with oneself. Know that direction is more important than speed. Good results for One's mind and body take time; they do not happen overnight. Create the vision for a more improved version of oneself and enlist the support of other people to help One along the way.

If something fails or fails to happen, remind oneself that One is not a failure. Never give up and never surrender to One's own self-limiting doubts or negative self-talk. Learn to rise above the noise of One's ego and encourage oneself to think, be and act positively. Life is lived in the moments that One is alive now, not in some arbitrary number or figure to be attained in the future. Be proud of where One is and how much One has overcome, endured and achieved so far.

Every challenge in life is a learning and every personal obstacle is feedback to use to grow, change and develop into the new and improved version of oneself.

SOL DAY 169
17 June

What One does today co-creates One's future reality for tomorrow. What matters most is that One does One's best in this moment and on this day. This is all that One can ask of oneself. If One is unwell, take time out to relax, heal and recover. Know that One is not a machine but a living entity in this magical and marvellous universe.

Use One's life and living energy on Earth to honour One's spirit and the divinity in all.

Ask not what this world can do for oneself, but what One can do for the people of this world. In this question lies One's answer to One's way in life and on this planet. Work out what One can do today to serve others in a way that is consistent with One's 'Mission Directives', then do it with all of One's heart, passion and spirit.

One is worthy, One is whole and One deserves peace, love and harmony on Earth.

One did not come here now to be part of a mass mindless movement driven by One's ego. One's preferred lifestyle is not to live in systems of perpetual egoic virtual slavery, working until One exhausts oneself completely and finally drops dead at work. As the fog of ego clears from One's mind, One will see an enlightened truth in this world. One will notice with great clarity the rhetoric of unawake individuals who fear prosperity and abundance for all. Egoic driven people promote a globally shared illusion of unending suffering and fear – a world without hope, only collective economic enslavement and socio-political servitude. People who operate with egoic programming have no real intention of bringing about meaningful and sustained change, prosperity or abundance.

But One does have a choice to change and become all that One can be – an enlightened and awakened Being of the universe or 'Bright'.

SOL DAY 170
18 June

Know that One is smart enough, attractive enough and worthy enough to be loved here on planet Earth. Being here on Earth is justification enough that One belongs where One is now. One's divine presence is a beautiful blessing in this world, One simply needs to see it, feel it and believe it with all of One's Being. Let this be One's truth and radiate this positive life-giving energy into the world and universe. Co-create this reality today.

One need not do anything special in this world to be of value; simply existing is enough. With One's spirit and manifested human form, One has the potential to do and be anything that One chooses, in cooperation with other sentient Beings. One's destiny lies not in the opinions and validation from others but within oneself now. Stand tall and, if One has to, stand alone for the things One believes in.

Know that with One's great realisation comes One's great awakening. One is imbued with infinite potential to co-create any reality or living experience in the universe.

Never be swayed by One's mind's doubt or the limited thinking of One's divine spirit and presence in this world. One has a gift and it is time to share it with the world now. Learn how to continually prioritise One's life's priorities and extract One's life from the modern busyness that pushes and pulls at One. It is not what life throws at One that is important, it is how One reacts to it in the moment that creates the path for One's life.

Remove the temptation to be less and rise above the ordinary to be more. More virtuous, more kind, more compassionate, more loving, more caring and more aligned with One's inner spirit and the flow of the universe itself. This world needs One now, more than ever before.

SOL DAY 171
19 June

It may seem like the world is drowning in a sea of information, yet starving for wisdom at the same time. But have no fear, for within One is an eternal divine light of conscious knowing and intuitive intelligence. Do not be fooled by past storytellers of promises of fame and fortune or the modern media drug dealers whose only wish is to have One addicted to a diet of sensationalism and hopelessness, sprinkled with fear and fantasy.

Turn off this electronic stream of dysfunctional and disempowering thoughts and images. Turn on the light within One's spirit and tune into the intuitive silence with which One's spirit speaks to One in this world. To hear this inner spiritual voice, One must be still and quieten the mind. This is the way out of the constant noise of modern day living and to be free. It is a gateway to being totally present in everything that One does and will ever do now.

The flow of information is not One's concern. What is important is that One realises how to switch off from the noise of modern living and become present with One's inner spirit, soul or cosmic consciousness. Meditation and mindful living offer One a way to be still, calm and quiet. Allow oneself time and patience to align with One's divinity, then One will know an infinite peace that is ever-present within One's inner Being.

All problems are illusions created within One's mind. Realise this truth and freedom.

Whenever One is confronted by any issue, concern or choice, know that the answer will always come to One. Pause, breathe and be patient. Meditate and knock on the sky. The answer will echo from the cosmic voice of the universe within One.

Everything happens according to the universe's divine timing and synchronicity. Little by little, everything always falls into its perfect place. As the world changes, so does One.

SOL DAY 172
20 June

From this day on, look upon One's life as a series of unfolding learning moments and living opportunities to know One's inner spirit, soul or cosmic consciousness. It is time to realise One's true potential on Earth. Everything that One has encountered, endured and survived has assisted and shaped One's growth, development and progression to this point in time. All things are in motion and everything is changing in this world. Look around oneself and take the time to notice the signs of One's life and living transformation.

Be open to anything and accept everything in One's life. Use each moment to facilitate One's personal transformation, higher purpose and life goals.

The more One honours the divine spirit in each and every person on Earth, the more One will be in tune with the oneness of the universe itself. Look beyond the surface and superficialities of the masks that others wear. Gaze deep into another person's eyes and bear witness to One's inner spirit. No matter where people are in the world, or whatever One's appearance, language, culture, race, tribe, nation or function in society is, One is the same as everyone else. Learn to see One's inner light and know that this light of eternal awareness and presence is the same in all Beings in the universe. It is only One's ego that separates one human identity from another by comparing external differences. Know that all human identities are false truths and simple projections of One's egoic perceptions.

Even the idea of being a spiritual person is misleading, as One is spirit and host of a human form.

When One changes One's perspective in this world, whatever One observes will also be changed too.

SOL DAY 173
21 June

Let all of life be all it is today. Accept the reality of this world before One. Do not waste any energy trying to change what is, only try to realise the truth – all of life is an illusion and there is no reality but that which is co-created by oneself.

The more One embraces and aligns with the natural flow of the universe, the more One will experience an effortlessness and ease in One's life. This may seem like a simple way to look at things, but trust One's inner knowing and intuitive sense of reasoning to discover this living awareness for oneself.

Know that One's life on Earth did not come with a rule book or a master plan. It is all a process of self-discovery, self-realisation, self-transformation and self-awakening. Learn to read the signs and trust the process of life, the universe and everything.

The only person who can awaken oneself and bring the ultimate paradigm shift to One's life is the person reading this sentence. No other person on Earth can cause another to be enlightened or awaken from One's state of unconscious living. It is a path and a process that must be undertaken alone. There is no special place, ritual or rites of passage that will hasten this quest for inner wisdom and divine enlightenment.

One is already enlightened. One simply needs to remove all the obstacles from One's mind–body in order to realise One's own divinity and experience One's inner truth in this world.

No magic potion or spell can or will cure the egoic prison within One's mind. One must look beyond the illusion of the door to One's freedom and realise that there is no wall that can ever contain One's inner light, love and oneness in this world and universe.

SOL DAY 174
22 June

Embrace the uncertainty of life today. Even though One may not be able to predict all that may happen in One's life, choose not to be afraid. Say to oneself, 'Today is going to be a good day, no matter what happens in One's life.' Look at this day and One's life with a sense of unconditional positive optimism. Promote a feeling of acceptance that everything will work out well. Make the unknown a friend by looking at it with a sense of wonder and curiosity.

One's life is a grand adventure, so live it fully in the moment. One never knows how long One has on Earth before One's life and time reaches its expiry date. There is so much beauty in this world. Open One's mind and see for oneself.

When One's mind is not being lead or driven by One's ego, One can see the beauty in the simplest things – the early morning rays of sun on a colourful flower, a coastal sea breeze on One's face, birds singing in the trees. Life is truly beautiful, so stop for a moment and appreciate where One is now. Life is a miracle worth living.

Step into the light of One's inner joy and do not be afraid to live. Spend time with loved Ones and make new friends and connections. Step out of One's comfort zone and get excited about experiencing something new. Take a journey that One has always wanted to go on. Stop running away from oneself and embrace a new life today.

As scary as it may be to take the first step, just do it. Lean into One's fear and learn with every step that One takes in life. Slowly but surely, One will get there. One will conquer One's fears and overcome any and all obstacles in One's life. Be patient and ask the universe for help, guidance and support. Do everything with a great sense of love, passion and gratitude.

SOL DAY 175
23 June

Before One was born, One was spirit, soul or cosmic consciousness existing in an infinite continuum of beingness. One was pure awareness itself. When One realises that birth and death are only doorways to and from One's human experiences on Earth, One will realise that all is an illusion and that the only reality is within One now.

Upon knowing this truth and understanding it completely, One will experience divine peace within oneself. One's human desires will fall away as naturally as leaves from a tree. There will be nothing to be gained from the outside world by acquiring it as a possession. One will only require necessary functional items for One's survival, but this will be limited if One is mindful about living a spiritual life on Earth.

The temptations of material objects will be looked upon as an unnecessary oddity and the people who try and obtain 10,000 things or more will be seen as living a futile egoic lifestyle. One's relationship with oneself will be paramount and hold a high degree of importance. One will come to value One's spirit and alignment within One's mind, body and spirit as a great accomplishment and worthy life goal each and every day that One is alive.

There will be a point in One's life where One realises that within the cosmic ocean of existence, there is and will ever only be One.

One is already free, so how can One be bound by any human thought or social construct. Wherever One goes in life, on the planet or in space, One will be able to align with One's inner joy and radiate it to the world and the universe.

The more One lives a spiritual life, the more One will be free and able to remove pain and suffering from One's life on Earth or among the stars.

SOL DAY 176
24 June

Today is a day to co-create One's new reality in the image of One's divine Being. Know that the universe is not withholding anything from One. One simply needs to strip away the ignorance of One's ego and remove this mental fabric in One's mind like used clothes. Burn these rags of prejudice and judgement from One's mindscape immediately. Learn to get rid of these layers of thought and egoic reasoning from One's inner self-image without hesitation or mercy.

Know that One is not One's thoughts. One exists beyond anything that One has ever created or put in One's mind. Every belief that One has ever held in One's head was put there at some point in One's life. They can be deconstructed, dissolved and discarded as easily as dust blowing in the wind.

Everything of divine importance that One is seeking in this world is available for One's direct knowing in life. Be still and it will come to One in One's time of need and asking. Be patient and ask the universe – it always responds in silence and in kind.

No other human being on Earth has any magic or mojo that One needs in order to be the best version of oneself. One is an incredible sentient Being of the universe with unimaginable gifts, insights and wisdom.

With every new day comes a new opportunity to remind oneself of just how special a Being One is. While the rest of world gets caught up living in a psychotic illness of ego, One can practice social distancing in favour of living a life that is in harmony and balance with One's spiritual alignment, mindful wellness and positive wellbeing.

The more One practices self-care, self-awareness and self-alignment with One's mind, body and spirit, the more One will co-create a better way of living and being on Earth.

SOL DAY 177
25 June

Use each day as an opportunity to train One's mind to be clear and calm. Clear of any distractions, temptations or desires One has in this world. Calm about any and all issues, concerns or worries in One's life.

One of the easiest ways to be calm with a peaceful mind is to practice mindful meditation and focus on One's breath. Sit quietly in a place where One will not be interrupted and focus on One's breath. One breath in. One breath out. Slowly, calmly and quietly … just breathe. Notice how, with every breath One takes, One's body and mind falls into sync with this natural body rhythm. Do this for at least ten to twenty minutes a day, or longer if One feels the need.

Sometimes it may feel as if One is missing out on things in One's life. Be reassured that One is not missing out on anything. Whatever was meant for One will come and be present in One's life. Relax and be patient. Everything is working in perfect synchronicity with all things.

When One meditates, One will find that thoughts arise in the mind. This is what the mind does. The rising of thought is not an issue during meditation, it is the attachment to the thoughts that often causes One's anguish, anger or anxiety. Be an observer of One's mind as the thoughts come and go. Pay no particular attention to any thought. In time and with practice, One will learn not to feed the thought or give it energy. It will simply and naturally dissipate back into the nothingness from which it originated.

Eventually, after some practice, One will be able to calm One's mind with ease and centre One's living present within One's natural breath anywhere One is in the world. Nothing will bother One or be of particular concern. One will feel a great peace and inner joy within every breath that One takes by oneself.

SOL DAY 178
26 June

One's ego lives in fear and seeks validation and approval. This is not who One truly is. The outward role or human avatar that One plays in life is a concealing mask for operating in a society that is afraid of One's divine self. Many are so frightened to look within One's spirit, soul or cosmic consciousness that One will do anything, no matter how stupid, to avoid coming to terms with One's inner Being and divine presence in this world.

Countless individuals and communities around the world work, live and play in a false egoic economy. Most are pretending to be something that One is not. Playing the game of ego and being a character on the stage of life gives rise to the futility of living a fake life.

One dare not speak One's truth for fear that One will be labelled 'insane'. To speak One's truth is a sign of bravery and courage.

One needs to unlearn all the egoic lessons that have been taught to One since birth. All these false truths have trained One's mind with the belief that to be valued and worthy in this society One must achieve, acquire and assert ownership over things of recognised modern contemporary Western value. One must show One's wealth through external symbols of power, control and material objects. One must continually and relentlessly work hard and never question the purpose of the materialistic mindset or corporate consumer culture in which One lives. One needs to be mindless in One's passage through this world, working until One drops dead of effort and exhaustion. One's purpose is to be a slave to money, endless debt and controlled by One's ego. Many in leadership positions want One to believe that One is not here for the greater good of humankind, the Earth, the universe or simply existing and being.

It is time to listen to One's inner spirit and wake up now.

SOL DAY 179
27 June

Make a commitment to oneself today to be attentive, aligned and aware of One's place in this world. Too many people on this tiny planet are rushing around each and every day, trying to get something or go somewhere without ever realising that there is nowhere to be but here on Earth. Be truly present and radiate One's light, wherever One is in this world.

Put oneself first and give oneself love, kindness and compassion to be the best version of oneself. One does not know how long One will be here, so make the most of each moment and living a virtuous life every day One spends in this world. One's presence here is a divine blessing.

People and circumstances will always challenge One, but do not give into this frustration. Rise above it and take on a lighter way of looking at the world. Everyone is wading through the stream of life at One's own level of conscious awareness. Some are bogged in the mud of pain and suffering, some are caught in the quick flowing currents of temptation and desire, and others have risen to the surface and realised the lightness of living life without attachment, judgement and resistance to change.

Then there are those who have become a 'Bright', choosing to experience an existence on Earth that is lighter than air itself and live life in a euphoric state of divine enlightenment. These Beings are truly awake.

Without struggle in One's life, One would not grow, develop and transform into a better version of oneself. Welcome all challenges as opportunities to be a better person and awaken to One's true inner oneness or divine existence here on Earth. The more One spends mindfully with oneself, the more One will realise the wholeness and completeness of One's divine Being.

SOL DAY 180
28 June

It does not matter if it takes One 100, 1000 or 10,000 steps to reach One's life goal or vision. Simply face the right direction, then take the next step. All One must do is move in the right direction to be the best version of oneself. One is already on the path of positive self-improvement. Have confidence in oneself. Learn to lean into One's fear and move with self-assurance in the directions of One's dreams and future vision.

Direction will always be more important than speed in One's life on Earth.

By the divine light of One's Being, know that One is destined to be all that One can be in this world. What society fears the most is One realising who One is and becoming fully awake in this world. Imagine a planet of fully awake divine Beings co-creating a unified spiritually based Type 1 civilisation. All going about One's business mindfully with conscious awareness and a shared sense of a global purpose. The way the world would work would be very different to the way it is now. Know that this is coming soon. The planet is experiencing a change in the way that people relate to oneself and others on Earth. Many are beginning to question the old paradigms and egoic systems of social control. More and more people are realising that there is something messed up about how the world currently works. People are waking up to One's divine essence and inner spiritual truth.

Repetitive, mindless work–life cycles will eventually give way to mindful awareness, loving kindness and healthy habits. Look within oneself and see the beauty of One's divinity for oneself. One need only realise One's spiritual sovereignty and surrender to it. There is so much more to life when One becomes a 'Bright'.

SOL DAY 181
29 June

True friends help One become the best version of oneself. A good friend encourages One to look inside oneself and see the divine Being that One truly is in this world and universe. People like this naturally encourage One's personal growth, wellness, self-care, mindfulness, healthy habits and inner mastery of One's thoughts and feelings.

A true friend honours the spirit within One and all others in this life.

These friendships promote a sense of proactive positivity about being alive on Earth. Through conversation, One is gently nudged to stay on track in looking after One's own wellbeing and being the best version of oneself. These friends often shine a light on One's harmful addictions, negative self-talk, limiting beliefs, unhealthy habits and closemindedness. Honesty is a trademark for being in One's company and there is a sense of comfortableness about how One chooses to live One's life on the planet.

These special human beings often radiate a life-giving aura of positive energy and love.

If One is surrounded by people who enable One's unconsciousness and promote living a life of ongoing pain and suffering, know that these are not One's true friends. One must dig deep within oneself and summon the courage to seek out new friends and friendships in life. One needs to break free of One's current unhealthy friendship circle and co-create different connections in the community. It is in One's best interests to co-create a wellness circle of friends who promote love, kindness and compassion.

When One changes One's own inner vibration to a higher level, it will naturally attract others of similar positive energy. This will become One's new friendship circle, vibe or tribe in life. Focus on One's overall wellness and positive wellbeing – let the universe guide One.

SOL DAY 182
30 June

Every path that One chooses to take in life leads back to 'the One' or divine oneness of the universe itself.

Make this the day that One chooses to dissolve and cleanse oneself of all of One's past mental conditioning, social expectations and relationship conformities. When things happen in One's life, know that One has a choice between taking specific action or simply reacting. Ego will always want One to senselessly react by lashing out, being aggressive or running away as fast as One can. Instead, step back and choose a different response to this or any situation. Pause and take a long, slow, deep breath. Learn to be a witness or silent observer of One's mind at this moment in One's life. Make a pledge to oneself to do no harm to oneself or others on Earth. Take the time to create space, stillness and silence.

Too often, people react to situations and circumstances with One's emotional auto pilot engaged. Turn off this automatic response to life and learn to master One's emotions (thoughts and feelings) differently. Find One's inner key to co-creating change.

One owes it to oneself to be a better person and not overreact, or not react at all.

As hard as it may seem, it is okay to take no action. People will often want to draw One into different perspectives about One's personal pain and suffering. Respond by saying, 'That's interesting. Why does One think this way?' It is not One's job or responsibility to agree or disagree with anything that another person says or does in life. Everyone's behaviour is a reflection of One's own internal mindscape and level of conscious awareness.

What is important is to stay centred within One's inner peace. Be spiritually present without attachment, judgement or resistance.

JULY
Sol day 183-213

One believes in love, light and oneness within all sentient Beings living on this beautiful planet now. A time is fast approaching when all will realise the need to wake up to a better way of living and being on Earth. The old ways do not serve anyone any more as the world transitions to a unified, spiritually based Type 1 civilisation.

It does not matter what One has thought or done in the past. What matters is that One embraces One's divinity and spiritual sovereignty. Do not compare oneself to others; focus on being the best version of oneself now. The moment is here and the time is right for One to realise the greatest within One. The more One frees oneself from the restrictive shackles of social conditioning, entrenched egoic thought patterns and unhealthy learned behaviours, the more One will be able to embrace freedom in this life and within the world.

A new way is coming and it all begins when One chooses to be free now.

SOL DAY 183
1 July

Today is a good day. It is important to find and discover something positive about each day that One is alive on Earth. Show gratitude for all the wonderful things in One's life. Aim to be the best version of oneself on this wonderful day. If One is alone, accept this aloneness time by oneself. Know that the universe is always on One's side. Laugh, love and live joyfully within this moment. Radiate a great sense of loving kindness and joy into the world.

One does not need to be in the company of another individual to feel loved or valued in this life. Learn to be a loving, kind and compassionate person towards oneself first. Take care of One's mind and body. Practice living in alignment with the **seven key states of consciousness** within One's spirit, soul or cosmic consciousness. Dive deep into this space of infinite peace and tranquillity. Experience the serenity of One's inner Being through the stillness of quiet and calming mindful meditation. Make time to co-create a space for One to immerse within the timelessness of One's spirit. Open a gateway into the infinite beingness of One's existence and realise just how awesome a divine sentient Being One is now.

No matter what One does or does not do on this day, the Earth will continue to spin and rotate around the sun. It is okay to take time off and be kind to oneself. If One's body is tired, rest it. If One's mind is busy with too many thoughts, calm it. Switch off and slow down. Unplug from the pressures of modern life and pause with peaceful patience.

Often the simplest solutions in life are the best. Do not overthink or overdo things. Just flow with the river of life as it happens. Know that whatever is happening is happening in synchronicity with all other things. Repeat this simple phrase: 'Life goes on, this is life.'

Be content and patient with small steps in the right direction, because this is all that life is.

SOL DAY 184
2 July

Do something today that frees One's mind, so One can naturally align with One's spirit. Realise that there is nothing to hold on to in this life, because all things change. Walk in peace, love and harmony with life and 'the way' of the universe. Remove all things and people in One's life that no longer serve oneself, One's living wellness or positive wellbeing.

It is vitally important to keep nourishing and nurturing oneself daily. Know that a garden will only thrive when it is well attended and watered with care and kindness.

Always choose to live in the light. With this intention in mind, things will get better and better. Make One's life as effortless as One can. Choose to flow with change and life. Embrace the unknown and welcome the opportunity to be the best version of oneself. Changing One's perspective is one of the easiest ways to changing One's behaviour. All thoughts precede actions on Earth and elsewhere in the universe – imagine a new reality and manifest it now.

Every great leader at some point in time has thought about giving up or throwing in the towel in defeat. But during these moments of self-doubt, unworthiness and lack of confidence, One realises that One is an indomitable spirit and that nothing or no-one can stand in the way of One's spiritual path of success.

One must rediscover this spark of inspiration and let it guide One's way in life. Fan the flames of victory by giving oneself a burst of brilliant, loving thought energy. One is and will always be powerful beyond measure in this life or the next. One can achieve anything in this lifetime with the cooperation of other sentient Beings on this planet.

With great intentions comes even greater outcomes. Believe – imagine – act in alignment.

SOL DAY 185
3 July

What if One truly realised that everything that One had been taught from birth was a lie to satisfy the collective ego of the society in which One was raised? It would be a total shock. One's first reaction would be denial, then disbelief and perhaps anger and, finally, acceptance. A statement of this nature would generate important questions about One's overall life, plans, expectations and destiny.

Mainstream media has been manipulating information to the masses since it acquired the technology and capability to do so. Successive social frameworks and governance stakeholders have been keeping One's thought processes busy and conditioned by an egoic meme of separateness, selfishness and social slavery. While 'old world' physical slavery is now abolished, it has been replaced by a more insidious form of economic slavery.

Currently, everything in this world is set up to promote division, divisiveness and dependency through continual competition and comparison to each another in One's local community. Any ideas, dialogue or discussions related to One's spirit, soul or cosmic consciousness has been steadily suppressed and drowned out by the white noise of egoic voices that emphasises, fear, greed, power and control.

Global unity and freedom for all Earth citizens is frowned upon. It is socially and economically discouraged on a worldwide scale. But things are changing. Not because the system has broken down, but because people are beginning to wake up.

The tide is turning and there is nothing that current governments or nation states across the world can do about it. With the reach of the internet and flow of information around the planet, people are reaching out to each another to ignite a shift in global consciousness.

SOL DAY 186
4 July

Begin each day with a positive outlook on life. Start by seeing things as they truly are and not how One wants or desires them to be. Let go of One's frustrations about oneself or others. People only change when One is motivated to do so by oneself. Most people are never taught how to change or be the best version of oneself, so it is up to One to learn and teach oneself the skills of continual quality improvement. One can never fail if One's intention is to be One's best in life now.

Yesterday is gone forever and tomorrow will never arrive because it is always in the future. Today is the only day to be 'the One'. Choose to be awake and spiritually present now.

Be the One who nurtures and nourishes One's mind, body and spirit. Be the One who co-creates and constructs new realities that align with One's spirit, soul or cosmic consciousness. Be the One who gives oneself unconditional love, attention and affection. Be the One who builds healthy habits and relationships in One's life. Be the One who lives a virtuous life and sees the best in people. Be the One who is open, accepting and understanding of others. Be of service to oneself, other people and the universe. Be mindful and an awake sentient Being of the universe. Be joyful and compassionate in every aspect of One's life on Earth.

Radiate One's inner peace, love, kindness and compassion into the world by simply being oneself.

When One believes that One can change the way One thinks, One will experience this reality now. Be patient with oneself as One reforms and reshapes the neural pathways in One's brain and retrains oneself how to 'think mindfully' with a positive outlook on life.

SOL DAY 187
5 July

One exists beyond One's human physical form, mind and space-time reality. One is a nameless, timeless and limitless Being of the universe. There are no 'real' words that accurately describe One's state or states of existence as spirit, soul or pure cosmic consciousness. For all intents and purposes, One is immortal, eternal and infinite.

This may come as a shock, but One's true identity is not a 'human being' at all.

This is a very profound statement that One may need time to come to terms with while living on Earth. Most humans only think of oneself as being human, when in reality One's mind–body is only a human avatar with which One experiences life here on the planet.

Every sensory input that is absorbed by One's human form influences One's signature energy. The reverse is also true. One can generate One's signature energy and aura by simply shifting One's perception, thoughts and beliefs. If One chooses, One can become a galactic generator of positive and mindful energy in this world. There is nothing stopping One from rising above the negative noise and toxic talk in One's life and operating at a higher frequency. All it takes is a profound belief in who One is and the will to make it so.

It is not One's fear that scares One the most, it is One's love, light and oneness to be all that One can be in this world.

There has never been a better time in life to realise One's infinite potential to change, transform and awaken to One's divine destiny. Many may think One has gone 'insane' or lost One's mind. But the truth is, most unconscious humans are living life in a zombie-like psychosis. It is these people who are operating with a mental illness, thinking that One is sane being a slave to One's ego and egoic thoughts.

SOL DAY 188
6 July

Somewhere, deep inside One, exists the divine free will to change and transform oneself completely into the best version of oneself.

Every person has the power to change the world by changing oneself first. One need not look outside of oneself to see this, One merely needs to realise that what is inside One's spirit is greater than anything on Earth.

Know that people can only meet One at the level at which One has chosen to look within oneself. Take a moment to dive deep within One's spirit, soul or cosmic consciousness. Look into the void of nothingness and step into the unknown with courage and confidence. Let One's inner light shine as brightly as One can and burn away any fears One has in the cleansing flames of spiritual enlightenment.

It is time to realise One's true divine nature and become awake now.

Only One's ego, false truths of personhood and illusions will be burned in the flames of spiritual realisation to reveal One's true essence and divinity.

There has always been 'the way' to self-realisation and self-transformation.

One's journey along this inner path of spiritual alignment started a long time ago and will continue endlessly into the future. Finding One's true path in life may require One to become completely lost along the way. Only then will One's spiritual compass point in the right direction, true to One's inner light, peace and oneness.

Make no mental demands on this present moment or insist that it give One something or remove something from One's life. When One can do this, One will discover a sense of living freedom without pain and suffering. Then just flow with life as it is now.

SOL DAY 189
7 July

Today is the perfect day to give One permission to change One's life story.

Know that One's story is not fixed and can be rewritten as many times as One chooses. In addition, One has the power to change every aspect of One's human experience on Earth. There is nothing as powerful as being the hero of One's own story.

Be brave, kind and loving to oneself on this amazing adventure called 'life'.

Train oneself to be efflorescent – in a state of blooming, flowering and development. Wherever One goes in life, go with all of One's love, passion, heart and kindness. Align with the oneness of One's spirit and never give up. One has so many beautiful reasons to be alive today. Make every day a joyful adventure so that it adds to One's amazing story. It is time to fall in love with living One's journey on Earth.

Whomever One chooses to be, be committed to being a champion of compassion and kindness throughout One's own story in this world. Surround oneself with people who imbue a similar positive energy of joyful delight and positive optimism. Invite the universe to assist and support One in co-creating the best version of oneself. Develop a vision board of where One seeks to be in a year, five years or ten years. Enlist the help of others to manifest One's new reality in One's lifetime. Anything is possible with the cooperation of other people.

One is and will always be a divine light in the universe. No person, thing or process will ever extinguish One's inner glow and spiritual radiance.

One has no obligation to anyone on Earth to be the same person One was five minutes ago. One is capable of rewriting the script of One's life and changing the ending at any moment. Changing One's intention will change the trajectory of One's life now.

SOL DAY 190
8 July

One of the most simple, courageous and important things that One can do in life is to show up and be present.

Stand up for oneself first. This means being fully present in One's own life without the drive and desires of ego. This is the year and decade to act with loving kindness, care and compassion for oneself, loved Ones and others on Earth. Look oneself in the mirror and say to oneself, 'It's time – time to co-create a loving space and place in One's life for oneself.'

This is not about being selfish, it is about being sensitive to supporting One's mind–body and aligning with One's spirit. It is about giving time and energy to co-creating a sacred sanctuary for living a spiritual life in balance and harmony with all things.

When One gives oneself unconditional love and affection, One raises One's own vibrations to a higher level and thus, by default, also serves all of humanity. Just by focusing on One's wellbeing, One is co-creating a higher frequency of wellness in One's life and the lives of others in One's family, friendship circle, relationships or the community in which One lives.

The more One can be there for oneself, the more One can be there for others. It may seem difficult, but it is not. In order to quench the thirst of others, One must first replenish the water of life from which One draws One's own sustenance and survival. When One removes the guilt from One's mind and makes oneself a loving priority in One's life, wonderful, magical and amazing things begin to happen. One begins to discover that One can tap into an endless and infinite stream of cosmic loving energy. It is like an internal tap has been left on and things flow endlessly from within oneself, as if One is directly connected to the source – which One is.

SOL DAY 191
9 July

Let today be a day of review, reflection and renewal. Look at the menu for One's mind and all the things that One has been feeding it to date. Has One been filling One's mind with junk ideas and toxic thoughts, or has One be nurturing it with a calming, kind and compassionate stream of thinking? Thoughts are like clouds in the sky – they come and they go.

Whatever One vibrates in alignment with, One becomes in life. Be mindful in choosing One's thoughts and setting the intention for One's day and life on Earth.

Do not blindly learn things just because they are being taught. Use One's intuitive powers to look beyond the surface of information being offered to One. Upgrade One's lifelong learning goal and adopt this simple phrase: 'Educate oneself to be the best version of oneself.'

Learn to question that which does not sit comfortably with One. Go into a deep state of inquiry and seek out the truth about the issue, concern or worry. With great doubt comes an even greater discovery of One's true nature and higher self. Be open to One's intuitive spirit.

There will be times in One's life when One will question One's thoughts, mind and path. It is perfectly okay to not have everything all figured out right away. Remember – One's life is a living process. Things are always changing. One is a beautiful work in progress, so go easy on oneself. Simply flow with life now.

When One looks for an answer, One will surely find it. Every problem ever created is solved at a higher level of conscious awareness than that which created it in the first place.

Releasing One's attachment to the issue will often be the catalyst that frees One's mind and allows One to directly experience the infinite wisdom that dwells within One's Being.

SOL DAY 192

10 July

Make the most of One's time and living moments today. Enjoy all that life has to give and offer One on this gorgeous day. Time is like any other resource on the planet. It is important to maximise it for the benefit of One's life. But do not think for One second that One has ever lost time itself, because One never really had it to begin with.

The funny thing about time is that it may appear to be always passing, however it is just an elaborate illusion within an infinite space–time continuum. One is already a timeless Being.

When One can realise that the wealth of One's spiritual existence is in a dimension or realm of beingness, One will begin to appreciate the timelessness of One's true existence. Do not seek to attach oneself to people, places or possessions. They are but momentary manifestations in the world. All things will eventually dematerialise into the emptiness of nothingness from which they initially arose.

Know that there is no time. There is no three-dimensional physical matter, only a convincing space–time illusion that makes it appears as though it is all 'real'.

One's ego thrives on certainty and control. It will always try and convince One that there is not enough time to do this or that. In reality, time is all around One and nowhere at the same moment. What One perceives as time is merely a reconfiguration of matter and energy or the shifting of altered consciousness in the universe.

Time is not important – being awake and living mindfully is.

The more One focuses on time, the more it will appear that One is limited by it. Instead, focus on co-creating One's life and living experiences by simply being in the moment. Forget about time and live for the joyful and loving moments in One's life.

SOL DAY 193
11 July

Today is an exciting day to be positive, brave and courageous. Being courageous is not about acting in the absence of fear within One's mind. It is acknowledging the fear and then leaning into it so One can conquer and rise above it. Any fear that One perceives is a construct and illusion of the mind. It does not actually exist. Learn to see One's fear for what it is and One will be free to do, say and be anything and go anywhere in this world.

To make a great positive difference in One's life, begin with small, simple, achievable steps. All great things that have changed the world forever were accomplished by people with a simple idea and flowing process. Follow through on One's vision with easy, incremental thoughts and actions. Some of the greatest achievements of humankind have been accidental discoveries and unintentional innovations. One is a great Being – believe and it will be so.

Be open to discovering the best that life has to offer by simply being oneself. Seek out people who inspire One and surround oneself with other positive people in One's life. Grow One's friendship circle with like-minded individuals who aspire to co-create a better world on Earth. Allow things to come to One easily and effortlessly. Keep things small and simple. Aim to do One's best and then become better with each day One is alive.

Adopt the UP ('Unconditionally Positive') theory as part of One's personal perspective and operating system for life. In everything that One thinks, says and does in life adopt an UP attitude towards it. No matter what the situation, circumstance or whatever life throws at One, be UP about it. Being UP is about training One's mind to express gratitude, thankfulness and positive emotions in response to anything or anyone in One's life. One will always rise and shine when One radiates an UP aura.

SOL DAY 194
12 July

This is a wonderful day to be mindful, grateful, positive, true and kind. If One can imagine it, One can co-create and manifest any and all experiences here on Earth.

Nothing is out of reach if One believes in oneself and the universe. Belief is like a celestial fire – the more One feeds it with raw energy and focused attention, the more it will burn brightly for One to see One's vision in this life. As One looks up at all the amazing stars in the night sky. One begins to realise that One is an integral part of a vast and endless universe. It is a humbling and gratifying experience just being in this moment.

Know that all the paths that One has gone down in One's life have led One to this point in time. One is here now. One is right on time too. One is not here because One is a 'bad' or 'good' person. One is here because this is the right place for One to realise One's divine self and awaken to One's inner way, spiritual voice or true self in this life.

There has never been a better time than now to be where One is.

Whatever One does, thinks or says from this moment onwards – always believe in oneself, never, ever give up. Have faith that everything will work out perfectly for One. Know that One is not alone in the universe.

It is reasonable to imagine that in ten or twenty years from now, One will be a vastly different person with a shifted life energy signature. Do not waste One's time living someone else's life or imitating another person. Be authentic and true to how One is now. Even if One makes a million mistakes along the way, be genuine in One's efforts to be the best version of oneself. After all, One needs to live One's life for oneself and not try to meet the expectations of family, friends, a life partner, First Nation, community or nation state.

SOL DAY 195
13 July

One exists in an infinite field of possibilities. One's divine self-worth is not to be based on the ideas and opinions of others. One's path belongs to One and One alone in this world.

Learn to clear and cleanse One's mind of all negative and toxic thought patterns by changing One's core beliefs and letting go of everything that no longer serves One in this life. Hit the pause button on One's life, so One can see clearly in this moment and what the future deeply holds for One now. All of One's conditioned thoughts since birth can be reconfigured. One has the ultimate power to change everything in One's life. One's spiritual rebirth, transformation and awakening begins the moment One's changes One's perspective of who One really is in this world and the universe.

By destroying, deconstructing and dissolving One's ego, One will open an inner way to One's states of cosmic consciousness.

Know that One's journey will not always make sense to others. That is okay, because One is on a path that only One can live to become the best version of oneself. Give oneself credit for how far One has come and all the challenges that One has met along the way. One's life and story are not over yet. Everything unfolds at the right pace when One surrenders to the divine in One's life. When One opens a gateway to source, One accesses the divine universe.

Once One has finally crossed the bridge of enlightenment, One will never be able to go back to what One was previously. One's life will have changed forever. One will be awake.

One will see the world from a totally new perspective. The magic of wildflowers, rainbows and the silence of the stars will all become an integral part of One's life. One will feel as if One has been touched by a cosmic powerful divine force itself and, guess what, One has.

SOL DAY 196
14 July

One is not born a 'Bright' or divine warrior of the light. One must become it as part of One's journey of enlightenment and cosmic quest on Earth.

When One chooses to embrace One's inner destiny, One is saying 'Yes' to the universe to become One's higher self or best version of oneself in this lifetime. Be gentle with oneself, as it takes time to grow, change and transform. It is only by breaking free of the conformity and conditioning of One's egoic beliefs, thoughts patterns and behaviours that One will begin to see One's true essence.

Do not struggle to be free of One's past, simply realise that it does not exist in this present moment. Everything that One has ever said, done or thought is but a tiny ripple on the cosmic ocean of consciousness as One knows it.

No matter what One does or does not do, people will always judge or feel the need to critic and review One's actions. Fear not the opinions, views and comments of others, because One's life is One's own business. Create a positive shield of impenetrable blue light to safeguard oneself from all low-level frequencies or self-limiting negative energy. Protect One's mind space from corrosive, cutting and scathing criticisms that unconscious individuals automatically generate.

It sounds simple, but One must train One's mind to not be swayed by those who would seek to negatively influence One's inner peace, loving kindness and divine wisdom.

When One moves One's awareness to One's heart centre in the middle of One's chest and takes some slow deep breaths, it allows One to align with the energy of love and be in alignment with the oneness within One's spirit.

SOL DAY 197
15 July

Remember that it all could be gone tomorrow, so it is important to enjoy everything in One's life today. Look at all the good things in One's life and be grateful now. Expressing One's gratitude sends a message to the universe about the prosperity and abundance in One's life. The universe can and will respond by giving One more of the same. It is simply a natural harmonic reflection in response to One's current vibrational energy and consciousness.

Many people choose to delay One's positive thinking and feelings of joyfulness because of the fear that One may miss out on something else. FOMO – the fear of missing out – is an ever-growing symptom of a society that is more concerned with what may happen in the future than actually living in the present moment. Living in expectation that something may or may not happen in One's life only shifts One's focus and energy from being present now. This creates anxiety and nervous apprehension.

Know that what is coming to One is already on its way now. Everything works in divine synchronicity with the universe, so do not be fretful, anxious or distressed. Instead, imagine whatever One desires already being an experience of One's life. Hold this feeling in One's mind and let the universe manifest it in One's life. One still has to enable oneself and do the work, but do not be anxious about living One's live.

Get out there and get on with living and being now. Co-create a beautiful life for oneself.

Free oneself of any expectation and apply oneself to simply move in the direction of One's desires and dreams. When One faces the right direction in life, all One has to do is to move or take the next step forward. As One steps into the great unknown, the universe will catch One.

SOL DAY 198
16 July

Today is a wonderful day to surround oneself with people who leave One feeling positive, uplifted and inspired about One's life. Pay close attention to the people in One's friendship circle and the life energy with which One radiates, because it is a direct reflection of One's inner mental landscape, mindfulness and level of awakened consciousness.

Does One feel recharged and enthusiastic about life or does One feel drained and demotivated after being in another person's company?

It is not up to other people to set One's intention, mood or energy level for the day. It is One's responsibility to design and co-create One's best outcome for the day. Be mindful of One's perception and attitude at the beginning of each day. Sometimes One simply needs to smile at oneself, life and the world.

Realise that the right intentions along with the right actions create a better place and world for all citizens of Earth. Know that One is not alone in the universe.

One is already enough. One does not need to prove One's worth or value to be a human being. Just by being here on Earth, One is already an integral part of the universe expressing itself as a host of a human form. What One does today on Earth is enough for now.

One's existence is not to be liked, beautiful or desirable. This is not why One is here. It is the purpose of all sentient Beings on Earth to awaken and live a virtuous life. When all of One's thoughts and feelings have left oneself, what remains is One's true and purest inner self.

Invite positive, lovingly kind, compassionate people and experiences into One's life. Be guided by One's spirit to co-create a reality that aligns with One's higher self.

SOL DAY 199
17 July

Lately One has been thinking about how One can be the best version of oneself and what meaningful experiences will value add to One's life here on Earth. Part of this process is realising that 'Now' is all One ever has in the universe. Every other moment in One's life will pass through the timeless window of 'Now' and flow into the infinite stream of beingness within One.

To be a magnet for love, peace and harmony or attract anything in One's life, One needs to become the thought, feeling and vibrational frequency for that which One is asking and inviting to experience. Believing that One deserves and is truly worthy of this manifestation is vital for being in alignment with it. This is the first step in welcoming a positive change into One's life. The second step is to let go and trust the universe to work its magic in One's life. When One consistently visualises One's projected manifestation with the accompanying thought and underlying belief that it will come easily and effortlessly to One, One is setting a cosmic intention for this experience to manifest in One's life now.

The more One believes in oneself and trusts the universe, the more quickly it will happen naturally as part of the universe's divine synchronicity. This might sound counterintuitive, but it works incredibly fast when One's mind, body and spirit is in alignment.

Focus on the positive outcome and how it will be a natural part of One's present living experiences on Earth. Create a vision board or journal and write down this new experience that One wishes to receive and manifest in One's life. Be visually and literally very clear and concise about One's thoughts and feelings. Be patient. It will come to One.

SOL DAY 200
18 July

All things must come to an end, so that they can begin again. This is how the universe works. Every moment that One has ever experienced in life was in relative synchronicity with every other moment throughout the cosmos. This day has a beginning and an ending and so will One's human life on Earth. There is a natural rhythm to all things in the universe. No relationship is ever permanent in this world, except for the relationship with One's spiritual self.

As One's mind–body ages on the planet, One becomes quieter and can hear the inner voice of One's spirit, soul or cosmic consciousness. The egoic noise within One's mind from others and generated in society begins to soften. One learns how not to react to people, situations or circumstances that appear in One's life. One consciously chooses not to get upset, but to stay calm, peaceful and spiritually centred in the moment. One knows that there is nothing to be gained by letting One's emotions or ego be the drivers of One's life experiences. Instead, One chooses a more virtuous and enlightened path of prosperity thinking with a free-flowing abundance of loving kindness, care and compassion.

Life has a deeply humbling effect upon One as One lives longer. One learns to recognise and value what is really important in One's life and what is not. One becomes more discerning about the positive people and quality experiences in One's life. One looks out to the future with a sense of awe and wonder about what may be on Earth for all future generations.

One knows that there will come a day when One's mind and body will have reached its expiry date. In this moment, One will become One's pure divine consciousness again. But until this day happens, One will burn as bright as One can in this world. One will positively influence all Earth citizens with One's life force and living present to be One's best.

SOL DAY 201
19 July

Like a tree in a rainforest, know that One is beautiful, lush and interconnected with all other life on Earth. Even if One does not feel it or see it, know that One is an integral part of the web of life on this planet. It is important to learn what nurtures and nourishes One's mind and body. Use this information and knowledge to promote One's positive wellbeing and healthy habits of wellness in every aspect of One's life.

To live is to grow, change and transform. The universe is constantly shifting, moving and evolving into something new. Everything is changing. Always has been, always will be.

Sometimes growth is slow, gentle and easygoing. At other times it can be quick, intense and shockingly confronting or even raw, harsh and maybe even aggressively brutal. Whatever the experience in One's life, use it for One's own personal transformation to be the best version of oneself. There is nothing as empowering as taking responsibility for One's own self-development, self-learning and self-transformation. Everyone likes a winner and the only person that One is truly in competition with is oneself. Give up competing and comparing oneself with others and focus on One's inner health and enlightened inner way in life.

To be the best, One must think the best of oneself first. This is critical if One desires to achieve something wonderful in life. Having a great inspiring vision for oneself is key to setting an intention that will motivate and encourage One to do One's best on the planet.

Do not try and live One's entire life in a day – this is just silly. One's life is an incremental and gradual process. Be patient, kind and gentle with oneself if One stumbles, breaks or makes a mistake. Realise that, with lots of positive personal energy, One can rise to meet any challenge in One's life.

SOL DAY 202
20 July

Orient One's sense of self with One's inner spirit, soul or cosmic consciousness, not One's position, place or possessions in life. Being detached in the present moment is about allowing oneself to be free of current conditions or the social circumstances in which One finds oneself.

There is often great relief when One releases oneself from the thing that One desires the most or the outcome that One is trying to manifest or experience. When this happens, One's mind is free of any particular thought. One can just exist in the moment. One does not have to think to be. One can just be and enjoy the beingness of One's Being.

Just because One has a person or material object in One's life does not mean that One must be completely obsessed by this manifestation of reality. It is much better for One's mental health that One's mind is free by practicing 'relative detachment'. With little effort, One can discipline One's thinking to become still, calm and quiet through simple techniques of breathing and focusing on One's heart centre and breath.

One can influence One's mind by resetting, retraining and renewing One's learned thoughts and behaviours to become more positively detached in One's life. Setting an intention for the day or One's life does not mean that One's mind needs to be desperately attached to this thought. The true source of joy already exists within One's cosmic consciousness now. However, happiness is a temporary pleasure and fleeting experience primarily reliant on an external source. Pleasure is transitory and inner joy is eternal.

The more One can be a source of joy for no particular reason in One's life, the less One's mind will be tempted or attached to any external source to bring pleasure into One's life.

SOL DAY 203
21 July

Play with the idea that One is immortal, eternal and infinite. Realise that, as a sentient Being of the universe, One's true essence is spirit, soul or cosmic consciousness. One is powerful beyond measure and more magnificent than anything One can imagine or conceive. One is and will always be an integral part of the universe. One exists, so One is always now.

Most people on Earth currently belief that One is a human being who may from time to time have a spiritual experience living on this planet.

Know that One is not human. Say it silently to oneself. 'One is not human.' One is spirit and host of a carbon-based human life form.

This statement goes straight to the heart of the matter and most likely against everything that One has been taught since birth. It is the real truth of One's existence in the universe. This spiritual information and divine knowledge is what One's ego and unconscious people do not want One to know about oneself. It is time to open One's mind to One's divine truth.

When One can completely come to terms with this statement and fully embrace this new reality, it will change One's perspective and life forever. One will be able to see a new way of living and being on Earth. One's view of the world will alter in such a dramatic way that it will shift One's outlook and, most importantly, One's relationship with oneself entirely. One's future will now stretch beyond the horizon and into an infinite continuum of existence in the universe.

One will look at One's life and time on Earth with new eyes. One will ask 'What now? What is all the point of this mindless doing? Be patient. All the answers will come to One.

SOL DAY 204
22 July

Today is an exciting day to be alive on Earth. It is the perfect opportunity to recommit to being the best version of oneself.

Make a mental note to stop limiting oneself with One's thoughts, beliefs and behaviours. One is truly capable of achieving One's wildest dreams with the cooperation of other sentient Beings on Earth. The right people will appear in One's life when One is open to receiving the gift of positive people. Be open and ask the universe for assistance, help and support. Do not be afraid. Consciously choose to be humble, grateful and thankful.

Every new successful adventure in life is achieved and built on the foundations of failure.

Go deep inside oneself. Find the courage, strength and resolve within oneself to dare to rise to the challenge and go for it. Do not be discouraged by what others may say or think about One's wild and wacky ideas to change the world. One's vision to make life on Earth a better place is an evolving process of living life itself. Believe in oneself, the universe does.

One can achieve amazing things in One's lifetime. Go beyond any expectations that One may have of oneself in the pursuit of living and being the best that One can be. One is already an enlightened warrior of the light. When One becomes a 'Bright' or an awakened Being, One will create a divine living positive presence here on Earth now.

There is no higher quest in life than awakening from One's dreamlike state of unconscious living and becoming truly awake in this present moment. It is like walking out of a dark room and stepping through a doorway into the light of day for the very first time. The key to opening this internal prison is knowing that One is both the prisoner and the prison guard. Realise that the door to One's prison cell has no locks, and the walls are just an illusion too.

SOL DAY 205
23 July

Sometimes One's life or daily living experiences on Earth may feel like One has been pushed to One's breaking point or limits. It may appear that the world is folding in upon oneself and that nowhere is safe or a way to a place of peaceful sanctuary. Fear not, for all things pass in life. No rainstorm, flood or bushfire lasts forever. Everything rises and falls in synchronicity with the natural rhythm of the planet. The universe has its own way of working everything out in perfect timing with all other things happening around the world.

When One is confronted with these moments of cosmic chaos in One's life, it is natural to feel frustrated, fearful and confused. Take several deep, long, slow breaths and put One's life on pause. Take a temporary time out and detach from the thoughts in One's mind. Disconnect from external situations or critical life events that One is in the middle of at this moment.

Put One's hand or hands in the middle of One's chest, over One's heart centre and just breathe. Breathe calmly, quietly and slowly. Say to oneself, 'All things pass and so shall this.' With every breath One takes, focus One's attention on the rise and fall of One's chest. Just breathe, easily and naturally. With practice, One will be able to calm One's mind and clear One's thoughts in response to any and all events in One's life.

One is resilient and One will get through this moment of uncomfortableness, whatever it is. Know that the universe knows that One has 'got this'. The universe only gives One what One needs for the transformation of One's higher self.

With a little prompting and positive reinforcement, One will realise that One can meet any challenge in One's life. The first step in being able to overcome or resolve any perceived disaster, tragedy or heartbreak in One's life is knowing that One can and will survive it.

SOL DAY 206
24 July

On this day, learn to switch off One's ego and not be offended by anything someone says or does that irritates oneself. Know that if One reacts easily, One is easily manipulated too.

Let things come to One in the moment and allow One's emotions to easily flow through One like a gentle breeze on a summer's day. Be not attached to anything or any thought that may harm or hinder One's path in life on Earth. Look around oneself now and enjoy the land, the sea, the water and the clouds in the sky being true to themselves. Take on no-one else's issues, concerns or worries in life. Be free of that which troubles others. Remind oneself to be mindful in a lovingly kind, caring and compassionate way.

Learn to be peaceful, soft and gentle, as well as flexible and adaptable. Stand tall with all the strength of a magnificent mountain range and have a calming presence like a free-flowing mighty river. Step back and stay out of others camouflage conversations and situations of conflict. Do not be drawn into ego's fight, fear and retribution responses. Respectfully decline to be a part of other people's protests, which are principally driven by greed, gluttony and self-indulgence.

Approach life with an easygoing attitude whose inner positive wellbeing and glowing wellness enriches the lives of other people in One's company. Think only of how One can shine a light on being One's best version of oneself. Then share this living energy with the world.

Use One's time on Earth wisely and in a way that brings a greater sense of good, basic human dignity, decency and kindness to One and all. If One is able to help only one other person during this day on Earth, One has done well. It is these simple acts of kindness that make the world a better place to live in now.

SOL DAY 207
25 July

When One is really open on the inside, One is free to experience the prosperity and abundance of the universe. Living a prosperous life on Earth begins with prosperity thinking. It is not dependent on what One currently has or does not have. The same can be said of abundance.

How does One change One's life to align with this experience? Firstly, One must believe in a new way of living life. This process is about shifting and reorganising the mindscape of beliefs within oneself so that One's neural pathways aligns with these thoughts. When One changes a thought in One's mind, the vibrations of One's mind–body automatically adjust in alignment with this belief. The universe then naturally responds to One's new reality and harmonic frequency with what is in One's mind by manifesting it in One's life.

This may sound too simple to be true, but trust oneself — it works. There have been too many times to mention when One was thinking about something and it magically appeared in One's life. The more One believes, the stronger the thought will become and the quicker the manifestation will occur in One's life.

One is not saying that just because One thinks something, it will instantly appear. One still needs to put in the work of removing all the blockages of unworthiness, self-doubt and self-limiting internal dialogue. Then imagine the vision as if it were real and as if One is living the experience in this moment. Hold the essence or feelings of the vision within One's mind–body and spirit, not as an expectation but as a manifested eventuality of living One's life. Clear space in One's life and be open. Do everything to enable this reality today.

What One believes directly reflects One's relationship with the world. The inside co-creates the outside. Realise this, and One is on One's way to a better space and place in life.

SOL DAY 208
26 July

Pay no particular attention to those who may judge, shame or belittle One at a family or social function, workplace, business meeting, community gathering, outing or public space. There is nothing to be gained in life by slurring One's character, looking down upon or gossiping about One. Know that the opinions of others are a direct reflection of the internal relationship that these people have within oneself. When One tries to devalue another person through word or action, One is only causing self-harm to One's own mind and body.

One cannot serve others with kindness and compassion when One is an egocentric slave to One's own ignorance, prejudice and personal bias.

Be kind, gentle and loving to oneself. Stay calm and do not react. Give only loving kindness, caring advice, helpful information and compassionate support in these situations. Know that people are operating at the level of consciousness with which One is awakened to at this moment in time. Only hurting and fearful people harm others. This is the lesson that One needs to learn in these situations. One must look beyond another's pain and suffering so One can see One's divine spirit and honour it accordingly.

Be genuine in One's approach to others, no matter what another person says or does.

Have confidence in One's ability to influence life, the universe and everything with One's inner peaceful presence, loving kindness and harmonic healing energy. Let the beauty of One's spiritual truth shine as brightly as it can in the world today.

Aim not to change others or fix the world that One lives in. Simply bring One's spiritual presence and positive perspective into play. Let things unfold naturally and effortlessly without expectation in the moment. Observe the difference One's presence makes.

SOL DAY 209
27 July

It is perfectly okay if others think that One is insane because One perceives, sees and thinks significantly differently to everyone else. Know that One is not insane, One simply has a more open mind and interesting way of looking at the world in which One lives.

All great thinkers, visionaries, artists and leaders had to break free from the chains of conventional thinking in order to do or discover something different. One needs to dissolve the barriers of social conformity and limiting self-beliefs within One's mind in order to co-create something entirely new in this world.

If One continues to think what One has always thought, One will always get what One has always got. It is time to break free of One's old habits, outdated thought patterns and dysfunctional ideas about life, the universe and everything.

This is the moment to write a new chapter in the story of One's life. It is not just about turning the page, it is about beginning at a new starting point and changing the entire arc of One's life here on Earth.

Say to oneself, 'It's okay if others perceive One as insane, it's okay if others look upon One as slightly weird, unique or eccentric, it's perfectly natural for others to not get where One is going.' One's life journey does not need validation from others or permission to undertake this adventure. The only person that One requires investment and ongoing commitment from is oneself.

Let One's passion inspire One, let the eccentricity of living in the moment fuel One's fire for life and let the universe's cosmic creative chaos fan the flames to manifest One's new future vision and reality today.

SOL DAY 210
28 July

Practice being oneself today. Do not try to imitate or pretend to be someone else on the planet. Being oneself is the best way to honour One's divine spiritual sovereignty. One can only be that which One is now. Everything else is an illusion in this world.

Remove all the layers of One's human identities, characters and roles in the society in which One lives. Cast these fake skins of individual distinctiveness away so One can focus on One's true self. It is time to dive deep within One's cosmic consciousness and realise who One truly is on Earth.

Know that One is not One's human form. One exists beyond the layers of skin, tissue, muscle and bone. One is the watchful presence and beingness behind the mask of One's mind. Anything that One can imagine or think of in this world, One is not this thought or idea either.

In undertaking this inquiry within oneself, One's ego will create enormous resistance. It will do everything in its power to prevent One from removing it from the equation of One's inner knowing. Ego never goes quietly. It will defend its image of self-importance to the death. One must dismantle or destroy it for One's own peace of mind, in order to create a spiritual sanctuary and sacred space in One's life.

In activating this process of self-realisation and self-transformation, One may lose close friends or family along the way. Do not fear this change. What lies ahead is an even greater reward, which is far more than what One could ever imagine.

When One focuses on oneself and loves oneself unconditionally, One will realise the value and importance of being oneself in this world. This decoupling of One's ego may result in some existing relationships being lost due to One's higher vibrational energy field.

SOL DAY 211
29 July

The universe always speaks to One in silent messages when One is still. This occurs as coincidences that One experiences from time to time and in the synchronicities of living life on Earth. It gently, patiently and reassuringly reminds One to stop, become aware of One's surroundings and be present in this very moment.

Life is not a battle, a war or a conflict to win. It is an opportunity to become the best possible version of oneself by being the Master of One's own life and destiny. There is nothing to fear in life, because all fear is an illusion created in One's mind. One has the ability to change One's reality with a single thought and with this thought, also change the world.

Know that One is powerful beyond measure and infinite beyond One's imagination. One is capable of achieving anything in this world with the cooperation of other like-minded and cooperative sentient Beings.

Never underestimate the things that can be accomplished in the name of love. The power of One's love for oneself and others has the potential to move mountains and shift the consciousness of everyone living on Earth. Focus on this inner oneness within One's Being and what One loves to do in life. When One does this, no task or activity will ever feel like work or a chore. Be a spiritual mentor or human avatar of loving kindness, care and compassion.

When One is truly open, One creates space in One's life for love and loving others. The more One is open to unconditional love, the more it will be part of One's shared living experiences. At the same time, One is also aligning with the oneness of One's Being. It is this oneness within One's spiritual consciousness that enables One to connect to One and all.

SOL DAY 212
30 July

When One is able to truly surrender to One's inner light and cosmic consciousness, One will be able to clearly see the duality of the world in which One lives. What was real will become unreal and 'the truth' about One's existence that One has been taught since One was a child will become a 'false truth'.

One will be intuitively guided in One's life to be where One is now. One will realise with absolute certainty that One is neither One's mind nor One's body. It will become very apparent to One that One is spirit, soul or cosmic consciousness itself and a host to One's human form on Earth. One will not fear death because One was never born. One has always existed in a state of infinite beingness within a continuum of unending timelessness within the 'Now' of One's existence.

One will spontaneously begin to live and be in the 'eternal now' of One's life. However, One's egoic mind will always create a gravity well to pull One's awareness to the past or the future. When this happens, it is important to gently guide One's mind back to the present moment. It is the nature of One's ego to use One's mind for its own selfish and self-centred issues of control, separation and importance. Ego's primary job is to continually assert its power through the false identity of One's imagined, conditioned and constructed residual self-image. Whoever One's egoic mind believes that One is on Earth, One is not.

Keep reminding oneself that One is spirit and not One's mind or body.

One's true nature is pure consciousness, an emptiness of divine oneness, an intuitive all-knowing sentient Being. One's divine truth exists within oneself, not in any human-made quantum theory of the universe, human law or religious concept of existence.

SOL DAY 213
31 July

Take a moment to completely, unambiguously and intentionally let go of the thought that the world is real. Give up the idea entirely if One wishes to find, learn and realise the truth about One's existence on planet Earth.

One is aware that this concept is most likely an incredible and totally consuming shift in One's core beliefs, personal perspective and current living experience or perceived reality. So take a moment to process this information. Be still in quiet contemplation with this new way of looking at the world in which One lives. When One can strip away all the superficialities of One's illusion, One will begin to see directly into the heart of One's existence and divine source.

If One does not release One's mind's attachment to this thought, One will always be grasping, wanting and desiring something in this world. If One becomes lost in the illusion that the world is totally real, One will never know One's true self.

It may feel like One has been deceived about One's reality, but it is all just part of realising the truth and becoming awake to it.

The way in which One perceives the world also changes it. What One once thought of as solid, fixed or immovable is now a manifested flowing field of infinite possibilities. What One thinks or imagines, One can co-create into a new reality for oneself on Earth.

Knowing that the world is not real will make a significant, positive impact and important difference in One's life and the lives of all other people with which One is consciously connected to on the planet. As One fully embraces this new truth and reality, it will release One from One's past perceptions and create a new conscious awareness of all life on Earth.

AUGUST
Sol day 214-244

One believes that One is not human and that the world is an illusion within divine consciousness itself. One reaches out across space and time to other sentient Beings on Earth who seek an alternative and better way to live life. One extends a warm hand in friendship and invites others to join One on a new life quest right here on the planet. A vision which embraces all Earth citizens as One. A reality which will be the foundation to co-create a new, spiritually based, unified Type 1 civilisation. A unifying oneness of spiritual consciousness, where One honours One's spirit, soul or cosmic consciousness and the divinity within all Beings. In the vastness of One's beingness, there is no relative direction and it is easy to become lost along the way. Let's celebrate One's life journey on Earth together. It is time for One to manifest a new way of living and being here now.

SOL DAY 214
1 August

One has always existed in the universe. One is indomitable, unbreakable and indestructible. Even after the eventual implosion of the sun in this solar system and the extinction of all life on Earth, One shall continue to be. One exists in a continuum of infinite beingness beyond space–time. Following the destruction of Earth, the illusion of living on the planet, which most people refer to as One's current reality, will naturally cease to exist. However, One's spirit, soul or cosmic consciousness will still exist in the universe. It is the only true reality that will remain in perpetuity.

Everything that changes in this world can be described as an expression of self-organising theory and subject to the universe's perpetual reconfiguration and ongoing repurposing. By its very nature it is 'not real' but is always in a state of change or cosmic flux.

Everything is connected and all is One. All that is manifested in the universe exists as an expression of altered consciousness and is integral to an infinite field of pure potentiality. One knows that whatever is or will ever be already exists in one form or another in this moment. One simply needs to enable the right conditions for it to manifest into One's life or living experiences. Arising out of the nothingness of emptiness, anything imaginable and everything conceivable is co-created within this space–time virtual reality.

Know that there is nothing to cling or hold on to in this life that will save One. It is only by letting go of all that One has grown accustomed to and known as 'real' that One will be free. As One releases One's grip on certainty, One will free oneself to simply flow with life as it is now.

To truly know oneself is to realise that One is a sentient visitor to Earth with a space–time temporary planetary visa in order to experience One's human form and manifested reality.

SOL DAY 215
2 August

When One first wakes up in the morning, stop oneself from turning on any electronic devices or having a cup of tea, coffee, juice or water. Train One's mind to sit quietly and undertake a process of gentle inner inquiry. Ask oneself this question: 'Who is "One"?' – meaning spirit, soul or cosmic consciousness within One's Being.

Notice that the term 'I' has been omitted from this question. There is no 'I' when there is only 'One'. One spirit, One Being, One sentient entity, One source, One divine consciousness in the entire universe. As raindrops are to an ocean, so too is spirit to source.

In silence, allow oneself to align with One's spirit and dive deep into this endless spaciousness. All the answers One is seeking will naturally flow and come to One. Clear and free One's mind of any thoughts. Resist turning One's mind onto 'active ready mode'. This is the time for One to reflect on One's place in One's life, the world and the universe.

Look at One's body and ask, 'What is this human form and how will One proactively, positively and purposely use or experience this body today?'

Look into One's mind and ask, 'What is this human mind and how will One mindfully and virtuously set One's intention for today?'

One's mind will naturally want to jumpstart One's day so it can take action. It is important to manage the thoughts in One's mind and discourage One's ego from trying to take charge. Be the witness or observer behind One's thoughts. See One's thinking for what it is and take note. Then come back to One's spirit. Learn to see oneself as a spiritual Being who is a host for One's mind and body. One's primary directive or mission is to live a prosperous, abundant and awakened life on Earth, with honour and virtuous actions.

SOL DAY 216
3 August

Just because One has had a difficult and challenging past does not mean that One's future will look or feel the same way. With an all-consuming inner belief in One's spirit, progress along a path of positive prosperity and know that the universe is on One's side. One is capable of co-creating a wonderful, exciting and successful new future today.

Every sentient Being who has ever lived on Earth has required the support and cooperation of other people to successfully live life. Despite the subtle egoic modern media messaging over the decades about 'greed is good', 'take more – give less' and 'consumption creates wealth' to millions around the world, the Earth is everyone's life-support system. This planet is still One's only home in the universe. If the collective use of Earth's resources by all of humanity pushes the natural ecosystems beyond the tipping point of environmental sustainability, there is nowhere for humans to go while Earth heals itself. Take a moment to deeply think about this. Earth is everyone's only home in the solar system.

If One's individual beliefs, old thought patterns and self-sabotaging behaviours significantly change, it is only logical that so will One's life. There has never been a better time in One's life to adjust, amend or modify One's thoughts, habits and the way that One perceives oneself in this world. Nothing has ever prevented oneself from being the best version that One can be 'Now'. One just needs to believe in oneself, do the inner work and stay committed to the outcome that One seeks in life.

When One positively changes the way that One sees oneself and how One lives life on Earth, One will also change the current wellness trajectory for all ecosystems on Earth.

SOL DAY 217
4 August

It is okay if One feel likes that One does not particularly 'fit' into One's family, community, First Nation, society or world. This is probably a good time to realise these feelings of uncomfortableness. It probably means that One is on the right path in life.

What seems very strange is that most people on the planet have accepted the work–rest–sleep cycle without ever questioning what exactly humanity is doing on Earth. Very few people around the world have a burning desire or passion to discuss this important issue. This leads One to the conclusion that most people are still so egocentric that One is only concerned with surviving in an illusion and not thriving at a higher level of consciousness.

However, have faith. One also believes that each and every day more and more people are beginning to wake up all around the world now. With this awakening comes a new questioning of One's life and living purpose on Earth. People are looking at oneself and asking One very simple mindful question: 'Why?' Why is One doing whatever One is doing here on Earth? What is the purpose of this human work function? Is it to help co-create a better version of oneself or help other people do the same? Or is it to only make money, promote and propagate economic slavery and feed One's ego? Is there a better way to live and be so One can fulfil One's higher purpose in life on Earth?

Know that with great questioning also comes great awakening.

One eventually realises that being on the path of enlightenment is the goal of an awakened sentient Being of the universe. Only then will One genuinely enjoy the natural beauty of living life as One flows with it. The effortlessness of life will become an ecstasy of experiences in each and every moment One is alive on Earth.

SOL DAY 218
5 August

Loving and accepting oneself is the quickest way to heal and help oneself in life. There is little point in taking medicine if One still continues to 'dislike' or 'hate' One's mind and body. One will only treat the symptom and cover up the underlying belief. One's mind-body pain and suffering will inevitably return as part of a self-generated hurt–heal–harm cycle.

Be quiet and listen to One's inner spiritual wisdom within One. This voice whispers, 'One is already whole – a beautiful divine spirit of the universe.' 'One is worthy of self-love and affection as much as anyone else on the planet.' 'It is okay to take good loving and gentle care of One's mind and body.' 'Being kind and compassionate to oneself is a sign of great wisdom and inner strength.'

Know that the more One turns inwards towards oneself, the greater One's alignment with One's spirit and the entire universe will be.

There is nothing One cannot heal within oneself, with the right thought, right treatment and the right way of living life now.

Too many individuals are tearing oneself apart in order to serve One's ego and meet the expectations of others or standards in society. It is shocking to see another person moving along a self-destructive pathway in life when all One can do is watch this disaster unfold before One's eyes.

Sometimes all One can do is stand by and wait to help One pick up the pieces of One's life. It's about helping One to dust off One's self-respect, then encourage One to begin again with loving kindness and compassion.

SOL DAY 219
6 August

Look up 'Now'. Today is a day to be overwhelmingly positive and optimistic about One's life on Earth. When One has a clear sense of who One is in this world, One will naturally and easily attract the right things and people into One's life. As One flows with life, so too will One's life flow.

Despite all the mistakes and shipwreck relationships or experiences One has had in One's life, set sail again with an unshakable belief and a willing wind in One's sails. Whatever One does today, it will be enough. Wherever One goes today, One will be alright. Whoever One meets today, One will be okay with. One's path in life is not chiselled in stone, written on a secret sacred map or scarred permanently onto One's heart.

One is a free spirit of the universe. As a divine free spirit, One can go here or there, anywhere in the world. But know that, wherever One goes, One's true home will always be within One.

No other person on the planet can accurately define who One is in this moment. Every person that One will ever meet in One's life is a reflection of who One is now. Be as kind and compassionate to others as One is to oneself. When One truly realises that all of humanity is One, One can no more harm or kill another person than stab oneself in One's own heart.

Look with eyes of wonder and intentionally invite magical moments into One's day. Be upbeat and excited about the amazing things coming to One. Broadcast to the world that One is a beacon of everlasting positive energy and cosmic divine radiance. Nothing will or can ever diminish One's enthusiasm for life and eternal spirit.

SOL DAY 220
7 August

The first step in living a peaceful, lovingly kind, compassionate, harmonious and balanced life is knowing of its existence.

Keeping the right mind with the right thoughts, the right practice with the right habits and the right company all go a long way to co-creating the right space in One's life. The most immediate reward for setting this intention is that it will naturally align with One's inner peace and divine state of pure consciousness. One will have signalled to the universe a shift within oneself, due to positively vibrating at a higher frequency.

The more One can remove worldly distractions and desires from One's life, the greater the chances One will be able to co-create a place of sanctuary where One can experience One's contentment and tranquillity with life itself. This is not about running away from the world; it is mindfully co-creating a living wellness space and place for One's inner and outer wellbeing.

Do not underestimate One's ability to influence One's immediate surroundings and manifest future life experiences. One has the capacity to co-create anything in this world.

When One frees oneself of One's personal pain, past trauma and ongoing suffering in the 'right way', One is also liberating others in the process. Give oneself permission to heal in harmony with the natural soothing rhythm of One's mind and body. In addition, co-create healthy mindful practices and habits each day, like meditation, a healthy diet and gentle exercise. Know that One will never heal oneself if One is tearing oneself apart from the inside or pushing oneself beyond One's limits.

Take comfort in knowing that with a positive mindset, outlook, practices and healthy habits, One can co-create positive experiences and manifest a positive future today.

SOL DAY 221
8 August

If One is significantly invested in absolute security, safety and certainty for oneself, it means that One has a mind that is attached to these egoic thoughts. One's mind is effectively a prisoner of this point of view, attitude or perspective.

There is a great difference between moments when One is in survival mode and when One is simply thriving as a natural part of living life.

One needs to realise that when One has egoic thoughts, One has unconsciously occupied space in One's mind with this way of thinking. Every egoic thought supports and reinforces One's egoic perception of the world in which One lives in. In turn, these thoughts attract more similar experiences into One's life.

Holding these thoughts in One's mind implies that One is so fearful about the future that One is trying to future-proof oneself against anything ever going 'wrong' or negatively impacting on oneself. The future does not exist, so all One can do is influence One's life now.

Know that whatever is going to happen will happen in One's life and there is nothing One can do about it other than fully accept it in the moment when it does eventually happen. Being on high alert or continually looking out for danger will significantly drain One's mind and exhaust One's body of energy. This may also cause One to experience despair and depression.

The alternative to this situation is to flip the script in One's mind with regard to all this fearful, scarcity and unsafe self-talk. One needs to completely change the narrative in One's mind. The founding principle that One needs to realise is that the universe is abundant and so is Earth. Just because this abundance is not directly in front of One at this very moment does not meant that it does not exist. Believe in a world filled with prosperity and abundance now.

SOL DAY 222
9 August

There is a great mental unwellness in the world. It has been happening for many decades. It affects millions of people around the world and is passed from one generation to the next. One is not talking about the COVID-19 pandemic. One is speaking of all the negative, toxic and poisonous egoic thoughts within the minds of the citizens of Earth. The pollution of the planet's lands, seas and sky begins with the contamination of One's mind with hurtful thoughts, self-harming behaviours and unhealthy actions.

The wellness of Earth is a direct reflection of the collective sum of all human activity on this planet.

The only way to cleanse oneself of this illness and become the best version of oneself is to take the time to look directly at One's mind. Look deep inside oneself at all the hurtful and unkind thoughts that One's mind is attached to now. Unhelpful thoughts of judgement, greed, control, power, selfishness and separation. Only in undertaking this process of self-inquiry will One begin to be able to reflect upon and uncover what One's life is really all about.

It is vitally important to realise that Earth is a living lifeboat and it is in the best interests of all citizens to keep it afloat. To do this, One must re-examine One's relationship with Country (land, sea and sky) and live more in harmony and balance with all life on the planet. The social messaging and common saying for the next hundred years should be 'Less take – more give'. One needs to proactively encourage partnerships of positive prosperity and promote investment in holistic wellness, positive wellbeing and spiritual social capital.

When ego is purged and filtered out from the collective human minds on the planet, Earth and all its life forms will continue to survive and exist. This is a shared responsibility.

SOL DAY 223

10 August

One has lived One's life in a world surrounded mostly by unconscious people with egocentric minds. It would be great to live the rest of One's life in the company of enlightened, awake, sentient Beings on Earth.

Let go of the fight against One's fear, anxiety, hate, jealousy, unworthiness, resentment, envy, ignorance and rage. It is time to transcend all of these negative and self-crippling emotions by realising who One truly is now. One is pure consciousness or spirit. One is also divine awareness itself. Imbued within One's divinity is One's eternal presence. Go to this space of enlightened tranquillity within oneself and rise above any thoughts and feelings in One's mind that do not align with One of the seven inner core virtues.

Truly value oneself (mind–body–spirit) and One's virtues for living and being on Earth.

One has most likely been living in a dream world and it is time to wake up now. Realise that One's mind has been hijacked by One's ego. To be free, One will have to remove One's ego from the driver's seat of One's life with meditation and mindful practices. One's individual false self-image does not belong on One's enlightened path of self-realisation. The solution is to permanently deny it control of One's thoughts and emotions ever again in One's life.

Know that when One aligns with the oneness of One's spiritual Being, One will become part of the great awakening that is happening in the world today. Beyond the hypnotic trance of One's past life awaits a wonderful, exciting future filled with infinite possibilities.

The things that One thought were important will become trivial compared to how One perceives the world now. One will look at material items as objects of One's manifested reality and see these as part of the One matrix of cosmic expression within the universe.

SOL DAY 224
11 August

Boundless freedom lies in knowing and believing that everything is connected and all is One. Everyone's spirit, soul or cosmic consciousness of every human alive now on Earth originates from the same source consciousness as every other sentient Being in the universe. It is like the individual drops of water from the same ocean. How can One call it different when its essence is exactly the same?

It is estimated that there are approximately 7 billion people living on the planet at this time. Over a year, about 56 million people die and about 80 million are born. At this trajectory, Earth will be overpopulated in the near future. However, with mindful awareness of this situation and considered, careful and corrective action, balance and harmony can be restored to all life on the planet.

Every new sentient Being arriving on Earth and hosting a new human form originates from source consciousness. There is only one human species on the planet with one cosmic consciousness from a single source. In summary, all is One. This truth is undeniable.

To see everyone as different, distinct or dramatically dissimilar is to only look at the outward appearance of human beings living on Earth. The distinction in language, culture, DNA, First Nation's customs and rituals, community of practice, laws, lores, social rules and behaviours or society are merely external superficialities or surface trivialities. One needs to look beyond the initial outer layer and honour the spirit of all Beings living on the planet.

Learn to look at the world from a new spiritual perspective and inner awareness. View life on this planet as if coming here for the very first time. Open One's mind and truly see now.

SOL DAY 225
12 August

Radiate the energy of prosperity and abundance in One's life. When One is naturally in the emotion (thoughts and feelings) of abundance, One easily and effortlessly attracts more of the same into One's life. As One would expect, this is how the universe works. It aligns with One's harmonic frequency and matches it.

Be a person who shines with and emits a high vibrational energy into the community and world. Allow oneself to be an inspirational spark for others in One's life and a beacon of encouragement for all.

There is no competition in One's life when One's life has no finish line. The only quest One is on is to be the best version of oneself in this moment. Stay true to oneself and everything will work out. One is unique and special in the way that One brings One's abundance energy into the world. One is also serene, sensitive and sharing in everything that One thinks and does. One is not defined by the regulations or standards of societies and governments that have no vision for the future wellbeing of each citizen of Earth. One operates in a mindful way that brings the best of One's inner joy, cosmic bliss, infectious laughter, overflowing creativity, exciting inspiration, positive pleasure and helpful healing into the lives of people within One's living consciousness.

One's sparkling vitality is a magnet that attracts people from all over the world, because others can see the worth of living and being this way. It is not in One's nature to lose sleep over people who choose to not like One or who operate at a significantly lower level of consciousness on the planet. One's journey of abundance begins with a belief in One's living abundance on Earth. Everything that flows from this are grateful gifts to be shared with all.

SOL DAY 226
13 August

When someone triggers the thoughts and feelings of love, kindness and compassion within oneself, it is because this resonates with what is already within One's mind–body–spirit now. There is no denying it, One is a divine Being of love, light and cosmic oneness.

Whatever expectations One may have about others and the world being a more loving, kind and compassionate place, let go of and release into the cosmos. Everything that One wishes to attract into One's life requires One to become it now. If One seeks love, be love. If One seeks kindness, be kind. If One seeks compassion, be compassionate. One's mind will create and believe whatever One thinks about the most. Believe – and it will be so.

Do not choose to be frustrated because something did not work out today or in One's life. Look at life not as a series of tasks or targets that must be achieved by a certain date or time, but as interconnecting moments to be enjoyed and mindfully lived in the 'Now'.

There will always be pain and suffering in the world. This is how humans learn, grow, change and transform. One can choose not to make ongoing suffering part of One's life now. Any concept or idea One has about how the universe should be is false and will never align to how it truly is. Learn to live in this world as it is and be the best that One can be in this moment. Every step towards improving One's way of living and being on the planet is a move closer to co-creating a better Earth for all citizens.

One's best future on Earth requires One's best effort today. Remember that the universe is on One's side to co-create the best version of oneself. It will always support One, especially when One's vision quest is pure of heart and virtuous in nature. Keep moving forward in a positive direction. What will be, will surely be part of One's life.

SOL DAY 227
14 August

If One asked the whole of the humankind if it believed in slavery, the vast majority of people would reject it outright today. It is not something that has great appeal or support in society. If One was offered an exclusive individual contract to live One's life in perpetual slavery until One dies, One would refuse to sign up to this way of living life on Earth.

However, most people alive today are living life in a form of artificial slavery. One's ego is the Master and society is a form of egoic plantation built to support this living servitude. One may significantly disagree with this overview. But ask oneself this question: How does what One does or experience in society advocate, support, promote, invest in, encourage or co-create freedom for being a citizen on Earth?

Freedom is a paradox. To be truly free, One must be free of the desire for freedom itself.

One's spirit is free and One was born free. But most people's lives on Earth are about surviving in a social system of intangible modern economic slavery based on fear and scarcity. To transcend this archaic and obsolete egoic arrangement is not to play the game at all.

When One realises that within One is One's eternal freedom, One will know the way forward. One will not buy into the hype and hysteria of corporate consumerism and competition. One will seek out like-minded individuals who have not been hypnotised by the stream of hopelessness and fear in society. One will begin a different kind of conversation, questioning how to improve humanity and co-create a sense of freedom for all Earth citizens.

Thriving in this world requires One to co-create freedom from judgement, freedom from attachment and freedom from resistance to change. Freedom especially from One's own ego in mind, too. Let the winds of eternal and everlasting freedom be forever in One's life now.

SOL DAY 228
15 August

Life is a cosmic game. Realise this and learn how to play it well today. One's cosmic existence and spiritual presence on Earth is just another way that divine source consciousness experiences itself through oneself (mind–body–spirit) and One's point of view. This is the only way in which One is able to truly know One's divinity and itself in the universe.

One lives in a world full of miracles that can be seen each and every day that One is alive on Earth. One also exists in an ever-changing reality with infinite unfolding possibilities. When One is truly aware of the boundlessness of One's Being, One will be in awe and amazed at One's divine place in the universe. One exists beyond space–time and in a continuum of eternal beingness. The universe is an ever-evolving matrix of matter and energy or altered consciousness in perpetual expansion and exploration of itself.

One was never created and therefore can never be destroyed. One is pure divine consciousness. A formless, timeless, ageless, everlasting, eternal, sentient Being. One has limitless potential in life to design, co-create and manifest any imaginable reality to experience in this world. One is also imbued with the free will to make any and all things happen with the cooperation of other sentient Beings on Earth. One's life can move in any direction One wishes or morph into any conceivable concept that One seeks or desires to live.

All is impermanent and everything is temporary in this life. Life is a very sophisticated and yet simple illusion, capable of manipulating and moderating One's mind into believing wholeheartedly in it.

Being what One chooses to be is about becoming all that One can be in this moment 'Now'. One is an expansion of source and an expression of the unified field of life.

SOL DAY 229
16 August

Embrace uncertainty and accept the unknown in One's life. Learn to lean into One's fear and perceived discomfort rather than trying to avoid it or resist change. Whatever One escapes, evades or runs from will eventually be met along the path that One is on.

Treat One's life as a direction, not a destination to be arrived at on a certain day or time at all costs. Be patient and refrain from punishing oneself for all of One's past mishaps and mistakes. Life is not a race. One is not here on Earth to kill oneself as a consequence of living life the fastest. Relax, breathe, slow down and enjoy the process of everything unfolding at the right time, in the right way and with the right people in One's life.

Do not be afraid of how others may perceive or see oneself. What is more important is how and what One thinks about oneself. Affirm who One is now. Just because others do not see One's value, path or worth does not mean that One must sink to this low level of vibration. Stay focused and always be positive about oneself, One's path of enlightenment and One's life.

Go confidently into the unknown. Invest in creating a space in One's life that celebrates One's inner joy. Enrich One's life with healthy habits, positivity, contentment and peacefulness.

Give oneself unconditional love, attention and affection. This kind of love is truly authentic and shows genuine kindness and compassion for oneself. This self-love is unbreakable and untouchable by any stormy relationship or traumatic incident in One's life.

Know that when One totally loves oneself, it reminds oneself that One is whole, complete and worthy. Another person's love can only add value to that which already resonates from within oneself and which One knows to be true.

SOL DAY 230
17 August

It takes courage, bravery and commitment to grow, change and transform. One's path of enlightenment, self-realisation and awakening will not make sense to everyone in One's life. One must be okay with this eventuality. One is most likely going to lose friends, family members and life partners along the way. Not everyone will wake up at the same time and it is only natural that One will lose harmonic resonance and personal connection with those who choose to operate a lower level of consciousness and mind–body vibration.

All One's talking and conversations will be useless when trying to convince an unconscious person about One's own spiritual presence or cosmic consciousness. It is like expecting an emu to fly when everyone knows that it is a flightless bird. It is just not going to happen, no matter how much One explains the concept to another. Let others be as One is and focus on One's own path of enlightenment and spirit-centred life on Earth. Let others see One's light and let this light shine as an example for others to follow or join One.

With every step that One takes along 'the way', learn to be grateful, graceful and genuine in One's thanks and appreciation of other Beings in the world. With every encounter, express One's gratitude and be humble. When kindness is shared, it brightens the lives of others, just like lighting a candle from a flame that is already burning in the dark.

It may seem that a daunting responsibility and enormous journey lies ahead of One. Especially if One realises that One is and will always be the One to whom One is accountable to. Have faith in One's future and begin by taking a single step forward, then another. Eventually, everything will be revealed in time. The fog of One's ego will lift and One's path will become clear with patience.

SOL DAY 231
18 August

Let One be unequivocal and perfectly clear about One's interstellar purpose here and now. One did not come to Earth to play the game of ego. One arrived on this planet with the great cosmic intention of completely changing the life trajectory of all sentient Beings within this part of the galaxy of the universe.

The not-so-good news is that One's life and interstellar purpose are not going to 'fit' in with everyone else. The great news is that One is meant to shine like a star.

The right people will come and the right way will unfold before One's very eyes. Many will look on with disbelieve and wonder, 'Why change?' Many will desperately cling and hang onto an egoic mindset and 'old world' egoic ideas, ideals and infrastructure. People who are delusional will be too scared to look within oneself and learn the divine truth about One's inner spirit or Being. Many will have no clue about what to do. Unconscious individuals will want, insist and demand to be told, how to think, what thoughts to upload in One's mind and what action to take. They will share a fixed egoic illusion of fear, darkness and negativity.

For those who believe in a brighter cosmic future, nothing and no-one will be able to sway One from expanding and exploring the divinity within One's own Being. One is a free spirit and, as such, can express One's freedom in ways that are beyond One's wildest imagination.

As One begins to truly grasp the idea of an unprecedented paradigm shift in cosmic consciousness on the planet, One realises that co-creating a spiritually based, unified Type 1 civilisation from a united spiritual oneness of mindful sentient Beings is actually possible. People may scoff at the idea; however, the vision is clear and the path is free to all now.

SOL DAY 232
19 August

Trust oneself, One's spirit and the universe. When One takes a leap of faith into the unknown aligning with One's higher purpose in life, the universe will always be there to catch One.

Know that One is whatever One believes oneself to be in this world.

One is spirit, soul or cosmic consciousness. One has infinite potential to be whatever One chooses to be in this world. One's human energy field of life expands and expresses itself to its highest vibration and manifests these living experiences in One's life. One can align with One's virtues and any of the seven states of One's spiritual consciousness in any moment of One's life. One is love, light and pure oneness. One is open and receptive to any and all spiritual wisdom and guidance in the universe. One knows that 'Now' will only ever be the time in which One will live One's life on Earth. All is an illusion and One exists beyond any and everything that is subject to change. One has the capacity to co-create and manifest any reality in space–time on this planet. One flows with 'the way' of the universe in everything that One does, says and actions in this life.

One chooses to be free of judgement, attachment and resistance to change. One is mindfully committed to being the best version of oneself during this moment, year and decade. One's life is unfolding effortlessly in the right direction. One is exactly where One needs to be now.

The universe will naturally reveal things to One at the right moment and in the best way to support living a life aligned with One's higher self. One's inner work is to remove the blockages and dissolve all the obstacles in One's mind. One's path of enlightenment is a journey of loving kindness, care and compassion. Be all that One can be today.

SOL DAY 232
20 August

In a world where One can choose to be anything, be kind, caring and compassionate today.

Learn how to talk with the universe about oneself, One's vision, hopes and dreams for a better world. Discuss the desire to become the best version of oneself. Converse about the simple things in life, along with some of One's successes. Share the excitement, love and joy One experiences on a daily basis. Speak about the gratitude in One's heart or anything that comes to mind in the moment. Even share One's struggles, concerns and challenges.

Know that the universe is forever listening, it is always on and ready to respond at a moment's notice. There is nothing too big or too small that it cannot handle in One's life.

The universe is on One's side and always working in One's best interests and higher self. Without doing anything, everything is done. Things will naturally happen for One when One is aligned to 'the way'. Trust the path and the process. Get comfortable with this new way of life.

Speak openly and honestly from One's heart or in silence. The universe is fluent in all languages and cultures on the planet. One does not need any special training or vocabulary to have a conversation with the universe. Just begin where One is now.

The universe is omnipresent and operates beyond the space–time continuum.

Talking with the universe relieves stress, co-creates peace and builds an invisible bond. The more One invests in this cosmic partnership, the sooner One will realise that it is there for One at any juncture or moment of One's life. It might seem a little silly at first, but One will find great comfort in knowing its unconditional love, endless support and intuitive wisdom.

The universe will also reflect and manifest One's deepest desires, ultimate successes and greatest fears. It will show things to One that One could have never imagined possible.

SOL DAY 234
21 August

When One wakes up today, thank the universe for simply being alive on Earth. Genuinely say, 'Thank you universe, One is so grateful for being alive on this wonderful, amazing planet.'

There are many things in One's life One can show gratitude for: breathing, feeling, seeing, talking, tasting, reading, listening, singing, dancing, creating, walking and moving. The items that One could write down could also include a bed, shelter, food, family, kin, friends, life partner or lover, as well as the opportunity to work, create and aspire to dream or even co-create the best version of oneself. The list is endless. Pick three things each day and write them down in a gratitude journal. Soon this practice will become a habit and One will automatically be showing thanks and being grateful for many things in One's life.

For everything that One is grateful for in One's life, the universe responds in kind.

Take a moment to smile at oneself in the mirror in the morning and say to oneself, 'One is grateful for this human form (mind and body). One sets the intention to be free of all judgement, attachment and resistance to change. One honours One's spirit today and will be the best version of oneself. One is alive and One is grateful for all the experiences of being a host of a human form on Earth now.' Write this down on a sticky note and put it somewhere visible for One to read each day.

When One is truly awake, One is truly alive and living in the present moment.

All great sages, Masters and awake people were born with a sense of spiritual sovereignty and divine wisdom. Over time, egoic social interactions, conditioning and grooming have validated and reinforced ego beliefs, practices and habits as the 'norm'. One must unlearn these false truths and relearn an inner way to experience One's living spiritual reality.

SOL DAY 235
22 August

One can only become the best version of oneself by letting go of what One's mind–body believes and thinks it is now. It is time to focus on improving and not inflating One's ego to impress other people in One's life or this world.

Be mindful of nurturing and nourishing One's life, dreams and aspirations with positivity, optimism and a star-like brightness. Always look for solutions to cultivate success and an attitude of uplifting inspiration for One's outlook on life. One's future can only be lived in this present moment and not at some far-off distant time. Learn to live now and cherish each moment that One is alive today.

Do not wait for tomorrow to be joyful and feel alive. Create a sense of self-worth and wonder today. Enjoy life as a spiritual Being and host of One's human experiences on Earth.

Some people can stand in a desert of beautiful, blooming wildflowers and only see the sand. Others can hold the desert sand in One's hand and yet only see the beauty of the wildflowers. One's perception of the world that One lives in has a lot to do with how One experiences it on a daily basis.

When One looks at the world through the heart of One's spirit, One will see a world unfolding and manifesting before One's spiritual presence. This is the key is to shift One's centre of perception from being mind-centred to become spirit-centred in this moment.

Change takes time, so be patient with oneself. Begin by adjusting One's perception of oneself and embrace a process of continual quality improvement from the inside out. Look at everything that has occurred in One's life as a blessing or gift. Use every challenge and crisis in One's life as a chance to change and become better and better.

SOL DAY 236
23 August

Let go of the difficulties of yesterday and embrace the opportunities of a new day. Each day brings with it the chance to do something different and be someone new. One's life is continually evolving and so is One. Give oneself a pat on the back for making it through another day. Today is the perfect day to live One's life well and focus on what matters most.

Always make One's life a priority, not just an option for One to invest in today.

One may not be a perfect human being, but know this: One's current relationships, be it alone, with a friend, life partner or lover, is perfect for One now. Things are not always going to be sunshine, rainbows and unicorns – they do not have to be for One to be content, satisfied and joyful in this life. Every peak has a trough and every low has a high. Learn to flow effortlessly with the current that runs through One's life. Pause, be patient and positively progress in the direction of One's calling and with the guidance of One's spirit. The universe encourages One to rise and shine in the best way that One can now.

Many have tried to meet the expectations of One's ego and failed miserably. It is time to stop looking for the keys to One's life in the dark and find them using the light within oneself.

Be a champion of One's life. Be a hero who has faith in One's future but lives it with unconditional love, openness and oneness in this moment. Others may look upon One as if One has seriously lost the plot. But One is designing, developing and delving deeper into being the hero of One's own life story.

The current collective chaos of the world is essentially an artificial construct manifested by many people with minds filled with similar egoic thoughts. It is okay to stand up, speak out and shine brightly like a star. Always be true to One's spirit and inner way in life.

SOL DAY 237
24 August

Give light to One's path of enlightenment, mindfulness to One's way and presence to One being here in the moment. Perfume One's life with the flower of change, growth and transformation. Be genuine, honest and realistic with oneself about what lies ahead. Improve One's 'people reading skills' so that One is able to easily and quickly discern and spot fake people. Do not be tempted or fall victim to the false promises that these egocentric people offer. Nothing these people pretend to give will ever be of true value or meaningful substance.

Whatever significant life event One encounters will change One. However, it is up to One to decide how this change will be undertaken. Will it be embraced as an exciting opportunity and delightful gift? Or will One's mind see it as painful punishment that is likely to create ongoing suffering for the rest of One's days on Earth?

Know that One can break One's own mind or build it up into something wonderful, amazing or incredibly beautiful. One can set an intention within One's mind and choose which path One's life progresses along. One is capable of changing One's mind by altering, adapting and reconfiguring the current neural pathways in the brain. Through meditation, mindful practices and healthy habits, One will be able to flip the script on any and all negative, addictive thought patterns, unworthy beliefs and dysfunctional behaviours.

Some may say that One is simply tricking the mind into perceiving something different about oneself. This is exactly what One's ego does. Ego tricks or deceives One's mind by hacking into One's current thinking or programming and repurposing it. It is as if One has uploaded and installed a sneaky, clever, devious, cunning virus of fear, separation, power and control in One's mind without One ever knowing about it. Let everyone delete it now.

SOL DAY 238
25 August

If One believes One will or One won't, One will always be right. Set an epic intention for One's life, to not just survive but to thrive on this planet. Never have any remorse, guilt or shame about being a person with a divine spirit and spiritual perspective. Know that the 'right kind of people' will always find a way into One's life. On the other hand, egoic self-limiting minds will always try and limit limitless thinking. Everything about oneself should inspire people to look within oneself and say, 'One is enough, One is worthy and One is whole.'

There is no real reason for anyone to be hungry, without medical care or homeless on Earth. There is no legitimate justification for engaging in any conflict or war between people or nations. There is no single legal argument or rationalisation for the killing of a human being by another. The legal sanctioning of murder by existing nations is an egregious act of self-harm on the planet. It is not widely spoken about in the community or society, but to recklessly harm another living sentient life form is an act of great unkindness upon oneself and humanity.

The first directive for all human beings is 'To live a prosperous, abundant and awakened life that serves and honours One's spirit, oneself, other humans, animals, planet Earth and the universe in a virtuous way without harm or, through inaction, allow harm to come to these living entities.'

This directive should be taught in every school and learned by each child on the planet. It needs to be the go-to phrase and principle for living life. If every child knew this, it would change every human interaction and the trajectory for all citizens on Earth.

This idea, concept or life principle, is a way to embrace a new life and future on Earth.

SOL DAY 239
26 August

Life is short and days can sometimes feel very long. Learn to see and live life as an infinite Being. Look at every new day that One is alive on Earth as a fresh start and an opportunity to begin again. Reset One's life clock with the rising of the sun and refocus One's life and inner way on being the best that One can be today. Even though time is an illusion, use this Earthbound resource to enhance, enrich and infuse One's life with only positive, loving, kind thoughts and energy.

Force nothing; flow with everything. What is meant to be, will be.

Making a difference in other people's lives begins with first making a conscious difference in One's own life. Never let One's ego's fear and frustrations overpower One's passion for living and being the best version of oneself today. Know that deep down inside One's eternal cosmic consciousness, One is love and One is truly loved. One is always changing with life. Even if One feels tired, weak, confused or perhaps broken at times, One can renew, refresh and reenergise oneself. Take time out to love oneself with warmth, love and affection. Pamper oneself if One needs it – it is okay to be kind to oneself so One can shine even brighter tomorrow. One is always stronger, wiser and more capable than One thinks.

Let the light shine from One's inner spirit and positive energy flow from One's mind and body. One has the ability to heal any part of oneself and make oneself whole again. It is never too late to align with the joy of One's spirit and radiate this feeling of inner bliss, eternal contentment and joyful lightness into the world. Be a 'Bright' – an awake Being.

Be receptive and welcoming of good things in One's life. Commit oneself to living life with cheerful optimism, energetic enthusiasm and embracing every moment One is alive on Earth.

SOL DAY 240
27 August

Today is a good day to be joyful for no reason at all. When One believes in oneself, One opens a doorway to infinite possibilities in One's life. Set One's sights on being the beautiful divine spirit that One is. Stay grounded in the moment and be centred within One's Being and eternal beingness now.

Surrender to One's cosmic consciousness and be a brilliant light in this world. One exists on Earth to be here now. Today is One's time, this is One's moment. Do not get caught up in the anger and anxiety of society or on social media platforms. See the beauty in everyday things, like the sheltering trees on the land, crashing waves at the beach, flowing water in the rivers and moving clouds in the sky. Smile to oneself as One enjoys the natural beauty of Earth in all its wonder. Say to oneself, 'Earth is beautiful and so is One.'

Do not try to control anything. Allow everyone and everything to be as it is. Let oneself flow easily and effortlessly with life. Existing in this present moment is enough.

One is a magnificent Being and worthy of beautiful, loving, kind and amazing experiences in One's life. Whenever One feels drawn into a lower level of vibrational living, gently remind oneself who One is and return to the spiritual centre of One's Being. Whatever thoughts or feelings may be dragging One down, do not dwell on these things. Break the cycle of current conditional thinking by writing it down, talking it out, gentle exercise, meditation and a good night's sleep. Be a change maker and co-creator of One's life.

The world has many noisy, busy minds all talking about a lot of numbing nothingness. It is not One's job to listen to it all. Find the silence within oneself. Learn to listen to One's inner voice. Regardless of what is happening in the world, focus One's attention inwards now.

SOL DAY 241
28 August

Everyone is and will always be an eternal luminous Being of the universe. The light that shines through One's mind can only be stained or darkened by One's egoic thoughts of judgement, attachment and resistance to change.

An unconscious person is incapable of seeing the reflection of One's own mind and will not necessarily cultivate a practice to improve it. The way to freedom is to free oneself of all the things that have been uploaded or created in One's mind and set the intention to be free. Practice the habit of leaving things be. Let the land be the land, the sea be the sea and the sky be the sky. One does not try to change the colour of the land, sea or sky, so why would One change others? Simply focus on improving the practice of One's own mind and life on Earth.

One does not need to keep up with the latest fad or fashions in the world. No 'real truth' will ever be found outside oneself. One is the student, the teacher and the Master – all in One. No number of holy words read and spoken from spiritual texts or books of enlightenment will do any good if One does not embrace and act upon the message in One's life.

Be firm in One's gentleness with oneself and others. Be strong in One's kindness with everyone else. Be attentive to One's own human daily requirements. Be present in One's awareness of others. Embody One's enlightened and awakened practices in the way One talks, walks and gives. Be virtuous in every aspect of One's life, today and always.

When One becomes awake, One will realise One's wakefulness in every part of One's life. With every step and every breath One takes, One's path will be a freeway of calm contentment, quiet contemplation, peaceful patience and simple serenity.

SOL DAY 242
29 August

It is okay to break away from the soul-crushing confines of social systems that support and promote glutinous greed of multinational corporations and unending economic slavery. It is alright to walk away from the people who have conditioned One's mind with egoic negative thoughts, self-limiting beliefs and dysfunctional addictive behaviours. It is fine to carve out a new path away from the social stigma of not fitting into the 'mass group think' that everything is fine in the world and nothing needs to change.

One is spirit and host to One's human form. With One's mind–body, One can co-create and manifest a new reality today.

One is free to break the bonds of One's past and seek out a new way of living and being on Earth. One is not bound to the mistakes and misguided thinking of previous generations. One can change and, with this change, change the world.

When One acts with compassion towards oneself, One is wisely acting with a sense of empathy in regard to the thoughts and feelings within One's mind–body. When One can transcend One's human identity of 'the self' and others, One will be able to align with the oneness within all Beings in the universe.

The easiest way to save everyone is for One to realise who One is, transcend One's thinking and wake up now.

It is important for One to get back to the basics of One's spiritual existence in this world. Cultivate a profound awareness of One's spirit by looking within oneself and at One's internal thought processes. Be the observer of One's mind and life. Wipe away the dust of ego from the mirror of self-reflection and look directly into One's spirit, soul or cosmic consciousness.

SOL DAY 243
30 August

One is whatever One chooses to be today. One becomes what One thinks about the most. All that manifests arises out of One's individual and collective human thoughts. Everything in the built environment was once a human thought and intention.

If One speaks or acts with a mind-body that is muddy with the impurities of One's ego then so shall One's life be. If rain falls from dark stormy clouds, it's likely that One will get wet. If One desperately clings to things and people in life, One is likely to drown in disappointment.

It is the same for a self-organised calm, serene and peaceful mind. A mind that is pure, clear and still is like a freshwater lake that holds nothing and reflects everything, including the entire sky, in its presence. The more One learns to be silent, the easier it will be for One to let One's emotions pass through One, like clouds moving across an empty sky.

Know that One is not alone on One's life journey and path of enlightenment. The universe and other Beings are always guiding One, encouraging One to be the best that One can be. As One wakes each morning, be grateful for One's human life and set an intention to use it wisely and with divine wisdom. Use One's energies to bring loving kindness and benefit to others on Earth, as well as the Earth itself.

Dissolve and discard any egoic thoughts or feelings of negativity, hate, harm or separateness from oneself or towards all others in this world. Say, 'One sets the intention to be lovingly kind to oneself and others today. One will flow with life and honour One's spirit and One's human form in this world. One will be open, receptive and welcoming of good things and positive experiences coming to One now. One is a magnet for manifesting that which One is aligned to in this moment. One is worthy, whole and enough. One is a free spirit.'

SOL DAY 244
31 August

Being oneself is and will always be the most valuable investment that One will ever make in One's life. Do not ruin a new day by reliving an old memory from the past again and again. Turn this looped scene off in One's mind. Stay present and focused on One's breathing. Enjoy living One's life in the current moment where One is now. Know that death is eventually coming to everyone on Earth; it is inescapable. Choose to be cheerful, joyful and kind today.

Think, say and do great work or simply rest and relax. Discover what One loves the most about life and immerse oneself in it with all of One's heart, passion and beingness. Be mindful about completing the simple tasks and let the big things naturally fall into place. Think highly of oneself because this is important and builds One's resilience, resolve and reliability in life. It is essential to stop over-analysing, second-guessing and questioning oneself. One cannot positively progress forward in life if One is continually paralysed with fear and indecision. Learn to tame One's multi-headed ego dragon with a magic potion of loving kindness, care and compassion from within oneself.

It is okay to let go of a messy, mixed up and mistake-riddled life, especially if One has spent a lifetime making it. Just because One has done something for most of One's life does not mean that One has to continue doing it. Have courage and be proud to be different in a world where many want to have and be the same as everyone else.

Take care of One's emotional, mental and physical health. Invest in One's overall positive wellbeing. Be fearless in manifesting and acting with One's own best interest in mind. One's self-talk is a powerful tool in the promotion of One's wellness and wholistic health.

SEPTEMBER
Sol day 245-274

One believes that the world is on the precipice of significant spiritual realisation with the awakening of humanity on Earth. One's intention is to inspire the evolution of all humankind to align with One's divine sovereignty and enlightened divinity. There has never been a better time on this planet to raise the level of harmonic vibration and alignment with One's cosmic consciousness now.

Every day, more and more people are beginning to realise that this world is not quite right. An intangible, egoic, viral pandemic has infected billions of people around the world. This self-perpetuating destructive illness has a cure and it resides within every living person alive today. The only antidote is self-treatment to calm, clear and cleanse One's mind of its ego thoughts, beliefs and behaviours. One is the key and the cure to changing One's life and future on Earth.

One invites all of humanity to answer every spiritual call. Honour every divine commitment within oneself. This is 'the way' to a new reality and new future on Earth.

SOL DAY 245
1 September

Never get so busy 'doing life' that One forgets how to simply be with life as a spiritual Being hosting One's human form. Take time to celebrate all of life's beautiful living experiences.

The perfect life is found in living simply with all of life's imperfections in the moment. Do not fight the flow of life, just go with it. Begin where One is now and One will be on the way to co-creating One's perfect life. Treat everyone and Country (land, sea and sky) with dignity and respect. Learn to honour the spirit within all Beings on the planet and in Country. How One treats others is a good indication of the relationship One has with oneself.

Be One's own best company and rejoice in One's aloneness when One is by oneself. Count One's blessing, people and places in One's life. All that One has to do is be fully present in the simple moments of One's life.

If One wants to live simply, in harmony and in balance with all life, One will find a way.

To end One's suffering, look closely at One's pain. It is the universe's way of telling One that something needs One's attention. Unpack whatever is causing One concern, angst or grief. Sometimes the best thing that One can do is slow down, be very still and listen to One's inner voice. The way to live, act and be will come to One.

Stop oneself from distracting One's focus and positive energy. Learn to read the signs that indicate that One's mind needs quiet time and One's body requires rest. Never feel guilty for taking time out to recharge, renew and reset One's internal wellness compass for life.

Know that busyness is a learnt habit which has become a social disease and is now a common illness in modern society. Creating space for meditation, gentle exercise, positive people and healthy habits is key to a better life today. Repeat 'All is well and so will One be.'

SOL DAY 246
2 September

One has tilted One's head up towards the stars for so long, waiting for a sign, that One has forgotten the divine light that shines within One's spirit, soul or cosmic consciousness.

What has most surprised One so far in life is not finding something outside of oneself, but rediscovering what exists within. Although One's life may be a journey across uncharted territory, One knows that, in time, everything is revealed to One in One way or another.

Buddha says, 'Three things cannot long be hidden: the moon, the sun and the truth.'

Do not confuse One's fear of being the best version of oneself with One's divine illuminating greatness in the world. It is time to get out of One's head and focus on One's breathing. Align with One's inner spirit and tune into what is happening right now. When One pays attention to One's breathing, One becomes more present. Through this present moment, One is also capable of infinite awareness and transcending time itself.

When One learns the 'language of spirit' or 'language of oneness' from an early age, it will change the neural pathways in One's mind and restructure One's brain. One will naturally become more spirit-centred and be able to think, speak and act in an enlightened way. One will be able to think from a spiritual perspective and One will perceive time differently. One will begin to move through time without ever travelling. One will be able to peer into the future as if it were present now. One will cultivate the gift of time travel by transcending the very nature and fabric of the universe itself.

Beyond One's thoughts is an infinite immeasurable beingness that already exists within One – an unbounded limitless continuum outside of One's current space–time reality.

SOL DAY 247
3 September

Talk with people who help One to see the world from an enlightened perspective and new way of being. Engage in conversations with others who are positive and excited about the idea of making the world a better place. Chat openly with like-minded individuals about One's inspiring thoughts, suggestions and direction in life. Have a heart-to-heart with a close friend about One's divine sovereignty and spiritual divinity. Invite a dialogue with the divine source and see where it leads One.

There are millions of ways in which One can enrich One's life, especially through the exchange of information and positive energy. Spiritually centred people are naturally mindfully uplifting and energetically encouraging.

Sometimes when One is least looking for something, it naturally appears before One. This is the synchronicity of the universe at work. Accept it and be thankful and gracious about it. Life is not meant to be all struggle, strive and stress. This is a very punitive way of looking at the world. Think of the world as a wonderful opportunity to manifest anything with the cooperation of other sentient Beings and the universe itself.

Whether One agrees with it or not, One is part of a spiritual evolution of all human beings on Earth. One's challenge is to raise One's level of consciousness right now. It is time to upgrade One's thoughts so One can change One's mind–body operating system to a higher vibrational frequency in the world. With an awareness of One's ego, One can transcend it now.

One is what One will ultimately become on Earth in this present moment. One's direction and path in life all lead to One's higher self. This divine destiny is 'the way' of the universe.

SOL DAY 248
4 September

Sit back, relax and breathe. Let the universe do its job. Focus directly on what is in front of One now – be completely present in this space. Just get on with One's life. Stop trying to control everything and everyone around oneself. What is meant to come to One, will come to One in synchronicity with the universe and what is not, will not.

Be open and receptive to all that One seeks, wishes or desires to manifest in One's life. Hold this vision of a new living reality as if it is happening now – then let it go. Know that the universe is always on One's side and is ever-present in One's life.

Only hold a space for that which One seeks in One's life. Believe in it and so shall it be.

Freedom will come when One learns to let go. Learn to never take anything personally in One's life. Everyone on Earth is operating at the level of consciousness that One has awoken to in this moment. Some people are more awake and enlightened than others. All are on One's own individual path of enlightenment, self-realisation and self-transformation. No-one can say for sure when One is going to transcend One's current matrix of egoic thoughts to become awake, only One knows the answer to that question.

The more One looks inside and cultivates an enlightened mind, the greater One's awakening will be on Earth. Let no person, process or principle dissuade One from the quest to become all that One can be in this moment and during One's life. Become a magnet for miracles in One's daily life. Learn to embrace One's spirit and cosmic consciousness as easily as One would greet a dear and loving friend. Dwell in One's beingness and be free forever now.

In order to positively influence oneself and the world, One must rise above it all.

SOL DAY 249
5 September

Begin today and every other day One is alive on Earth with these two words: 'Thanks universe.' Thanks for the air that One breathes, the food that One eats, the water that One drinks, the place where One sleeps, the friends, life partner or lover and family in One's life, the path of enlightenment One is on and the opportunity to simply be alive on this magnificent, glorious day. One is grateful for all these things and so much more in One's life. One is profoundly grateful for everything. One honours the spirit within One and all Beings.

The universe will always act and respond to what is in One's best interests and higher self. It works in One's favour. Whatever makes One's life joyful, blissful and peaceful, invite it into One's reality now. If One radiates love, kindness and compassion, or positivity, prosperity and abundance, guess what happens? The universe will reflect this back to oneself in One's life. Be mindful of how One chooses to live and be on Earth. One is the co-creator of One's reality.

Realise that no amount of worrying about One's past will change it or any amount of anxiety about the future will fix it. The only way to ensure One lives the life One chooses is to be mindfully present in this moment now.

Co-creating the best version of oneself is a way to generate success in One's own life. One will arrive at the destination that One's desires by realising that One has already created a space for it to be manifested in One's life. Focus One's attention on moving forward in a positive direction. Be intuitively guided by One's spirit and what resonates within One's heart. Step outside of One's comfort zone and realise that good things take time. Trust oneself and One's inner way to change oneself and the world for the better.

SOL DAY 250
6 September

There will be times in One's life when One will outgrow One's old version of oneself. It may be a slow, painful, shocking, confronting or even traumatic change in One's life. Whatever the journey, it is a sign that One is evolving. With this mind–body personal growth process comes an opportunity to realise One's divine spirit and inner transformation.

Shedding One's old personhood and residual self-image within One's mind can often have an external impact upon One's human form. When One lifts the veil of ego from One's mind and can see clearly for the first time, an important realisation will occur to oneself. One has been living in a dream world of unconscious living on the planet. Looking around, One will be able to view the world with fresh eyes, a shifted perspective and a significantly altered outlook. It may seem as if most of the people in the world are pursuing and chasing after intangible ideals, social statuses and seemingly superficial substances and experiences. One will begin to remove and withdraw from people who have a shallow, insincere or phoney sense of self. One will begin to crave and seek out 'real people' who are authentic and desire genuine meaningful interactions and conversations.

Do not be alarmed if this is the case. It is to be expected when One is awake or going through the awakening process within One's life. One is simply moving through and experiencing a natural shift or change in One's level of consciousness. It happens to all enlightened Beings.

Adjusting to One's point of view or frame of reference to be more spiritually centred will become easier as time goes on. One will be able to sit and centre oneself in One's infinite beingness and simply 'chill out'. In this space, One will be able to bear witness to all of life.

SOL DAY 251
7 September

Be willing to embrace the belief that anything is possible in this life. Spend time today raising One's vibration to be the best version of oneself. Imagine enjoying a better life and living in a better world now. Work gently and patiently with One's mind to reconfigure it into something loving and incredibly beautiful. Respond to everything and everyone in a lovingly kind way.

Breathe and allow oneself to be still, quiet and peaceful. Do not be drawn into the vortex of negative social media, conflict cultures, argumentative conversations and thought streams of unhealthy habits. Create a blue bubble of impenetrable light and positivity around oneself. Let nothing negative, undesirable or harmful into this sacred space.

Know that One's spirit is indomitable, indestructible and unconquerable.

One need only realise the truth to be free – there is 'no self'.

Know that today will never happen again, so it is important to embrace this living opportunity with joy. One is exactly where One needs to be now. If things are not working out for One, it may just mean that One is not looking at things in the right way to manifest the best outcome for One's life. When One alters the way One looks at things, this can be the catalyst for change. Be an agent of change and change One's entire life now.

It is easy to say that people are flawed and the world is broken. It is much harder to turn One's gaze upon oneself and confront One's own self-constructed problems, perceptions and lack of positive wellbeing. Fixing the parts of oneself that appear to be broken is the fastest way to create healthy solutions in One's world. There is nothing so big in One's life that a little loving tenderness, care and kindness cannot heal, made better or improve.

Be the person who takes care of oneself and, in doing so, also takes care of the world.

SOL DAY 252
8 September

Have the courage and kindness to be the person that One desires to be in this world. Reveal One's true spiritual identity to all with patience, peace and positivity. Step up onto the podium of One's life and choose to be the best version of oneself.

One does not need to pretend or wear a mask, just be true to oneself in this present moment. Living in this moment is not a dress rehearsal for One's 'real life' or some other time in the future. One is co-creating and manifesting One's reality right now.

Whatever One does, be proud of oneself. It does not matter if One has failed countless times in One's life. Failure is an opportunity for success – embrace it now. Know that One can never fail at being spirit. Awakening is an evolving process. One is a continual work of art in progress, a great masterpiece or mess in the making, however One perceives oneself to be now. One's greatest magic trick in life will be to manifest and make One's reality materialise before One's very eyes by transforming oneself in the process.

Billions of people wake up every morning, but today is different. Today, is the day that One realises that it is possible to transcend every self-limiting belief, negative thought and unhealthy behaviour that One has ever had in One's life. On this day, One can choose to set a new intention for One's day and life. One can create a new vision and reality where One is the most important person in One's life. A space is reserved exclusively for oneself and specifically for One's journey of enlightenment in this life. It is time that One invested in One's future by honouring One's mind–body–spirit.

One is already a winner here on Earth now. Among the many billions alive on the planet, One's inner way is the only true path to be the best version of oneself in this life.

SOL DAY 253
9 September

If One is unable to see the reflective sunshine in others, be the light in One's own life. Be mindful when giving rise to the thoughts One creates in One's mind today. One's thoughts have a way of rippling out into the universe. Stop blaming oneself for undesirable and dysfunctional thinking. Instead, focus on patiently training and skilling One's mind through self-reflection and meditation in a way that naturally and automatically promotes calmness, clarity and a sense of serenity in One's life.

When One is still, the entire universe will reveal itself to One in this eternal moment.

Some days, One may feel like that One is running around in circles, endlessly chasing after something or trying to relive the same experience repeatedly to no end. It is a sure sign of **insanity** to continue to do the same thing and hope for a different result. If One's mind–body has attached itself to an addictive thought or behaviour, and One does not break the underlying belief upon which the thought is built, the most likely outcome will be the same.

This life wheel of unhappiness is a contemporary curse for people living in the world. It offers no solution or salvation to One's presenting issues. It could also be called the circle of hopelessness. The fruits of any so-called success will taste like ashes in One's mouth. To free oneself from this modern insanity and social illness of perpetual promise, One must not play the game at all.

It is reasonable to assume that if One were to create One's own circle of spiritual sanctuary, One would have a better chance of setting One's own intentions, co-creating One's solutions and savouring the flavour of One's own sweet successes.

SOL DAY 254
10 September

In a past that can never be touched and a future that can never be reached, One will always be able to sit and see clearly when One is present 'Now'.

When death eventually comes to One, smile with brightness; when One's body decays, laugh with happiness; and when One's mind disappears from the world, sigh with contentment. One's eternal presence will always be within One's spirit wherever One goes in the universe.

In the absence of happiness in One's mind, One's inner joy will radiate from One's Being.

Know that One is just one of a limitless number of sentient Beings in the universe. One can experience inexhaustible realities in a field of infinite possibilities. One's mind, on the other hand, has difficulty processing the infinite beingness and limitlessness of One's existence. This is because it is basically a difference engine with pattern recognition software and sociocultural behavioural algorithms. It has an inbuilt survival program with an objective to maintain clarity by creating certainty and predictable inevitability. However, with the right guidance, it can be so much more.

One's daily living routines and life ways need to cultivate mindful practices that can observe without emotion or judgement all thoughts that arise in One's mind. When One looks at One's own death, see it not as an ending of One's life on Earth, but as a continuation of One's spiritual journey in the universe.

When One fully understands the enormous magnitude of the limitlessness of One's spirit, soul or cosmic consciousness, One will know the greatness of One's own divine Being. One's spirit is an integral part of the existence of everything – everywhere.

SOL DAY 255
11 September

There are two important life rules that One should remember. Rule 1: Do not think about what others may think about oneself, One's life or One's divine destiny. Rule 2: Forget Rule Number 1, then simply align with One's spirit and get on with co-creating the best version of oneself and One's life now.

It is easy to get lost in a world when people are continually comparing oneself to another person at work, among friends, in One's family, at social functions, outings or events. Do not become a victim to this social disease. Learn to insulate oneself from the opinions, perspectives and judgements of others. Be conscientious and attentive about keeping a free and open mind. Do not let it be muddied by someone else's words, looks, gestures or appearance. Steer clear of people whose mission in life is to bring others down to One's low level of vibration so that this person feels justified and not alone in One's life.

Do not engage with people who insist on turning every conversation into a competition. Step away from the noise of people trying to be important. This type of person is only interested in investing in topics and issues that support One's own self-interest. These people have an egoic agenda. The best way to respond is to get out of the way. Stay calm, remain peaceful and be non-reactive. Eventually, the right people will arrive exactly on time to be with One and it will be worth the wait.

Disregard the potential twisted and life-altering people in the world. Allow space and time in One's life to cultivate purposeful friendships that are kind, supportive and compassionate.

SOL DAY 256
12 September

One's goal is not to be better than someone else in the future, but to be the best version of oneself today. This is not about forcing oneself to be something that One is not or trying to comply with an ideal or perfect image someone else has in mind. It is about evolving, changing and transforming into One's true and higher self.

To surrender to 'the way' is to trust the universe openly with the outcome of One's life.

One's divine beauty already exists within One now. It is time to detox One's mind and body from negative self-talk, self-limiting beliefs, harmful habits and burdensome behaviours in One's life. At some point, One will realise that the machinery of thinking in One's mind is harming oneself and One will stop being unkind to oneself and start being kind.

Being in solitude will be a welcome sanctuary to relieve any stress and give oneself a chance to reset, renew and refresh oneself. Everyone needs time out to be lovingly kind and compassionate to oneself. Act in One's own best interest. Create a space or go somewhere that One can begin to be kinder, gentler and more loving towards oneself.

Helping oneself to be the best version of oneself is a great way to take back One's life. It is time to set a new intention for the rest of the year, decade and One's life. Just do it now.

Some days all One needs is to lie on the grass and look up at the sky. Not thinking about anything, just watching the clouds float gently by. Often when One looks at nature, One can see how things flow effortlessly. Clouds do not worry about what direction they go in, they let the wind carry them as it blows. The sky is not anxious because it has no clouds, it simply holds an open space and waits patiently for things to manifest when they happen.

SOL DAY 257
13 September

Allow oneself to sit quietly. Let oneself relax completely into this space. Promote One's calm, soothing and rhythmic breathing. Encourage One's mind to be silent. Reassure oneself that everything will be okay in One's life. When One does this, One's healing will occur naturally and effortlessly within oneself.

Trust oneself enough to let go and shift One's healing energy to where it needs to be. Give oneself permission to heal and be well. Allow One's mind–body to work in harmony with one another. Mindfully direct One's awareness to create an aura of wellness around One's mind and body. Within this wellness is One's way to a better life on Earth. Channel One's life energy to find, repair, renew and refresh oneself. With loving kindness, instruct each living cell to support the health and positive wellbeing of One's mind and body. In each waking moment of this meditation practice, One's healing is the only priority. One's mission is to heal One's mind–body completely and become the best version of oneself now.

One is and has always been a creator of One's own health and positive wellbeing in One's life. Know that One is the patient, the healer and the cure. Everything that One puts into One's body needs to nurture and nourish One's overall wellness. Carefully limit and be mindfully selective about One's physical and mental intake. Say to oneself, 'No junk food and no junk thoughts in One's mind–body.'

Serious illness and perpetual suffering are often caused not by the initial injury but by maintaining an ongoing attachment to it. One's road to recovery requires One to break the cycle of One's unhealthy attachment and create new healthy habits. To be mindfully and spiritually well, One needs to cultivate the practice of wellness in One's life today.

SOL DAY 258
14 September

Let go of the sorrows of yesterday so that they do not sour the sweetness of today. Remind oneself to set an intention to have a wonderful, exciting, joyful and beautiful day. The world is waiting for One to rise and shine in this moment. One has a standing invitation to bring the best of oneself onto the stage of One's life. Life is a performance piece and One is a continually moving and changing work of art. If One wants to change this living, working and breathing expression of life, One must actively inspire and change the way it is being performed now.

Know that One is the producer of this show and there is no script for One's life. One can literally rewrite every part of One's life repeatedly until One gets it right. Although it may seem that everything is on the move and at times it is hard to catch One's breath, One has the power to close the curtains to the world at any time. Take a break and switch off.

Never be hurried, pushed or pressured into doing something that One feels uncomfortable about thinking, saying or doing. Stage fright is a good thing if it is used in a healthy way. Everyone has nervous energy before a big performance and One's life is the biggest show that One will ever star in. As the leading person in One's life, it is up to oneself to give 100 per cent to One's role. One must be committed to being the best that One can be. Have the confidence to make mistakes and learn from any mistakes along the way.

If One is going to sing, sing One's heart out. If One is going to dance, dance One's legs off. If One is going to act, act with the deepest of emotions, the courage of a tiger in the wild and a spirit as vast as the universe itself. Life is a stage and One is the hero of One's own life story.

SOL DAY 259
15 September

When others think that One is 'insane', it just means that One is on the path of spiritual sanity in a world where billions of people believe in One's ego. It is perfectly okay to stop thinking like everyone else on the planet. Too many lives have been lost on Earth due to people blindly following egoic thinking and attached thought patterns of greed, scarcity, control, power, hate, harm, judgement and separation.

Leaders who have nothing of any substance to say or intuitive wisdom to share will always talk about fear. Fear is the go-to agenda of modern living and contemporary marketing. It is what feeds people's constant cravings for more and more. In particular, the fear of missing out on this or that – the fear of not wearing the right clothes, eating the right foods or being in the right place with the right type of people. Fear is poison to the mind and will eventually bring death to oneself and One's sense of divine purpose in this world.

It is time to free One's mind from this deadly viral infection and return to One's spiritual centre of being in the world. One's inner peace begins the moment that One decouples One attachment to fear and centres One's breath and life in One's spiritual heart. Do not let One's emotions be controlled by the actions of others in this world. Stay still, remain calm and be centred within One's divine presence of One's life.

Concern oneself not with other's thoughts, actions, beliefs and behaviours. Focus on being One's best version of oneself. Bring simplicity to the complexity and chaos of the world that One lives in. Imbue peace, harmony and balance into One's life today. Continually adjust and adapt One's way in the world by aligning to One's mind-body and spirit.

SOL DAY 260
16 September

Spiritual awareness and self-acceptance are the starting points for all positive changes within One's life. Begin where One is now. One will never become what One needs to be if One remains fixed in One's current image as only being human.

Have the courage to embrace being a better version of oneself. Make it happen today. One's life is far too precious to wish it away or waste it on pleasing others who are incapable of accepting who One is now. The greatest love story in One's life is learning to unconditionally love oneself. Make up One's mind to be a beautiful, loving, kind and compassionate sentient Being here on Earth.

Be confident in One's outlook that everything will work out okay. Value One's time, life and living experiences on this planet. Know that One truly is a remarkable spiritual Being. Be true to oneself and path of enlightenment in life. It requires nothing to have the same small thinking as everyone else, but it requires great strength to stand alone as One undertakes the ultimate inner quest of self-realisation, personal transformation and spiritual awakening.

When One opens One's eyes in the morning and is about to get out of bed, pause for a moment and realise that One is an incredibly capable person who can do anything in this world. As soon as One's feet touch the floor, hit the reset button on One's life. Activate One's courage, confidence and commitment to be the best version of oneself today. With One's consent, be a change agent for success in One's own life now.

It is vitally important that One believes in oneself, that One's new vision of reality is and will be a manifested certainty in this world. Know that nothing and no person can stop One's spirit from radiating light, love and oneness to everyone on the planet.

SOL DAY 261
17 September

Say 'Yes' to being unconditionally positive, 'Yes' to being the best version of oneself and 'Yes' to aligning with One's spirit and flowing with 'the way' of the universe. Free One's mind and open One's heart completely now. Learn how to confidently say 'Yes, yes, yes' in One's life. When One says 'Yes', One is consciously making oneself a priority and raising One's level of vibration at the same time. In addition, One is aligning to a state of oneness within One's divine Being and all things in the universe.

The simple act of saying 'Yes' reprograms One's mind and sets One's clear intentions. It sends an energetic positive message to the universe that One is ready, willing and open to receiving. It allows things, people and experiences to harmonise with whatever One is visualising and thinking about. When One uses 'Yes' to preface any statement, it is like changing paths from travelling a winding, bush track to a freeway heading to One's destination at light speed. Some may find this frightening. To those who are used to navigating life through using these hyper-spiritual gateways of thoughts, it will come quite naturally.

The rich vibrancy of One's vision is always contained, embodied and conveyed in the message. The universe reads and responds to energy, not the language One is speaking or the words One is using. Be mindful of One's energy and how One is communicating the message.

There are three important tools or qualities One needs to practice when using this kind of process: clarity, confidence and certainty. Step 1: Clarify the message. Step 2: Express overwhelming confident positive energy in the message. Step 3: Believe with absolute certainty that the message will be heard and will manifest into One's living reality now.

SOL DAY 262
18 September

One is living One's spiritual truth and being unapologetic about it. One hopes to inspire others to do the same on Earth. One's superpowers are patience, simplicity and loving kindness. One's super-sight is to see into the future and bring One's positive energy and living presence into this moment now. One's compassion is One's courage. One's belief is One's bravery. One's silence is One's strength. One's patience is One's power. One's gratitude is One's gift. One's simplicity is One's steadfastness. One's openness is One's shield. One's acceptance is One's ability to adapt. All these human qualities fuse into One and show One 'the way' to become the best version of oneself.

Live One's life not in fear or in the shadow of other's rejections but in the light of One's own divine inspiration and spiritual alignment on Earth. The universe only responds to what One genuinely believes One deserves and is worthy of in this life. The more One values and respects One's mind, body and spirit, the more the universe will as well.

Simply be a better version of oneself than One was yesterday. Realise that as One's life flows, One's job is to continually improve, not attain or achieve a certain point of perfection. At the end of the day, One must be joyful and content with how One lived, what One did and where One is now. Have no regrets about any aspect of One's life.

When One goes to sleep tonight, say to oneself, 'Today was a good day, tomorrow will be just as good or even better.' Be excited about One's life, like a child waiting for One's birthday to arrive, so One can celebrate it with One's friends and family.

Living joyfully means aligning with One's spirit, soul or cosmic consciousness. It is not the distance that One travels in life that is important, it is how One journeys to get there.

SOL DAY 263
19 September

Ninety per cent of being successful in One's life is simply about showing up and being present. With imagination and commitment, One is unlimited in what One can manifest as One's reality in the world today. There will be days when One may feel very tired, even overwhelmed or totally frustrated about One's progress. Have faith. One is on the right path. If it is not the right path, it is leading One to it, so One is still on the right path.

If One has a strong impulse to soar like an eagle as an expression of One's life, spread One's wings and take flight now. The sooner One learns to trust One's abilities, gifts and intuitive intelligence and flies in the face of One's own fears, the more One will realise that One is not bound by the weight of other views, ideas, opinions and perspectives about oneself. How other people in the world view oneself is none of One's business.

Know that great spirits have always faced fierce and fearful resistance from unconscious people desperately clinging to egoic thoughts in mind.

Be a creative and constructive force for kindness, mindfulness and enlightened living on Earth. Change can often appear incredibly challenging at first, but it is essential for One's growth, transformation and awakening. Every ending signals a new beginning in One's life. Take the time to talk to oneself as if One were One's best friend. To be a great person, One must abandon old ways of thinking, doing and living. It is time to be brave enough to stand alone with only the freedom of One's existence to comfort oneself in life.

The most powerful of sentient Beings on the planet do not crave or seek the approval of others. One consciously chooses cooperation over competition. Operating at a higher level of consciousness, One is above the frequency of limited mediocre minds.

SOL DAY 264
20 September

One's spirit, soul or cosmic consciousness recognises another by One's spiritual vibe and not any external human appearance. When One's mind is blind to difference, One will only see sameness in others. This is when the very nature of love and One's alignment with One's conscious oneness comes into being. One's mind's eye will be wide open. No perceived separation will exist within it, only oneness originating from the One pure source of divine consciousness.

At some point along One's spiritual journey, One stops believing in One's own fear and starts believing in love. Unconditional love for oneself, everything in the natural environment and all other humans here on Earth. One will know One has reached a tipping point when One demonstrates loving kindness, care and compassion for One's enemies. There will be no opponents, long-time rivals or adversaries in One's life. All will become just people living and operating at One's own specific level of consciousness on the planet.

Some may say that this is impossible. This kind of limited thinking is exactly what One's ego would have One believe. One needs to cast this false premise away and invite a new way of looking at the world in which One lives.

What spiritually unites us all is infinitely stronger than any fear One can have of it.

Give oneself as many moments as One needs to embrace One's personal change and inner transformation. One's spiritual path of enlightenment, self-realisation and awakening is a journey of many moments all leading oneself to 'the One'. The One idea, the One thought, the One realisation and the One moment of awakening that One is spirit, soul or cosmic consciousness. Everything is connected and all is One.

SOL DAY 265
21 September

Everything changes when One stops receiving and being imprinted upon by other people's negative energy and One starts vibrating and radiating One's own positive spiritual vibe into the universe. Never underestimates One's ability to influence One's own life and the world that One lives in today. To experience a new reality in One's life, One must first clear out what is not serving One anymore. Make space for something new and wonderful to manifest in One's life. Space is the key to inviting change into One's life and emptiness is the quality needed for One's mind to be free. Be open to everything in the universe. Create space, remain empty and stay open. Good things are already coming to One now.

There is an incredibly strong pulse of cosmic light within One. It is calling and drawing oneself towards One's own path of enlightenment. Do not ignore this eternal beacon of divinity within One's spirit. Do not get trapped into thinking that One can shop for One's spirituality as if One is going to the mall or shopping centre. Looking outside of oneself and touching the teachings of various Masters without ever embracing the message is like skipping a stone across the water. It is never immersed in the water until it finally stops moving.

Do not get lost along the way by thinking that this Master is better than that Master or that One needs to find the perfect Master who says things exactly in the right way which resonates within One.

To know a Master completely is to know oneself entirely – this is 'the way'.

Any true Master can quench One's thirst for spiritual enlightenment. It is like drinking water from a different source. It is all the same water that comes from the one sky above.

SOL DAY 266
22 September

Take time to notice things in One's life. Notice how the sun rises, the full moon glows and stars sparkle at night. Notice how waves continually crash on the beach. Notice the sand beneath One's feet. Notice the sun on One's skin and the cool coastal or mountain breeze on One's cheek. Notice how a pretty flower opens and gives off its fragrant perfume. Notice how birds sing brightly and cheerfully in the morning when One wakes up. Notice how the sun arcs across the sky. Notice how storms come and go, rain falls, creeks and rivers flow and dams and lakes fill up. Notice how life blooms and that everything lives in harmony and balance. Notice how nature does not demand anything from anyone and yet is at peace with itself.

This is a great, noble and selfless quality, worthy of emulating in One's own life on Earth.

There are endless opportunities in One's life for One to express all these qualities. The best way is by being virtuous. Virtuous in the way One thinks, says and does things in One's life. The **seven key virtues** for living an aligned and spiritual life are being compassionate, helpful, accepting, generous, simple, patient and open. When One practices these virtues, One aligns with the seven states of One's consciousness within One's Being: knowing, awareness, free will, joy, presence, peace and oneness.

To deeply hold a space for these virtues within One's mind is to invite a greater sense of spiritual alignment with One's divine spirit in this life. To become 'the way' is to know 'the way' in the universe. All the answers are within One and along One's journey in life. Let go and listen to the silence at the core of One's Being. Notice how One's spiritual intuitive intelligence is always guiding One, from moment to moment in One's life. Learn to listen and align to it.

SOL DAY 267
23 September

When One can get One's ego out of the pilot seat of One's life and push the automatic spiritual pilot, One will find that the plane of One's life will be naturally guided to the destination. This is the path of least resistance and effort. The more One can use One's intuitive spiritual guidance system within One's Being, the sooner One can stop trying to control the direction and the outcome of every encounter One has in life by using One's mind exclusively.

One will find that problems dissolve into solutions and the clutter of chaos in One's life evaporates into thin air. Of course, One must still do the work, but One now knows what work needs to be done. More importantly, One is aware of how to set the scene or living landscape for new experiences to change the outcome of One's life. One does this by purposely making One's spirit a priority in One's life now.

As a result of deconstructing the illusion of One's false egoic identity or 'the self', things will begin to flow much easier. In addition, One's life may become almost strange, weird or surreal. It may be like walking through a busy mall or shopping centre, surrounded by lifeless humans all standing still as if frozen in time. People may be stuck in One's egoic image of oneself, not knowing how to break free from the prison that One has created for oneself. One may feel a great sadness or compassion for all these trapped souls, but there is nothing that One can do to free these spirits. Everyone must break free of One's own self-imposed egoic sentence of virtual imprisonment.

All One can do is look on with hope, faith and trust, and encourage and inspire everyone along 'the way' of One's own path of enlightenment. One can only point 'the way' for another's escape and eventual salvation. It is up to each person to save oneself in this world.

SOL DAY 268
24 September

Rise above the 'profit before prosperity' mindset gripping the modern world today. Choose to not participate in this self-perpetuating poisonous process of thinking. Pursuing a path of profit motivated attitudes, actions and addictions only makes ego One's Master and spirit a slave to its fears.

The real treasure lies not in possessing a mountain of material objects or things but in One's ability to not be a prisoner of One's possessive thoughts.

It is important that One finds and discovers an eternal space within oneself that is so infinitely vast and unendingly silent it feels like home. Only in this space will One be able to sit in the serenity of One's own solitude and be soothed by it. This emptiness is absent of everything. Only One's perpetual presents exists here now. It is the only dimension or realm in the universe in which to experience One's state of pure divine consciousness and source.

To the One who knows this space, it is as familiar as the air that One breathes now.

There is nothing more intimate in life than being totally comfortable with One's spirit, soul or cosmic consciousness. This is One's true beauty, attractiveness and spiritual radiance. Having the foresight to see through One's human form and gaze directly into One's spirit or soul is a gift. It is looking without using One's eyes, perceiving without using One's mind and existing without experiencing life. Learning to live life in this way requires One to cultivate a meditative practice and mindful living habit. It is all within One and available at any moment.

If One's mind is attached to a particular thought about a person, perspective, possession or place, One will not be aware of One's divinity. Only when the chattering noise of must have, got to get, really need it, desperately want it has ended in One's mind can silence begin.

SOL DAY 269
25 September

Be curious about One's life on Earth. Imagine living life as the best version of oneself, moment by moment and day by day. Lean into the possibility that One's future is not fixed and that it can be changed with a single belief, thought or encounter with another person. When One imagines a future where One is whole, worthy and deserving, the universe will conspire and support oneself to make this a reality in One's life.

If One inherently longs for, desires or wishes to experience something or someone in One's life, begin by becoming that which One seeks first. If One seeks to attract love, a lover or life partner, be love itself. If One seeks positive people, connections and conversations, be positive. If One seeks good health, healthy habits and positive wellbeing, be healthy. If One seeks peace, serenity and calmness, be peaceful, serene and calm. If One seeks prosperity and abundance, be prosperous and abundant with One's thoughts and attitude towards oneself and One's life. If One seeks to enjoy living in an artistic world, be an artist. If One wants to experience being in a better world, be a better version of oneself first.

Whatever One vibrationally aligns One's mind–body–spirit to in life, One will manifest and attract as part of One's new reality. When One positively reconfigures One's thoughts, One co-creates new neural pathways in the brain that give rise to different harmonic energies being emitted into the universe. This new electromagnetic wave-like energy is akin to broadcasting new messaging, enthusiasm and excitement. This new thought stream is how One shifts One's life in a new direction and manifests a different reality today.

Learn to positively change One's life by changing the channel within oneself.

SOL DAY 270
26 September

Most people want things to change in One's favour without ever having to change oneself. This is not how the universe works. Many people seek a longer life without ever considering how to moderate One's current lifestyle so it can support the extension of One's living existence on Earth. When One changes the way that One looks at things, the things that One looks at also change.

A spiritual-centric outlook changes One's entire perspective of One's life.

Living life well is about enjoying the simple pleasures, like being in nature. Surround and immerse oneself within it. Bathe naked in the stillness of a tropical rainforest, open desert or calm sea. Sit quietly at the beach and watch the waves roll in or sit on top of a mountain and look out at the landscape. Walk gently along a winding river track or soak up the soft scent of wildflowers in springtime or flowers in bloom in a garden. Whatever One's preferred place to be, be there with all of One's presence. Some moments can feel like a lifetime. Allow One's mind to be free and unbounded by everyday thoughts, tasks and timetables for living.

Surrender to the silence of One's spirit and know that One is eternal, infinite and immortal. A quiet mind makes no noise and hears all. At the deepest depths of One's Being, One is an extension and expression of the universe seeking to experience its own divinity.

Learn to give more time and pay more attention to One's inner world. It is in this space that One's true salvation and only spiritual sanctuary exists.

Know that One's spiritual existence will continue long after One's mind and body has reached its use-by date on Earth. Even when One's human ashes have been blown away by the winds of change, One's spirit will always exist as an infinite sentient Being in the universe.

SOL DAY 271
27 September

Dedicate the quality and importance of all of One's virtues and positive actions to all sentient Beings in the universe. Merely be a vessel and vehicle for 'the way' of the universe to manifest itself through oneself. Take no selfish pride in what One has achieved or accomplished. Be thankful and grateful to be of service and to have served the world with One's virtues.

It is important to be mindful regarding what One thinks, says and does. Ensure that these things are for the benefit of all Beings. In co-creating anything new, One needs to be free of judgement, attachment and resistance to any idea, notion of self and concept of subject or object. In this moment of co-creation, dedicate One's efforts and energy to the enlightenment and benefit of all Beings.

Aligning with One's spirit, soul or cosmic consciousness will centre One's presence and One's mindfulness and guide One's actions in life. When One knows One's way, One will be able to positively progress along the path of enlightened and mindful living on Earth. Stay true, remain calm and be mindful in aligning to One's virtues and cosmic consciousness.

One is bound to make mistakes that will result in errors and learning opportunities in One's life. This is natural. All One can do is examine oneself at the end of the day, realise what One could have done better and commit to improving oneself tomorrow.

Asking for help is the first step along the road of inner change to be the best version of oneself. It is not weak; it is a sign of maturity. Seek out a teacher, mentor and Master or life coach to assist oneself to improve in any aspect of One's life. When the student is ready, the teacher, Master or life coach will appear. Openly welcome this opportunity to improve oneself.

SOL DAY 272
28 September

Being alone is a great way to know oneself. It is a perfect opportunity to be free and align with One's spirit, soul or cosmic consciousness. It gives One a chance to truly know One's inner spirit as well as One's mind and body. Create a loving kind space in One's life where One can be generous and giving to oneself. A space that is nurturing and nourishing to One's spirit and mind–body. Everyone needs a place where One can truly be oneself, where One can have an open, honest and heart-to-heart moment of introspection and self-reflection with oneself, away from others who may judge, cast doubt or fabricate false truths about oneself. It is okay to be with oneself, by oneself and for oneself today.

Sometimes being alone in the world can feel like the scariest thing One has ever done or felt in One's entire life. Have courage and stay with this feeling of fear and uncertainty. It will soon pass. Let thoughts arise and fall in One's mind. Nothing lasts forever.

This is the moment to open One's heart centre and mind so One can look deeply within oneself. Ask oneself these questions and wait patiently for the answer from within One's Being. Is One living a life in which One is satisfied or is One just going through the motions of surviving day by day? Is One's life on Earth a celebration of joyful living or a walk through the valley of death? How does One desire to live One's life? Will One co-create a lifestyle where One is spiritually centred and living mindfully or will One be emotionally pushed and pulled by One's ego as well as others' opinions and perspective about oneself?

An enlightened and mindful life requires One to stop dragging One's feet on the way to a decision. One needs to actively determine how One desires to live now. Will it be a life lived on One's knees or will One die on One's feet, living and being true to oneself?

SOL DAY 273
29 September

To be free, One must 'let go' of several things in life now. Let go of 'the self' or One's ego and align with One's spirit, soul or cosmic consciousness. Let go of reality and realise that all the world is an illusion. Let go of the concept that everything is permanent or fixed, and embrace the idea of a continually vibrating reality. Let go of the thought that One is a human and know that One's spirit is host to One's human form and thoughts. Let go of the suggestion that One is alone in the universe and be aware of One's spiritual entanglement with all sentient Beings. Let go of all judgements, attachments and resistance to change and empty One's mind. Let go of people, possessions, places and perspectives and hold a space for any intentional manifested experiences. Let go of negative toxic relationships and invite better friendships and positive energy into One's life. Let go of doubt and fear that may fill One's mind and be loving, kind and compassionate. Let go of the thought that One's life will never work out and have faith that everything will be okay. Let go of not being with the perfect person, lover or life partner and create a space to manifest the right person now. Let go of dysfunctional addictions, unhealthy habits and destructive behaviours and co-create a more positive loving relationship of unconditional love with oneself. Let go of negative self-talk, self-limiting believes and self-sabotaging behaviours so One can change and transform into the best version of oneself today. Let go of the idea that One is not powerful beyond measure and radiate One's divine greatness into the world. Let go of the proposition that One is not capable of achieving anything and live a successful life from moment to moment and day by day.

Everything must go from One's mind for One to transform completely. The only thing holding oneself back from One's inner awakening is whatever One is holding onto now.

SOL DAY 274
30 September

Greet each day with an open heart and an open mind. Welcome the new day into One's life as if One were greeting One's best friend at the door with a warm embrace. Hugs, kisses and other displays of affection show One's love for people and raise the positive vibration on the planet. One's joy, love, kindness, compassion and happiness can never be diminished by sharing these with others. Like the sun, this creates warmth and light in One's life.

All humans are creators and can transmute, transform and transcend anything in the world. Like a bird taking flight, One can rise above any issue, concern or worry in One's life and see it from an entirely different perspective. When One approaches problems from a totally new point of view, solutions often appear automatically, like an unexpected gift.

The mind-body biochemistry cannot distinguish between experiencing an 'external reality' and 'internal reality'. The mind-body treats both experiences as if they are exactly the same. This is also known as the placebo effect. One can trick the mind-body into believing anything One chooses to believe. For the average person, this means that One can reprogram or rewire the neural pathways inside One's cerebral soft tissue and synapses to support being the best version of oneself through meditation, mindfulness practices, healthy habits, positive beliefs and beneficial behaviours.

To put it another way, One's thinking and perceived reality are not fixed.

It is extremely important to learn how to align with and explore the essence and conscious states of One's spiritual existence. Even though One's mind-body function is within One's human form, One's spirit is a cosmic dimensional host to One's physical body and mental thoughts.

OCTOBER

Sol day 275-305

One believes that infinite possibilities exist in every moment that One is alive on Earth today. Even though every aspect of One's life on Earth is impermanent and in a constant state of vibration or flux, there is much love and loving kindness within One's heart that can be shared with others on the planet. While One's egoic mind may crave permanency and solid structures in the world, One knows deep down that One's spirit only seeks to exist in the moment. It is in these moments, when One is completely 'awake', that One is truly alive.

Learn to look without reason, see past One's logical or conditioned sides of the brain and think creatively outside the box of One's mind. Beyond this is a place where space–time reality does not exist and One can stare directly into the truth of One's own divinity. The only thing that One will find there is One's spirit, soul or cosmic consciousness looking back at One, reflecting the same intense love and loving kindness One carries in One's heart and the conscious oneness of One's Being and the universe.

Believe and it will be so.

SOL DAY 275

1 October

When One decides to become a 'Bright', a warrior of the light – have no fear. Be an advocate for One's divine spirit, an enlightened awake sentient Being and act to unite the spiritual consciousness of all Beings on Earth. Put any doubt that One may have to the side and focus on One's path of enlightenment and final awakening. Now is the time for the sleeper to awake.

A time is coming when the people of the planet will unite in a shared global consciousness. Be brave and fearless. Cast off the old egoic ways of One's ancestors and upgrade One's life so that it aligns with One's mind–body-spirt and 'the way' of the universe.

There are still billions of people in the world who are blind to One's own spirit and purposely ignore, disregard and overlook One's own divinity. They choose to continue to experience a familiar path of pain and suffering in the anticipation that all of One's hard work, blood, sweat and tears – along with a mean, aggressive attitude and stubborn relentlessness – will somehow pay off in the end. What One does not realise is that One is just harming oneself in the hope that One's mental viciousness will bring victory to oneself. All this will do is keep oneself from knowing the beauty of the light, love and oneness that exists within.

The warrior's way is to look directly into the source of One's fear and face it with courage, confidence and a coolness, knowing that whatever One does, One has already won. A great virtuous life and a good living death will always be the best reward.

One does not become a 'Bright' by beating One's fear of the unknown. One becomes an enlightened awake Being by being willing to go where others fear to tread.

Every person on the planet has the potential to become the best version of oneself.

SOL DAY 276
2 October

Relax into One's life today. Do not become a slave of the system, ruled by schedules for doing, constantly competing and always being busy getting things done. Learn to plan One's free time to just be and simply live well. Life is a journey that requires One to relax into every new day that One is alive on Earth.

No matter what One does or does not do today, One is enough. Know that the Earth will keep on spinning and the sun will rise again tomorrow morning. A new day is always coming. It arrives perfectly on time and at exactly the right moment in One's life.

It is only when One puts artificial conditions and constraints on oneself to conform and comply with certain expectations that One's stress levels begin to rise. Sometimes it may feel like the chaos of the modern world is consuming oneself and One's life entirely. Switching off from the noise of modern living is an important skill to develop and make part of One's daily routines. Cultivating a practice of mindfulness and morning meditation is a great way to start the day. Go for a walk to clear and calm One's mind, take a yoga class or do some other form of gentle exercise. Whatever One does, ensure that One is creating space in One's life for resetting One's mind and body at the beginning of each day.

The best way to have a great start to the day is to prep for it the day before. Planning and organising is key. However, it is important to realise that One's life can only be lived in the present moment. Eat healthy food, get plenty of sleep and be ready to improve oneself and support One's positive wellbeing in One's life. The sooner One can accept One's life as a wonderful, beautiful gift, the sooner One will be able to appreciate the magic of living life now.

SOL DAY 277
3 October

A peaceful mindful mind will always welcome being present in the moment, but a mind with egoic selfish thoughts will always fearfully grasp, desperately reach for and want something that it does not have now.

Be patient, grateful and thankful for the little things in life. Life is not to be forced, hurried or pressured into happening at a specific time. Let it manifests effortlessly into the present moment. Simply go with the flow of life.

To determine if an opportunity is meant to be in One's life and not just something filling the void of One's ego's selfish wants, desires and needs, ask oneself these questions:

- *Is One free of the emotion (thought and feeling) to desperately cling to or wantonly grasp at having this person, place, process, perspective or possession in One's life?*
  If One answers 'Yes', enjoy the moment as it arises.
  If One answers 'No', let it go.

- *Is One free of attachment, judgement and resistance to this person, place, process, perspective or possession?*
  If One answers 'Yes', enjoy the moment as it arises.
  If One answers 'No', let it go.

- *Is One's proposed action about this person, place, process, perspective or possession going to contribute to benefiting oneself and all sentient Beings?*
  If One answers 'Yes', enjoy the moment as it arises.
  If One answers 'No', let it go.

These prompt questions are good indicators to work out if One is on the right path.

SOL DAY 278
4 October

Today is a great day to be alive on Earth. Whatever weather is happening outside and in nature, be grateful for it. Do not dwell on past worries or future events that may or may not happen. Just enjoy living One's life as it unfolds today. Be in this moment. This is where One's life is, it is the place and space where One lives One's life today.

One cannot hide from One's destiny. One can only become that which One perceives oneself to be in this moment. Many may think that One's ego will imprison oneself for the whole of One's life. This way of thinking is false. One is capable of breaking free and escaping the constraints that imprison One's mind and body at any time One chooses to be free. One simply needs to realise that One's containment and conditioning is all an elaborate illusion created by oneself. When One does this, One will experience freedom like never before. A gateway to the universe will open to One like nothing that One has ever experienced in One's life.

Empty One's heart and mind of grief, greed and ego. Fill it with courage, kindness and compassion. Realise that One is a light warrior of the highest order and One is in a battle for One's own life here on Earth. One's spirit is indomitable, undefeatable and impossible to conquer. When One is directly aligned with it and the universe, One is truly invincible in this world. One can do anything One chooses to think, say and do. One simply needs to align One's seven core virtues with One's seven key spiritual states of existence. Upon unifying and aligning One's mind–body–spirit in this way, One will find perfect balance, eternal peace and unending harmony in One's life.

The way to where One wants to be, has and will always be within One now.

SOL DAY 279
5 October

Learn to centre One's mind and life in the moment. To do otherwise is to miss One's whole life by living in One's memories or imagining One's future life. Make a determined effort and conscious decision to be joyful for no particular reason and live One's future life of wellness today. Everything that One does to prepare, promote and practise wellness in One's life also raises the vibration of One's own sense of celestial and human wellbeing.

Practise taking care of One's mind and body. Intuitively think, say and do things that will support One's mental, physical and spiritual wellbeing. Create a welcoming space in One's life for wellness. Dedicate a portion of One's day to living and being well. Be good to oneself and nurture and nourish the temple of One's body and the treasure of One's mind.

Life is too short to be anywhere other than where One is now. A lifetime is very brief compared to the lifespan of other celestial objects in the universe. Surround oneself with proactive, positive, lovingly kind, caring and compassionate people. People with a sense of mindfulness give off a 'happy, bright, light, uplifting and calming' vibe that can be felt or experienced across great distances. The presence of One's energy aura can often precede One's presence in a room or shared space. People naturally want to be in One's company because of the vibrancy that One is radiating into the space around One.

Allow oneself to be, feel and experience One's inner joyfulness. Give oneself permission to create and flow through life with a sense of positive wellbeing in all that One thinks, says and does in life. Be genuinely happy about the simple things in One's life. Live in synchronicity with life and the universe. Flow with life and One's life will simply flow.

SOL DAY 280
6 October

Hard or harmful thoughts will not heal a wound. Rough or ruthless action will not remedy or soothe a broken relationship or heart. In the heat of conversation or a conflict between two people's ego's, know that the only victor is ego itself. It preys upon One's fears and insecurities. It feeds upon One's doubt and distrust of oneself and others. It knows One's weaknesses and uses it against oneself. Never underestimate the ability of One's ego to work against oneself to weave a web of lies and entangle One in untruths about oneself, and others.

The only way to defeat ego is to walk away and give it none of One's attention.

Whenever One feels anger, resentment or anxiety arising within One's mind, know that this is One's ego trying to take control of One's emotions and set One's mind on a collision course towards conflict, confusion and chaos. The first step in avoiding this outcome is to shift the direction of One's thoughts. The way to do this is to be mindful of One's mind and what One is thinking. Stop, pause and take a breath. Interrupt One's thinking processes by focusing on slow and gentle breathing, taking a break from the situation and purposely doing something else for a moment or saying, 'Let me think about that and get back to One'.

Find whatever works for oneself and practise using it now. The trick is to slow things down so One can process things calmly, clearly and caringly in the moment. Ego will always want to take immediate action. Ego is a fight-or-flight addict, so One must starve it of that which it seeks most – to act in the heat of the moment.

To disrupt, dislodge and dissolve One's old patterns of thinking and dysfunctional behaviours, One must consciously break the cycle of receive–react–repeat.

SOL DAY 281
7 October

Living life with One's mind wide open will reveal to oneself amazing insights and wonderful wisdom about the world in which One lives. There will always be tension between what is and what it is becoming. One is caught in this current of contradiction and oncoming wave of willing free will. As things change on Earth, One evolves and so too does One's own world.

Earth is a never-ending place of becoming. The evolving work of the planet is ongoing. Waves continually crash onto the beach, wind constantly blows across the land and water consistently falls from clouds in the sky. The more One can stand still in the wilderness, the better One can see and experience the wild side of life in all its majesty and magnificence.

A fully grown tree may stand tall and alone by itself in the rainforest, but it is surrounded by others reaching for the same sunlight above. Eventually, its time will come, and its once mighty structure and form will return to the forest floor to become nutrients for the next generation of trees, plants, mosses, lichen and ferns, adding to the biodiversity of life. All that is on Earth exists within a becoming process.

The best way to deeply appreciate nature in all its beauty is to bathe in it. Create space and time in One's life to go 'nature bathing'. Go for a walk along a bush track/hiking trail, sit quietly at the beach or visit One's local public gardens or park, nature or conservation reserve, national park or wilderness area. Spend time outdoors – it is good for One's mind–body and great for One's spirit.

Reset, refresh and renew One's inner way by realigning One's mind–body with One's spirit. Open a conversation with the universe about becoming the best version of oneself.

SOL DAY 282
8 October

The universe does not care how hard One works or how intensely dedicated One is to the task, job or exercise at hand. What matters most is what One believes in One's mind – the vibe One gives off and sends out into the world. Whatever One radiates from oneself to the universe is always received and reflected back to One. The universe is like a big cosmic pond of harmonic reflection.

Pay no particular attention to what everyone else is doing on the planet. Focus on One's spiritual path and mindful way. Get the inside right and the outside will naturally and effortlessly take care of itself. Know that One will be able to rise to any new challenge and meet it. One will also be able to adapt to any unforeseen changes in One's life.

When the small things work in One's life, so too will the big things.

Mindful management of One's mind is like watering One's tree of knowledge with love, kindness and compassion. After careful tendering and kind nurturing, it is sure to bear fruit. Be mindful that One does not water it with worry, concern or anxiety. This will stunt the trees growth and cause it to bear only sour fruit, or no fruit at all.

Be sure to keep a watchful eye on other people's toxic thoughts and negative energy as these will act like poison. If unhealthy thinking and low-level vibrations get into the soil or substrate of One's mind, it can be hard to cleanse and difficult to remove. It may even significantly harm or damage One's positive prosperity and joyful living expression.

To avoid this situation or lessen the risk of harm, it is best to limit One's exposure to anything that is likely to negatively impact upon One's mind–body. This may even mean that One needs to change the people in One's friendship circle or end close personal relationships.

SOL DAY 283
9 October

People will always say that something cannot be done until it is. The fears, doubts and uncertainties of One's ego will always speak up first in a crowd. Ego will purposely seek out attention, reaction and validation by others for its point of view or limited perspective. It is more comfortable talking things down than considering the unimagined possibility that whatever is being proposed could really work.

Doubters shout; believers stay silent.

Even when One is in complete darkness in One's life and everything seems hopeless, One's spirit will remain untouched, unstained and unconvinced of any external situation, condition or experience. It is only when One looks within oneself and observes One's mind that One will see One's thoughts clearly. Be a witness to One's way in the world now.

It is okay to have objectives and goals about One's life. It is an honourable aspiration to seek to be the best version of oneself today. It might not happen today, but with some proactive planning, persistent patience and continuous positive progress, it will happen. Living One's dream daily means learning to be flexible, adaptable and hold a joyful win-win attitude to life.

Some people need to see to believe, while others simply need to believe so One can see the way ahead. Know that One can never kill an idea. This is why ideas and thoughts are so powerful. Once an idea has been lit within One's neutral pathways, it can light up One's entire mind and life. It can also change the world in the most dramatic way.

Once One is awake, it will be impossible to return to One's unconscious sleeping state. One will have passed through an enlightenment 'lightgate' from which One can never return.

SOL DAY 284
10 October

Today, make a clear and conscious decision to be less like others in the world and more aligned to One's spirit or true self. It is okay to leave everyone else behind and set off on One's own inner way and spiritual path of enlightenment. Let people choose for oneself how One wants to be, exist and behave in this life. It is not One's job or duty to tell others how to live One's life. It is also not healthy for One to set expectations for others to meet in order for One to be satisfied, fulfilled, happy, proud or justified. Sometimes One just has to let it all go.

There is no shame, guilt or dishonour in letting people go from One's life.

Ultimately, it is up to every individual to realise One's own truth, transform oneself and awaken to One's spirit and divinity within. Painful as it may be, One's journey or path of spiritual self-awareness only has one outcome – to remove the current illusion of reality from One's mind and life. One will experience One's spirit, life and the oneness of the universe itself.

Life is not a complex test and the universe is not a complicated, multidimensional cosmic machine. One does not need to be granted passage to the afterlife or entry to access heavenly pearly gates. Life is life and One is just spirit. Life is a simple opportunity within a synchronising system of divine chaos or altered consciousness for One to be true to oneself, know oneself and align with One's spirit, soul or cosmic consciousness.

One's best life begins the moment One acts with the best of intensions towards oneself. The best way is simply flowing with 'the way' of the universe. No fuss, no hassle and no hurry.

Create a path that is proactive, purposeful and positive. One does not need to be liked by others if One already unconditionally loves oneself.

SOL DAY 285
11 October

One becomes everything that One believes oneself to be now. In this limitless, endless and abundant universe, One is unbound by space and time. One may perceive that One lives in a physical or material world, but it's all just a wonderful vibrating magical illusion. It is time to change One's current perception of reality and be the best version of oneself.

Citizens of the world once believed that Earth was flat and at the centre of the universe, until this idea was rejected, disproved and replaced by the current conventional belief that the sun is at the centre of the solar system and a spherical Earth spins around it in its yearly orbit.

There are countless other examples that demonstrate contemporary changes in thinking that altered or shifted humanity's collective beliefs. Some enlightened individuals living on Earth now are ahead of the wave of awakened consciousness on the planet, while others are still stuck in the insanity of One's ego matrix.

One must decide for oneself. Is One going to spend the rest of One's life trawling at the bottom of One's low level of human experiences? Or will One rise up high and freely surf the crest of the wave towards a new spiritual shore?

One can begin a new life here and now on Earth in any moment of One's life. This really is a 'no brainer' of a decision for any reasonably intelligent person. One does not need to be a genius to realise that living mindfully and spiritually is much better than clinging to the ongoing pain and suffering of an egoic lifestyle. Unfortunately, most people will choose something familiar, even if it means that One continues to suffer, rather than select a different path into the great unknown.

Believe that One will change to be the best version of oneself and so it shall be.

SOL DAY 286
12 October

Today is a beautiful day to follow the spiritual colours of One's dream. Not everyone will understand or appreciate One's spiritual journey in life. Just be okay with this. People will only meet oneself to the depth that One has explored One's own inner spirit or level of consciousness. Do not let One's fear stop oneself from starting where One is now.

Wake up each morning and set One's passion for living life on fire today. Realise that this day is a glorious gift, so use it well and enjoy it to the max. The sun is shining, even if One cannot see it. It radiates its cosmic energy into the solar system and beyond. It has no intention of ever limiting its capacity to burn as brightly as it can be. It illuminates the universe, until its time is at an end. There is only one way to live an amazing awesome life and that is by being an amazing awesome person. Let this divine quality within oneself shine now.

If One feels like One is living One's life on One's knees, take a moment to consider that eventually everything will be gone and life simply goes on. This may seem scary, but it is true. It is wise, gracious and appropriate that One is grateful to the universe for all the things in One's life. Saying 'Please' and 'Thanks' is a way to be grateful and show One's gratitude.

Invite prosperity and an abundance of love, light and divine oneness into One's life. Let go of the artificially constructed world outside. This is a false reality that purposely promotes people with egoic minds to enslave other minds on the planet. It is a world that people need to reconfigure now. See through the insane ego matrix, hypocrisy, insincerity and pretence of people. Remove oneself from the subtle, invasive, egocentric agenda of this false society.

Today is a beautiful day to follow the spiritual colours of One's dream and be free.

SOL DAY 287
13 October

Starve One's ego of life and enlighten One's spirit, soul or cosmic consciousness. To improve One's living experiences and life on Earth, remove hate, judgement, remorse, jealousy, shame, sorrow, worry, anxiety, distrust, forcefulness, negativity, control, certainty, expectation and possessiveness from One's mind. Watch how One's personal wellbeing and quality of life dramatically improves in this world. To lose these things is to gain One's freedom.

Sometimes One needs to take a wrong turn to get to the right place in One's life. One's path of enlightenment is not a straight road – far from it. There will be days when One thinks that One is totally alone and that no-one else understands what One is going through. One may even feel abandoned, or that One is standing in a neutral zone of nothingness. One might experience a sense of numbness towards oneself and others in the world. One will look around oneself and view the rest of the world as if it has gone completely insane. People may appear to be mindless human drones, senselessly doing without ever looking within oneself.

One may ask oneself: 'Why?' Why are other people so switched off to One's spirit? The answer is amazingly simple. It is because One is trapped within the matrix of One's egoic mind. These humans are possessed by an unconscious or unawakened mind that still believes in the illusion of reality and One's egoic human self-identity. Billions of people around the world still desperately and wantonly cling to this delusion of One's personhood or persona in the hope that if One fixes it, changes it, modifies it, develops it or strengthens it enough to fit in with others and society, One will be spared from ongoing pain and suffering or completely saved in One's lifetime. This kind of thinking only serves to reinforce an egocentric perspective and spiritless view of the world.

SOL DAY 288
14 October

A busy life is not necessarily a joyful, harmonious, balanced or productive life. It is not other people's job to align with One's inner spirit. This is something that can only be accomplished by oneself. Having a mature attitude to oneself and One's life means learning how to turn off One's mind to stop thinking and close One's mouth to prevent speaking. In this silent is where One will value being in tune or aligned to the divine source of the universe within One now.

Do not sit around waiting for things to become better in One's life before One begins to be joyful. Align to One's inner joy within One's Being. Take a deep dive into One's spiritual consciousness and allow oneself to be unconditionally joyful now. One's inner joy begins the moment that One believes in it. When One focuses on the joy in One's day and life, One begins to be more cheerful, sunny and glowing. There is a lightness and grace to One's energy signature that One is openly emitting and freely radiating into the world.

One's inner joy is far more important than One's outer appearance.

Making a conscious decision to be joyful today is one of the most valuable investments that One will ever make. When One sets a joyful intention for the day, One is also cultivating a powerful practice for One's success in life. One does not need to be the smartest person in the room, One just needs to be present. One's inner joy can never be diminished by sharing it with others on the planet.

The important thing is not to force anything, just let joy flow naturally from within One's Being and in One's life. When it works, it works. Learn to smile on the inside continually and effortlessly at One's spirit. It is okay to be different – radiantly joyful, enthusiastic and excited about life.

SOL DAY 289
15 October

Be open, accepting and hold a positive learning space and outlook about One's life. One is not always right. Teachable moments often arise at the time when One should be willing to listen, change or be taught. Everyone is One's teacher and every moment is an opportunity to learn, grow, change and transform. When One looks for the gift, One is sure to find it right in front of One. Often One will see that it was there all along, waiting patiently for One to shift One's perception and allow it into One's present consciousness.

To realise and awaken to One's true divine self and spiritual immortality is to transcend the mortal bonds and boundaries of One's human form.

Do not rush the process of living to get a desired outcome and arrive at One's destination as soon as possible. Take One's time, be with One's spiritual presence, live One's life in the moment. One's human death will come soon enough. It will come knocking at One's door at the right time and in the right way. Nothing will prevent One's spirit or Being from returning to source consciousness in One's pure divine state.

Little is needed to be joyful and content in this life. It is all within oneself. One's way in the universe is as simple as looking and aligning with One's inner spirit or cosmic consciousness. Wherever One is – be there. Whatever One thinks, says and does – believe it.

There comes a time in One's life when One needs to stop listening to suggestions and advice from others. It is time to know oneself from One's deepest truth. Learn to honour One's mind, body and spirit in One's own sacred space. Create boundaries of self-worth and wellness for One's life.

SOL DAY 290

16 October

Decide if One is coming from a place of trauma or truth today. If it is a place of trauma, immediately stop all actions that may continue to do any more harm to oneself. Take care to support One's healing journey first, before anything else that One thinks, says or does in life. Invest in nurturing and improving One's mental and physical wellness. Create space to proactively support One's positive wellbeing and living healing energy on the planet. One is unable to serve others if One's own whole-of-life wellness is empty. One cannot give what One does not have. This is the simple truth of the matter.

Pause and take a moment to hypothetically travel into the future. Imagine One is living a peaceful, harmonious, balanced and spirit-centric life. A life where One is more aligned with One's mind–body–spirit. One has a daily practice of meditation, healthy habits and a virtuous outlook on life. One regularly takes time out for nature bathing and simply being in the world.

One is not hurried, hassled or working under pressure. One's work is free of distraction from electronic devices and demanding profit-driven deadlines. Energy is essentially free with only a minimal access/maintenance service charge. Information communication technology is at its lowest rate ever. A variety of electric modes of transport benefit all citizens of Earth.

Prosperity and abundance is now the working culture of the planet. There is one global unit of currency. Flexible home and office space is common practice. Everyone has a universal living income and all forms of violence, in particular war, are prohibited and illegal on Earth.

Now ask oneself what would it take to live this lifestyle today? Open One's mind to co-create a new improved Earth today. Change the way One thinks and lives One's life now.

SOL DAY 291
17 October

It is never too late to begin living One's life in a more mindful and spiritual way. One is the only person responsible for being the best version of oneself on Earth. Just because One grew up in a culture, society and world that is unethical, separatist and egocentric does not mean that One has to take on these low-level vibrational frequencies. One can rise above it all and transcend these thoughts. One is truly capable of making an incredible difference in One's own life. One has the potential to co-create a better world for all Beings. It all begins when One pays it forward to the next generation on the planet – a living legacy for all.

Tap into One's cosmic conscious awareness, where there is no sense of separateness. Realise that One exists in a unifying field of infinite beingness. The way another person appears is like a wave on the sea of cosmic consciousness. Underneath it all, everyone is 'One'.

One is totally responsible for how One perceives and co-creates One's current Earthbound reality in space–time. If One instantaneously reacts to any situation, ask oneself, 'Why?' What is the motivation behind the reaction? Is One's reaction out of fear, hate or loathing?

Look beyond One's initial reaction or response and discover the reasons for One's beliefs and behaviours. Turn One's unplanned reaction into an act of love, kindness and compassion. Everything that One does is filtered through One's current perceptions and understanding within One's mind. As One turns the looking glass of self-inquiry and self-reflection on One's own mind, the greater One's awareness will become.

Consider the duality in which the world exists – good and bad, black and white, saint and sinner. Know that without judgement there is no duality in the world. This is the space that One's spirit exists in. It is free of judgement and duality – only thinking makes it so.

SOL DAY 292
18 October

This is a truly magical day to align with One's inner peace. Centre oneself within One's soothing eternal stillness. Flow with the infinite freedom within One's spirit. Stop sabotaging One's efforts for a peaceful, harmonious and balanced life by continuing to maintain an attachment to dysfunctional thoughts and feelings. Do not make excuses for what One thinks, says or does by blaming it on external factors, like One's childhood, bad parenting, education, training, job, relationships or friends. Luck has nothing to do with it either. Own the space and place that One's life is in right now and know that things always change.

Wherever One is, One can bring peace, love and harmony to the world. One does this by being peaceful, loving and harmonious within oneself first. This is the divine synchronicity of the universe at play and work within One's life.

One's destiny is not found on some distant shore or galaxy far away. Know that One's fate is not fixed; it never has been. It is something One co-creates with other sentient Beings each day on the planet. When One realises that One can change the direction of One's life completely with a single thought, One will become extremely excited or even overwhelmed at the idea of shifting One's direction in One's life. The possibilities are literally endless. One is only limited by One's imagination.

To live a different mindful and spiritual lifestyle on Earth, One need only imagine it now. One can manifest any experience if One honestly believes in it. One's clear vision, unshakable commitment and unwavering certainty to oneself and One's new reality is all the proof that the universe needs to make it so.

SOL DAY 293
19 October

Be the One who shines and radiates One's light, love and spiritual oneness into the world so that others may clearly see the divinity of One's own path. Be the kind of person who openly talks about and gives unconditional love, kindness and compassion to oneself and others in the world. Be someone who aligns with One's mind–body–spirit daily and cultivates a practice of mindfulness and virtuous living in every aspect of One's life. Be a person who is not afraid to speak One's truth or express One's joyful positivity to make the world a better place. Be free of judgement, attachment and resistance to change. Learn to always be flexible and purposefully adjust to situations, circumstances and events as they unfold.

This may seem like an impossibly high standard to aim for, but it is not. It is simply about getting in touch with and getting back to One's natural spirit centre. Too many people are lost in a world without love, care, kindness and compassion, living in a landscape devoid and denuded of spirit, conscious oneness and divine cosmic unity in One's life. A time is coming, when One will be called upon to dive deep within One's spiritual consciousness. It is a knowing or cosmic calling from One's spirit to be One with oneself and One with all.

If the people around oneself appear to be totally consumed by fear, negativity and chaos, resist the call of darkness, despair and depression. Change the tune and choose the living light within One's spiritual Being. Ruthlessly reject and refuse to be part of a process or collective hive mind that can only see what is wrong with the world. Negotiate with oneself to stand by oneself and stand alone if need be, with a different vibe and vision for One's life on Earth.

Bravery is not about putting oneself in harm's way or danger. It is about looking One's own fear in the eye and telling it clearly and with absolute certainty to 'Go away now'.

SOL DAY 294
20 October

One is safe, successful and divinely aligned with One's spirit and higher purpose here on Earth. One easily and effortlessly attracts wonderful and exciting opportunities into One's life. Other people and sentient Beings in the universe celebrate One's growth, change and transformation into the best version of oneself on the planet. Everything that One thinks, says and does, which aligns with One's inner virtues and spiritual consciousness, has a multiplying effect in One's life.

One is a beacon of love, light and oneness for all Beings on Earth. Whatever One can imagine, One can manifest in One's life with the cooperation of other sentient Beings. One can achieve and accomplish anything. One's connection with others in the world co-creates a powerful positive ripple effect in the universe. One's divinity is One's spiritual sovereignty. One is spirit now and always.

When One normalises this view about oneself, One will be able to shift One's perspective and experiences on the planet. One will understand that One is not separate from the divine source of all things in the universe. One can never lose One's connection to the divine.

To be that which One is, is to transcend all that One can be in this world.

One is a brave, beautiful and capable person with a gentle way, fearless courage and worthwhile life. One's patience and unconditional positive energy will always be a part of One's unlimited potential. One's spirit will guide One's spiritual and mindful path in life.

One knows that One's ego will seek to divide and separate with fear. One's spirit will consciously aspire to unify and unite life on Earth. It is not a trick; it is just how things work.

SOL DAY 295
21 October

Begin each day within One's spiritual presence. Relax One's mind and take deep, long, slow breaths. Be consciously aware of One's spiritual awareness within One's spirit. Notice the energy of One's body in this waking moment. Just let things be and sit quietly in this moment of self-awareness. Calm One's mind–body and let everything go. Do not pick up a phone or turn on any electronic devices. Pause, rest and be positively patient with oneself. Take as long as One needs to feel clear, calm and centred.

Set the intention for today to live One's life as deeply, peacefully and calmly as One chooses to be now. One does this by being mindful and mindfully being. Enjoy each breath, every step and all that life is today. Pace oneself and be patient with oneself. Today is the perfect day to be free, live free and experience freedom in every aspect of One's day.

Know that One's life is blessed with amazing people, wonderful opportunities and exciting experiences. There will be moments of pure joy and bliss in One's life. Embrace these when they happen. Celebrate life and living it well.

When One discovers who One truly is in the universe, One will be free.

One is enough, One is worthy and One is whole. Do not let anyone else say otherwise. One is a positive magnet who freely and consciously attracts positive people and positive experiences into One's life. One does this by being and radiating freedom and positivity from within One's own Being first.

To be all that One can be, begin by being true to oneself.

SOL DAY 296
22 October

Know that what One believes, One becomes. What One thinks and feels or the kind of emotional vibrating energy One radiates, One attracts. What One imagines, One manifests and co-creates in One's life on Earth.

Find peace in each moment of One's day. Let go of One's fixed plans and inflexible expectations for the day and One's life. Focus on doing the simple things well in a mindful way. All great achievements in One's life are made up of getting the little things right first. Take a breath with every task and remember to just breathe. Create space between every successful thing done and watch how it all just flows naturally with 'the way' of the universe.

One's life is not meant to be hurried; it is meant to be lived in the moment.

Cultivate a deep sense of trust about One's life and how everything will work out fine. Say to oneself, 'It's all good, all is well, so be it now.' The universe is always on One's side. Do what One can with whatever One has. One's virtuous actions are reward enough for One's efforts.

Learn to slow One's life down, not speed it up so One can cram more things, people and activities into it. Immerse oneself in the feeling of joy and simply being in the moment. Allow oneself to become lost in activities that bring love to One's life. Be passionate about living One's life now. Radiate this passion into the world and the universe today.

Be unconditionally positive. Do not let the current state of the world deter or discourage One from being the best version of oneself. The first step towards becoming a better version of oneself is realising that it exists now. All One must do is face the right direction and keep moving forward along this path of enlightened awakening. Focus less on doing and getting it right, and more on the right way of living and being now.

SOL DAY 297
23 October

One is part of something greater than oneself. One is an integral part of the whole universe. One co-exists as a fractal expression of divine oneness or source consciousness. There is a spiritual entanglement that flows through every sentient Being in the universe. An inter-dimensional synergy or 'wave consciousness' that One has with all spirits, souls or cosmic consciousnesses. It moves across space–time like gravity and transcends all reality. This is why One is able to align, tune in or connect with any spirit in any part of the universe, at any moment in time.

Affirm One's direct experience of One's spirit and not in the shifting reality of the illusion of the world. The constructed abstract ideas, colours and concepts of realism created in One's mind are a way to maintain certainty, control and predictability about the world.

When One can see the duality of the world in One's mind, One will realise that there is no hard and soft, good and bad, or black and white. There are only things or perspectives that give rise or birth to each other. The nature of One's perception creates the world in which One lives. Know that everything exists in perfect balance. Stop projecting One's perspective onto others and the world. Look at life with an open mind and free spirit. Allow that which is before One to simply be, like a rainbow in the sky. Attach no meaning to an object, place or person, which by its very nature has no meaning, only a dimensional form occupying space–time.

One's realness begins by really looking within oneself first. It is here that One can directly experience One's spiritual reality or divine existence. Learn to be still and sit in silence. Get comfortable with aligning with One's infinite spirit and intuitive knowing.

SOL DAY 298
24 October

Pause patiently before One thinks, says or acts today. Things are not necessarily always what they appear to be in life. Remove the impulse to react, and take a moment to observe and be a witness to whatever is happening in One's life. Just because something is happening externally to oneself, does not mean that One must act and respond straight away.

Breathe. Relax. Stay calm and clear One's mind of all distractions. Tell oneself that everything is going to be okay. The suffering in people's life is because of attachment to a desire for One's reality to be something other than what it is now. Learning to accept things as they are is the first step on the road to recovery and removing suffering from One's life.

Being intentionally present in One's life is a great gift. It allows oneself to reorient One's perspective and way of life to being in the moment. Although others will invite One to entertain the idea of countless mindless acts in society and the world, learn to filter these offers out from One's mindful options. Focus on cultivating and promoting helpful attitudes, habits and behaviours. If everyone was more helpful in the world, this would go a long way to co-creating a better place on Earth for everyone. Do what One can, where One is now.

Helping without harming oneself or others in the world is a healthy habit.

Understand that when One co-creates a win–win situation in One's life, it inspires One and all to do the same. Raising One's own vibrations also contributes to lifting the level of cosmic consciousness of the entire planet. The more One is aligned with One's higher self, the greater benefit One will be able to give to all Beings on Earth.

Helpful people have and share a harmonious healing energy.

SOL DAY 299
25 October

Be unconditionally positive and inspirationally uplifting about oneself and One's life on Earth. Let One's imagination, creativity and spirit guide oneself in life. Great people do not do what others have already done. One uses what One has seen as a source of divine inspiration for everything to come.

Too many people crumble under the weight of taking full responsibility for One's life and motivating oneself to be the best version that One can be right now. If this idea seems too big and overpowering for One to comprehend, let it go and think of something smaller, like flowing with the current of a river of inner and outer improvement in One's life. When One can immerse oneself in the waters of change, One will allow the current of improvement to bring One along 'the way'. Know that it takes time for a single raindrop of water that has fallen at the top of a mountain to flow all the way down and out to the ocean. One's life is like this.

As One consciously moves to the spiritual centre point in One's new life, One will directly experience an inner knowingness and spiritual cosmic pull. It will guide One on One's way in life. Pay close attention to this intuitive aspect of One's life. Focus on being flexible, adaptable and adjusting to continual change. The world is always shifting, turning and transforming.

The future will take care of itself. All One has to do is be present in this moment now.

In times of uncertainty in One's life, know that there is one thing that One can count on: One's spirit and the universe. One's shared humanity on Earth is not about being human and suffering all together as One. It is One's shared divinity in being spirit, soul or cosmic consciousness and living a prosperous, abundant and awakened life.

SOL DAY 300
26 October

Be mindful by practising living mindfully today. Make a commitment to oneself to live in a state of mindfulness throughout the day. This is not about dealing with the dilemmas, dangers or dysfunctional things or people in One's life. It is also not about conquering the challenges either. Being mindful is not some personal self-help strategy to be successful or make the unsustainable sustainable or the impossible possible. Some think that it is a life hack to reboot One's living mental operating system to the latest version, which may be closer to the truth. It is not applied from the outside, it is initiated from inside One's mind.

To be mindful is to be aware of the way One is thinking about life, the universe and everything. It is healthy and natural to be present in One's life as it is and how it is now. There is no 'right way' of doing mindfulness, only being self-aware of One's thoughts and thinking processes. It is about learning to look at One's mind in a non-judgemental, non-attached and non-resistant way. When One can openly, honestly and genuinely peer into One's thinking processes, it can often reveal great insights into why things are the way they are in One's life. Stop oneself from condemning or condoning One's thoughts. Just be present with One's thoughts and life as it is unfolding and happening in the moment.

Do not over-analyse things. Let oneself be free. Slow things down and be where One is, doing whatever One is doing. If One is working on a task, work. If One is resting, rest. If One is playing, play. The same principle can also be applied to other aspects of One's life such as drinking tea, eating, exercising, drawing, writing, painting, singing, talking, performing or sleeping.

Being mindful and mindfully being arises out of each other.

SOL DAY 301
27 October

More does not always mean better. Less does not always mean loss. Overturn One's thinking and perspective on how One looks at gain and loss in One's life. Take a moment to reflect on what really matters in One's life. What brings joy, peace and contentment to oneself? Is it being joyful, peaceful and content itself? Is it unconditional love, freedom, harmony, balance, good friendships, kind, loving and caring relationships, and meaningful conversations with others? Is it being in the company of a special person or particular people, a certain group or family members? Is it gardening, being at the beach, fishing, playing sports, being a creative artist, helping people, learning new things, experiencing nature or walking along a wilderness track? Maybe it is as simple as healthy habits, meditation practices and being mindful in the moment. It could be any number of things. Only One will know the answer to this question. The important point is to make it a priority in One's life today.

Whatever it is, make a note in One's personal journal to show One's gratitude for it. Often One will find that it is the simple things in life that bring the most joy, peace and contentment into One's life on Earth. Ego will try to convince One's mind otherwise. Get out in front of One's ego and set an intention for today. Imagine One's life as joyful, peaceful and content – then live it as if it is already a living certainty.

Nothing need be anything other than what it is now.

Being content with less in One's life means knowing just how prosperous and abundant One's life truly is now. The more One is grateful for the emptiness that everything is, the more One's life will be overflowing with inner contentment.

SOL DAY 302
28 October

Pursue everything with patience in One's life. Do not try and skip ahead or rush the very moment that One is in now. Allow time for time itself. Everything is coming to One in divine synchronicity with all other things in the universe. One's external goals may seem especially important for One to achieve or accomplish right now. Take a moment to realise the reality that One is already co-creating with oneself in this very moment. Enjoy the journey on Earth.

Act with clear and concise intentions when it comes to manifesting One's future today. Do not be persuaded from being true to oneself and living One's spiritual path or experiencing a new reality. Stay focused and emotionally unattached from it. See through other's ulterior motives or fictional fears that aim to distract One along 'the way'. One only needs to be the best version of oneself; this is enough for now. Let the universe take care of everything else in the world. One's human life on Earth is limited and bound by time. Keep moving forward in a positive way, one foot after the other. Eventually One will arrive where One needs to be.

No matter what happens in One's life, accept it, embrace it and learn from it. Use every experience in One's life to transcend One's current thinking and raise the level of One's consciousness. Know that everything will be okay in the end. Smile, breathe and gently flow with 'the way' of the universe. Release oneself from the need to struggle or fight against life, people and situations. See only solutions to benefit One and all other Beings on Earth.

Free oneself from One's own mind and the daily habits that prevent One from living a new life and becoming all that One can be. It takes only one new thought to change oneself and one new action to recreate the whole world. Life on Earth can be reconfigured into something uniquely beautiful. Know that One is the right person to initiate and inspire this reality now.

SOL DAY 303
29 October

Be light, bright and joyful today. Radiate cheerfulness and a glowing positive optimism about One's life and future today. Avoid taking oneself too seriously. Immerse oneself in the simple act of living One's life one moment at a time.

Most people have similar human aspirations – such as being free, loving and to be loved, a safe place to live, work and play, supportive friends and family, good food, clean water, suitable shelter, access to lifelong learning, education, training and modern health services to create a liveable, happy and sustainable contemporary modern life.

Life is about living well, not dying young with runaway debt and in spiritual depravation. One was meant for something more than this in One's lifetime here on Earth.

Modern life needs to enable One's ego being One's servant, so One can become its Master. The only way to do this is to take charge of One's life, One's purpose and One's direction now. Focus on being calm and patient and consistently devote oneself to being aligned with One's mind–body–spirit. Use One's whole-of-life energy in a way that will keep One's vibrations high and do not indulge in a pity party for any unforeseen adversity or significant life challenge. Subscribe to the idea of being free and living a free life that benefits other sentient Beings on Earth. There is every good reason to raise the flag of inspiration or wear the colours of divine enlightenment in the world.

Be unconventional, eccentric or weird if One feels the need to think, say or do something that is outside the normal mainstream acceptable cultural and social protocols. Know One's old boundaries and be open to breaking the mould of the person that One once was.

SOL DAY 304
30 October

Empty One's mind before One unloads One's opinions, comments or the dishwasher. If One's mind is free, so shall One's life be.

It is extremely easy to be sucked into the vortex of other people's agenda, views and interpretations. Do not become tainted by another person's or collective version of the perceived truth. One must wake up on the inside and come to One's own realisation about living life and how to be virtuous so One can think right, act right and do right by One and all sentient Beings in this solar system.

One's ego will always be called into action and act in its own self-interest. Learn to live One's life with One's spiritual autopilot on. This will remove the power and control from One's ego and bring a sense of peace, joy, harmony and balance into One's life on Earth.

No situation is ever static, solid or stays standing still. No future fear remains frozen, fixed or inflexible. Things are always changing in One's life. This is a good thing – trust oneself.

Experience is important, but One's imagination is infinitely more inspiring.

Free One's mind of the contemporary constraints of One's ego and the limiting self-beliefs of the culture, society and world that One lives in now. Look to the horizon for a new way of living and being on Earth. Every change that ever was began with a single thought. The greatest visions are created from the simplest ideas. Ignite the spark of divine existence within One now.

Getting where One wants to go means first being present where One is now. Find contentment with One's life as it is. True freedom exists only when One is free of One's own expectations.

SOL DAY 305
31 October

Keep a cool head and a kind heart, no matter what happens in One's life today. Cultivate the practice of mindful living and simply being present in the world. One's deepest sense of self exists within One's spirit, soul or cosmic consciousness. Do not sacrifice One's peace of mind or spiritual identity for social validation about One's work or way of life. Stay in alignment with One's spiritual sovereignty and the synchronicity of the universe. Surround oneself with like-minded and spiritually attuned people.

All good things take time to manifest in One's life. Be patient with the process and open to unexpected surprises. Often when One least expects it, things magically appear in One's life as if they were meant to be. As the sun rises each day, create space in One's life to become inspired to be the best version of oneself. Have the courage to try new things and face One's fears with unbridled bravery. Self-discovery is a solo act with significant rewards for One's mind, body and spirit.

One's path of enlightened realisation, self-transformation and spiritual awakening belongs only to oneself and no other. The only way to measure One's spiritual progress is to be consciously aware of it now. Give oneself permission to do less and be more on Earth.

Changing the external conditions of One's life for the better can help, but it will not necessarily fix what is going on inside One's head, relationships or life. However, when One changes One's internal landscape of One's mind, the outcome of this inner change can often be that the outside automatically aligns with it. One has unlimited potential to influence One's outside world by first changing One's inside way of how One perceives it, views it and observes it today.

NOVEMBER
Sol day 306-335

One believes in a blueprint for a better way of living and being on Earth. It all begins within oneself first. It is about co-creating a window of opportunity in space-time to inspire a new vision for all Earth citizens. A manifested reality that benefits One and all sentient Beings. A way of living life mindfully and spiritually aligned with One's spirit, soul or cosmic consciousness. Where One openly, effortlessly and naturally flows with 'the way' of the universe. A planet where people regularly cultivate a practice of mindful living, spiritual meditation and virtuous action in every aspect of One's daily life. It is a place where a new unifying spiritual language is taught worldwide, which raises One's consciousness and cosmic vibrations to such an extent that One is able to perceive space differently and transcend time itself.

On this new Earth humans will naturally be concerned with these important questions:

- Who is One?
- What does it mean for One to be 'awake' now?
- How does One live mindfully and purposely on Earth as an 'awake' spiritual Being or 'Bright' in the universe?

SOL DAY 306
1 November

Today is a special day to make profound positive changes in One's life. Sometimes these changes may appear to be hurtful, harsh or even hostile on the outside and have a negative impact upon One's life. Whatever the experience, do not judge what they appear to be. Instead, simply realise that space is being created for something new to emerge and manifest in One's life. For something, someone or some moment to exist, there must first be space.

It is a good thing that the universe is essentially a field of infinite possibilities. Anything that can happen will happen, given the right conditions for it to be manifested in this present moment. This is wonderful and exciting news for any person seeking to make profound positive changes in One's life now. It means that, with the cooperation of others sentient Beings and the universe, whatever One can imagine can be co-created and manifested in this world. The options to change and co-create the best version of oneself on Earth are limitless.

When One deeply embraces this idea, One realises that anything is possible in the world.

Imagine a time in the not-so-distant future. Imagine a new living reality on Earth. Everyone is connected by electronic devices. Every citizen of Earth is free. People live in a virtuous, ethical, mindful, principled, honourable and spiritually centred way for the benefit of One and all sentient Beings. The Earth is healed. There is no war, hunger or disease, only peace, prosperity and abundance. People are united as a single divine consciousness. Earth has a common goal to evolve into a spiritually based Type 1 civilisation to explore the solar system and beyond. All education, information technology, communication, energy and transport is free. Every person on Earth is allocated an affordable, basic living income from a single universal Earth currency. Imagine it as One's new life on Earth – so be it now.

SOL DAY 307
2 November

Today, be aware of the duality of the world in which One lives in. Within this duality, all that is perceived exists along a spectrum of good to bad, life to death, light to dark, enlightened to unenlightened, and so on. Things are not always what they seem to be in this world. As soon as One's mind grasps for a perspective, it becomes ignorant of the whole of life as a dualistic system. There can be no up without a down. Left does not exist without right, forward without backward, or positive without negative. Each gives rise to the other. Whatever perspective or judgement One's mind applies to the outside world, it is only looking at half of the picture.

As soon as One stops One's mind from judging and categorising the world, One begins to see more clearly. One realises that only thinking makes it so and therefore so it is.

On occasions, One will lean to a certain perspective more than the other side. This happens for many reasons. Sometimes it is conditioned behaviour and sometimes it is a conscious choice. Most people desire to be happy not sad, light not dark, joyful not joyless. Know that all choices are relative perspectives in the moment. A thing is just a thing and an experience is just an experience. It is only when One applies meaning to it that it becomes something else.

Where people get stuck is when One attaches to a particular thought within One's mind that something or someone must be a certain way. It is this unhealthy obsession about how One's life must be that gets people into trouble. It is not the initial thought that is the problem, concern or issue. It is the fact that it gets fixed in the mind. It hardwires the brain into believing that life must be this way and, if it is not this way, One's mind will make an assessment that there is something wrong with One's life. This is not true.

SOL DAY 308
3 November

Remind oneself that 'no self' is the best person or someone that One can be in life. Removing the ego-self, personhood or residual self-image from One's mind will significantly help One's journey along the path of enlightenment, improve One's life outcomes and enable One's divine awakening.

Most suffering is caused by a belief in the self and the need to protect and project this image of oneself to others and the world that One lives in today. The idea of the person who One thinks One is, or One's ego-identity within One's mind, can have a strong influence and power over One's life and living experiences on Earth. Many people throughout One's entire life will endlessly try to satisfy One's ego-identity in the hope that One will not feel empty, alone or scared. People will go to extraordinary lengths and do weird things in order to hide from One's spirit, soul or cosmic consciousness. Do not underestimate the things other people do so that One pleases and placates One's ego-identity.

To remove One's ego-identity from One's image of oneself, begin by avoiding saying 'I am ...' and replace it with 'One is ...' or One's mind or mind–body is ...' When One uses this kind of thinking, One shifts One's centre of awareness from inside One's mind to One's spirit. Decouple One's thinking about oneself from One's identity of oneself. Lose One's human identity – it is only a form, not One's true identity. One's true identity is spirit, not whatever DNA human form (male, female or transgender) One has or is host to.

With no self, One can truly know oneself.

When One looks within, away from One's projected self-image and One's form, One becomes aware of the truth of One's real divine identity and cosmic consciousness.

SOL DAY 309
4 November

To improve oneself is a daily habit and ongoing practice of being the best version of oneself. This is a well-intentioned goal – One is worthy of being the best that One can be in life. It is not about being perfect or attaining a high level of perfection in One's life. It is about accepting and embracing all of One's imperfections and being perfectly happy to work to improve oneself each day One is alive on Earth.

As a tree grows from a seedling and expresses itself in nature, so too should One. A flower does not compare its beauty to another, it simply allows the light of the sun to reflect all of its colours and gets on with being itself. It is important to care less about what others may think about oneself and more about how One views and perceives oneself in this world.

Waste no time trying to copy someone else's life or comparing oneself to other people. Be inspired by others' achievement and lifestyles, but never lose sight of being oneself. People will love One for who One truly is , not a fake version of One's true self. Pretending to oneself and others only serves One's ego and keeps One from being One's authentic and genuine version of oneself. It is okay not to be perfect, – no-one is on the planet.

Every mistake is a learning, every mishap is a lesson, and every misadventure is an opportunity to make a course correction to One's life. Keep adjusting the direction of One's life. Find One's moral, ethical and spiritual compass in life. Set One's intention to continually improve One's mind–body and alignment with One's spirit, soul or cosmic consciousness.

Every new day is an opportunity to begin again. Learn to positively praise oneself in the absence of any feedback from an external coach, mentor or Master. One may not ever hear it from others, but know that One is a special sentient Being. Believe in oneself now.

SOL DAY 310
5 November

Check in with One's mind and body before One begins One's day on Earth. Notice if One is feeling any stress, pain or discomfort within One's mind or body. Focus One's awareness on One's human form and give it loving kindness and compassionate attention. Adopt the simple practice of smiling with joy from the inside. Simply breathe if One is feeling stressed, pain or discomfort. Rest, relax, release, repair, renew, refresh and reactivate One's mind–body. Take time to nurture and nourish One's mind and body today.

Healing is an act of self-help that benefits oneself and all sentient Beings.

Sometimes One can become overwhelmed, confused and feel as if One's life is in complete chaos. If this is the case, just breathe. Discontinue the pattern of One's unhealthy lifestyle and just breathe. Disrupt the inner dialogue that says One must achieve results and a specific outcome at all costs and just breathe. Disable the increase in tension in One's mind–body by resetting One's work–life lifestyle so One can take time out and just breathe.

Reassert self-governance over One's life. Be fully present in the moment. Turn off the noise of judgement in One's mind about what One should or should not be doing at this very moment in time. If anyone asks, 'What is One doing?', reply by saying, 'Mindfully breathing'. If One is not breathing, One's human form will die. One can see how important the act of breathing is for One's life, balance and harmony on the planet.

Whatever One is doing today, check in with oneself and notice the condition of One's mind and body. Regularly come up for air from actively participating in a sea of doing and busyness. Nature does not operate in a state of emergency or ongoing crisis care. Neither should One. One's mind-body is part of the natural ecosystems of Earth, not a profit-making bio-machine.

SOL DAY 311
6 November

What if One is right? Pause patiently for a moment and take a long, slow, deep breath before continuing. One might ask, 'Right about what?' What if One is right about everything? What if One is right about being an infinite, immortal and eternal sentient Being of the universe? What if One is correct that One is spirit, soul or cosmic consciousness? What if One is accurate in describing oneself as a divine Being existing in a continuum of beingness beyond space-time?

Think about what this might mean for One's life. Limitless existence outside of One's human form, an unending and intuitive guiding spiritual intelligence and inner conscious knowingness with the divine oneness of source consciousness in the universe.

What if One were to extend this idea of 'rightness' out into the infinite field of possibilities in which One lives now? What if One is correct to imagine being the best version of oneself today? What if One is truly accurate in being able to manifest a new reality on Earth and live freely in peace, harmony and balance with all? What a thought. This is incredible.

What if One is able to change the world forever by changing oneself now? This is amazing, terrifying and overwhelming all at the same time. One's heart is pounding with excitement and One's mind is overflowing with positive enthusiasm for what might be. One does not need a time machine to go to the future – One can bring the future to this present moment now.

It is scary to think that One has the inherent power to positively change One's own life and the lives of every other sentient Being on Earth. One must rise with courage and kindness to conquer One's imaginary fears. Dedicate oneself, One's vision and energy in loving devotion to enable a better way of living and being for all Beings and future generations.

SOL DAY 312
7 November

Remind oneself today that One is worthy and deserving of all the good things and people in One's life. One accepts and receives of all the blessings and lovingly kind experiences coming to One now. One is open to every opportunity to be the best version of oneself. One knows that One attracts positivity, unconditional love and optimism. One is beautiful, loving, joyful, happy, healthy, honest, genuine, gentle, kind, smart, caring, confident and successful in all aspects of One's life. One is virtuous in the way that One lives One's life on Earth. One is a seeker of the truth and acts in the best interests of One's higher self. One believes unequivocally that the universe is on One's side. One is a beacon for others so that One might find One's way in this world. One never gives up and One never surrenders to the dark side or a low level of vibrational frequency or living consciousness. One is proactive, positive and purposeful in the way that One approaches life. One is mindful about how One's lives. One is all of these things and so much more.

One is here on Earth to make an incredible contribution to the lives of people and positively influence the world in ways One cannot even begin to imagine.

This is the right time to awaken to One's inner voice and see a new vision for oneself and this planet. Many lives are so caught up in survival and suffering that it is difficult to see the forest for the trees, let alone the light of One's own divine spiritual consciousness. A day is coming when One will have to make a conscious choice to continue to live in darkness and go aimlessly through life blind to the light within One's spirit, soul or cosmic consciousness or to realise that One is powerful beyond measure and step directly into the light of One's inner spirit and embrace being a 'Bright' or enlightened awake Being.

SOL DAY 313
8 November

Begin One's day with gratitude, loving kindness and joy. Know that most suffering is a way to bring about One's inner realisation and inside transformation. It is through this very personal and intimate process that One eventually awakens. Suffering can often crack or break ego's stranglehold on and control of One's mind. Sometimes a traumatic journey disrupts, deconstructs and dissolves One's pre-existing beliefs, thoughts and self-image. Suffering, as unpleasant as it is, has a divine purpose to enable One's freedom – if One chooses to be free.

The universe is giving One signs every single day that One is special, One is spirit and One is the universe itself. There is magic in One's life and it is up to One to become the magician and make it happen. Look around oneself now. Notice the synchronicities in One's life. The way things are, how life flows from moment to moment as One goes about One's daily life. Pay careful attention to the patterns of positive prosperity and amazing abundance, because the universe is communicating with oneself right now. Be open to listening and One will begin to notice the true magic in One's life now.

When One first begins to listen within and observes these signs it may seem contrived, a little bit weird or even difficult. One's mind may even be filled with a stream of doubt, but trust the process. After a while, when One has comfortably relaxed into the centre of One's spiritual beingness and present moment awareness, it will become easier and easier as time goes on.

Deprogramming One's mind of old thinking habits and a co-dependent belief system will take time – be patient. There may be many triggers that One will need to remove which are linked to past experiences and feelings of remorse, guilt, abuse, neglect or abandonment.

SOL DAY 314
9 November

Give oneself permission to be where One is now in life. It is okay, One does not need to be anywhere else other than here now on Earth. Take a moment and relax. It may feel like that One is missing out on something in One's life, but this is just One's ego's way of trying to get oneself emotionally invested in fear. Let all things happen naturally as One stays open and calmly unattached. Trust the process of life to unfold effortlessly in the moment.

One of the best parts about living One's life is that One has a new opportunity every single day to become the best version of oneself.

The universe is not in any hurry to do anything or be somewhere. Its only purpose is to exist and be now. The only agenda and timetable for One's life is set in One's mind. This is why One may feel disappointed, depressed or disillusioned with life as it is now. Learn to let go and go with the flow. Trust One's spirit, trust the process and trust the universe. Everything will work out. It always has, it always will.

Be gentle with One's mind and body. Praise oneself each and every day. Say to oneself, 'One is doing a really good job. Keep being positive, keep being thankful and keep being open to love, light and living the best life that One can on Earth.'

Use the best of One's imagination to co-create a new reality where One is mindfully living life in a way that is healthy, harmonious and helpful to all Beings. Know that every cell in One's body is connected to every other cell and it listens to all the thoughts in One's mind. When One sets a positive feel-good intention for One's day and life, One's mind–body goes where One's energy flows.

Earth needs One's positive and creative imagination to co-create a new future today.

SOL DAY 315
10 November

Nature will never disappoint, belittle or betray One. Nature will always be open, honest and reveal its true beauty without ever asking for anything in return. Nature is life and a good life is living naturally within and with nature. Immerse oneself in nature and it will speak to One in ways that will fill One's heart with immense joy and bring inner peace to One's spirit. Nature does not judge; it only expresses its real form freely to One and all. Nature is everywhere on Earth. It surrounds One, flows within One, it is part of One's mind and body. When One realises that One is part of nature and nature is part of oneself, the whole universe resides within One now. The infinite and the finite exist within One's Being here on Earth.

Stay close to nature or Country (land, sea and sky). Let it wash over One like a cool summer breeze or kiss One's cheeks like the early morning rays of light touching a beautiful flower. Let nature soothe One's concerns and worries like a gentle river flowing to the ocean.

All that One is now comes from nature. It sustains One, and it nurtures and nourishes One's mind and body. It gives life to all living things in ways too many to mention. From the top of the tallest mountain to the depth of the deepest ocean, One is surrounded by nature. One's home is nature and nature is One's home on Earth.

To harm nature is to hurt oneself in the end. Nature, and Earth, is a living entity and it requires One's love, kindness and compassion as much as anyone else in One's life.

To master oneself, rather than nature, is to know 'the way' of the universe. Within every living sentient Being alive on Earth exists the power to be One with nature and the entire oneness of the universe itself. When One heals oneself, heal with the natural rhythm of nature's harmony, balance and natural medicine. As One gives to nature, it returns tenfold.

SOL DAY 316
11 November

Today is a day to choose to be free and celebrate One's freedom. Freedom comes in many different forms, arrangements and practices. Freedom from hunger, violence, war, pain and suffering. Freedom from the tyranny of colonial powers, egocentric systems of governance and separatist policies or dictatorships. Freedom from anxiety, fear and depression. Freedom from self-limiting beliefs, behaviours and habits of addiction. Freedom from the opinions, perspectives and comments of others. Freedom from over-thinking and over-doing. Freedom from perpetual consumer debt and contemporary economic slavery. Freedom from feelings of unworthiness and lack of confidence. There are a million things One can choose to be free of in this life. It begins by embracing One single thought – the intention to be free and live free in this moment. Do not let One's excuses prevent oneself from being free now and forever more.

One was born free and One will die free. Everything in-between is a choice to be free or not to be free. No-one else can choose One's path for One. One is responsible for One's own freedom in life. Being free is an act of spiritual sovereignty and divine destiny.

Knowing that there is a life out there where One can be absolutely free is the first step in co-creating and manifesting a life of freedom as a reality today. Being free of material possessions and the need to constantly please people is a great way to start this 'freedom ride'. Meditation offers One a great way to let go and free One's mind of thoughts. Be open to One's path to freedom.

Begin a 'Freedom Journal' and write down the top three priorities that One is seeking to be free of at this very moment. Undertake a meditation session and come up with a mindful plan and sustainable way that will enable One's freedom as a priority in One's life.

SOL DAY 317
12 November

When One becomes awake, it clarifies who One is by dissolving the false identity that One is not. There is nothing scary about it; it is a natural process of realising the illusion within oneself and the illusion outside of oneself. This may seem like an incredible idea or point to reach in One's life. But it is all part of the universe revealing its truth to One – embrace it now.

What intrigues One is that very few people are wondering why One is actually here on Earth. Hardly anyone is asking, 'Why do all the things that One is doing on this planet? What is the purpose of it all? What is the overall planetary goal One is contributing to? How does whatever One is doing benefit One and all Beings?' These are simple questions and it is One's responsibility to have the courage to ask them of oneself today. When One does ask, listen in silence for the answer. Be the One with the oneness of a single divine consciousness and a common unifying vision for a new Earth today.

It is time to rise and shine as the brilliant 'Bright' One is on Earth. This is not about forcefully changing the world. It is about adjusting its current global trajectory to align with a higher purpose by spiritually evolving oneself in alignment with the universe.

This may sound farfetched, but be reassured. Take comfort in knowing that it is all part of the universe's grand plan to bring things to a point of *spiritual singularity*. Whether One realises it or not, One as spirit exists within a field of spiritual entanglement with all other Beings in the universe. This is a phenomenon where source consciousness is present in such a way that the individual spiritual states of consciousness exist independently until aligned, and the act of conscious alignment of One influences that of the other, even when at a distance from each other in space–time within the universe.

SOL DAY 318
13 November

Anyone can inspire oneself to be the best that One can be today. Empty all self-limiting beliefs and negative thoughts from One's head. Explore infinite possibilities that currently exist now. Aim to be better than One was yesterday. Ask the universe for help, guidance and support. Consciously invite inspirational people and creative opportunities into One's life.

One is not stuck where One is in life. One is always in transition to a higher level of conscious awakening and being in this world. Be the answer to One's own question: 'What will One be?' One will be the best version of oneself today – plain and simple. Life is not a competition; it is an act of cooperation with oneself and others in this world. This is a call to action and it is time to activate One's new life on Earth today.

Motivate One's mind and energise One's body. Set the intention to have a positive mind, positive vibes and a positive life. No matter what happens next, be fully focused in the moment. Be completely committed to an amazing outcome and get excited about engaging with One's life. Know that One's life does matter. Whatever One does today is enough. Never let anyone tell One that whatever One is aspiring to do cannot be done. Just go for it now.

One is truly a being of unconditional love and light. Stand in front of a mirror and repeat this: 'One has got this. One can do this. One will be the change that One seeks to be in this world.' Believe in oneself and One's life so much that the universe has only One choice to manifest it in One's life now. Embrace One's inner joy and endless enthusiasm to be the best.

One's new agenda for living life starts today. Begin where One is now and love One's path of enlightenment in this world. One's real-life journey starts the moment One stops listening to the fears of others and begins to believe in oneself. One is truly a great spiritual Being.

SOL DAY 319

14 November

One's goal must be to free oneself from the conditioning of One's parents, culture and society. In freeing oneself, One also frees other Beings and naturally extends a circle of love, kindness and compassion to One and all living things on Earth.

Learn to embrace the things that excite One. It is a path to One's true calling in this world. People's passions often connect One to One's prosperity in life. When One's actions benefit One and all Beings, One knows that One is on the right path. Welcome prosperity, abundance and freedom flowing effortlessly and continuously into One's life today. Know that the universe is on One's side, now and forever. Be at One with it now.

The biggest of dreams and changes in One's life often come from the smallest sparks of an idea or thought in One's mind.

Eventually everything comes full circle in One's life. Everyone returns to One's pure divine consciousness. The process of One's life is to truly realise who One is now. One's life journey on Earth is about shifting to a new level of consciousness. It is about dissolving One's egoic thoughts of fear about suffering and dying, living in judgement and separation, and resisting a change to empty One's mind. One is continually being drawn to transcend One's old life and outdated habits so One can align with One's inner spirit, harmony, balance, insight, intuitive intelligence, eternal contentment, cosmic creativity, infinite peace and higher self.

Centre One's life not on the outside, but to what is going on inside oneself. The moment One decides to believe in being the best version of oneself and commits to experience a better living reality on Earth, is the same moment that the entire universe shifts its synchronicity to align with One to manifest this new reality. Accept it. This is how the universe works.

SOL DAY 320
15 November

The way One speaks to oneself is how the universe hears One. One is responsible for One's self-talk and co-creating One's life on Earth. When One is loving, kind and compassionate or peaceful, patient and prosperous, this is how the universe responds to One. One can achieve and do anything. One is worthy of a great life with incredible experiences and wonderful people in it. Just because things are the way they are now, does not mean that they will not change for the better. Believe in One's higher self or divine spirit and in a brighter future today.

Begin with a single positive thought of gratitude and then another. Soon One will have a cascade of positive beliefs and thoughts flowing in One's mind. One's mind–body energy will radiate positive energy into the universe. Know that there are endless opportunities and infinite ways to improve oneself and enhance One's life on this planet. Begin small and imagine big. Reach for the stars and at the same time stay centred within One's spirit. Know that One is an integral part of the universe and One is worthy of being here on Earth.

Believe it when One says that One has the ability and spiritual intuitive intelligence to figure it all out. One is an indomitable, undefeatable and indestructible spirit. A divine spirit will always experience a divine life here on Earth or anywhere else in the universe.

The breakthrough that One has always been seeking in One's life is here now. Everything that One is aligned to is coming to One in the right moment, the right way and with the right people. Never doubt what and how the universe can manifest something in One's life. Be a believer and so it shall be. Every drop of belief contributes to an ocean of reality in One's life.

SOL DAY 321
16 November

Hold a space for One's honesty, authenticity and genuine spiritual self. It is okay to let things be as they are in the world for now. It is not One's job to fix fake people or buy into the falseness of other's ego identities. One needs to burn away One's own egoic illusion in the flames of purifying truth within One's spirit. From the ashes of One's old identity will rise One's divine consciousness.

It is time to connect deeply into One's heart space. Listen to oneself and bathe in the richness of One's inner wisdom.

Be honest about what is working and not working in One's life. Learn to share One's story of success and unlock the truth within oneself. Provide a guiding light for others as well. Integrate One's spirit into One's life. Allow all emotions to pass through One, uninterrupted by judgement, attachment or resistance to change. Learn to listen, feel and be still in this powerful place of empowerment. Do not react to life – learn and live with life as it unfolds.

Lift others up and rise together in unity in the world. Remember One's honourable creative power within oneself. Know the inner space where One can go to be whole, complete and true to One's spiritual sovereignty. In this divine place lies One's freedom to just be.

Incorporate a living, natural, active practice, to be connected, nourishing and nurturing of One's spiritual life on Earth. Be grounded in how One chooses to live One's life. There is always an understanding within and an understanding without. Teaching is in the conversation of life itself. There will always be a right time to hear what One needs to know. Show up with no expectations about One's life – just go with it now.

The only way to solve One's living challenges is by leaning into oneself.

SOL DAY 322
17 November

One's life and society is shifting and changing today, not because it has to, but because it simply is. It has reached a threshold or tipping point where it no longer serves One's spirit, soul or cosmic consciousness. People are beginning to wake up all around the world. There is only so much of One's life that can be lived in ignorance before One finally realises that enough is enough. One's spirit and spiritual life cannot be ignored any longer. To deny the truth about One's own spirit is to deny One's actual divine existence in the universe.

Sooner or later, One comes to the inevitable conclusion that life was not meant to be lived as part of an egoic culture on the planet. One begins to feel incredibly tired of people with egoic minds trying to enslave others with an unrelenting agenda of control, power and greed. Generation after generation have been brainwashed into believing 'money is God' and worshipping this illusion in blind faith. Most people are influenced from birth into thinking that money will save One and solve all of One's problems. One embraces an alternative idea and is totally convinced that there is a better way to live One's life on Earth. A new way, which honours One's spirit, everyone's divinity and the whole of Earth itself.

This is not about converting all peoples to a single religion on the planet. Religion is an interpretation of spirit by someone else, which One believes. Spirituality is aligning with and having a direct experience of One's own spirit, oneness and source consciousness.

The dawning of a new age of enlightenment is here now and it is not going away. It does not come with a bang or explode onto One's screens like a blockbuster movie trailer. It happens in the twilight of One's mindful and spiritual presence.

Change is coming and it is time to ride the wave of change in One's life now.

SOL DAY 323
18 November

One is always co-creating and manifesting One's reality on Earth. This comes naturally to One and happens daily. One has been a creator since birth. What One is learning now is how to consciously co-create that which One seeks to manifest in this world.

The more One gives with overflowing generosity, the greater the gifts One will receive.

With practice, a focused mind and aligned spirit, One can manifest any experience or reality that One desires or believes will benefit oneself and other Beings. The universe will always support One and act in the best interests of One's higher self. One is infinitely greater than any obstacle or problem that One perceives in One's life. Every challenge is conquerable, every question has an answer and every problem can be solved. This is the yin and yang or duality of life in which One lives now.

Remind oneself that if things are not changing externally for oneself, One might need to change One's internal perception of things first and see what happens next. It is worth helping oneself first and then others. Do not shy away from this approach to life. Learn to invest in and use One's gifts and creative abilities. When One does this, it will inspire others to do the same.

If One feels frustrated that things are taking too long to manifest in One's life, pause, take a breath and be patient. No-one knows exactly how long a thing is supposed to take before the experience, form or moment comes into reality. Life does not come with a dedicated timetable or fixed compass of certainty. The universe works in synchronicity with all things. The greater the light of belief within One, the more it will shine to illuminate One's path in life.

SOL DAY 324
19 November

A wrong turn in One's life can be the right path if One chooses to see it as so. Always be guided by One's intuitive intelligence within One's spiritual Being. Do not beat oneself up if One is not where One expected to be in life now. Look around One, be aware of One's surroundings and say to oneself, 'This is life, One is alive and all is well.' The closer One is to One's spiritual presence, the more One will align to living in the moment. Stay in the moment until it is no more, then move on like a cloud in the sky – be free now.

Encourage but do not criticise; praise but do not punish; engage but do not attach, judge or resist. One is the teacher and the student of One's life.

A good leader never acts in One's self-interest or forces others to follow One. A great leader simply invites others on a journey on which One will awaken to One's own light and truth in this world. Sometimes One's greatest challenges are the places and spaces where One realises One's most profound truths and inner strengths. This can be both a difficult time and the way to become the best version of oneself.

One must bring One's spiritual awareness into every aspect of One's life. When One 'gets it', One will bring benefit to oneself and all other Beings in the world. How successful One is in depends on how aligned One is to living a spiritual life.

The strongest of people are the gentlest when it comes to being loving, kind and compassionate to others in this world. One's inner strength is not an external force to be used to coerce others into doing what One wants. It is an unwavering belief in One's spirit and living resilience that One can meet any challenge in One's life, anywhere One is on Earth

Be confident knowing that every 'wrong turn' in life will always lead One to the 'right path'.

SOL DAY 325
20 November

Take a moment to relax into One's mind–body–spirit at the beginning of One's day. Let the tension melt away as One empties One's mind in meditation. Know that there is nothing to be gained, apart from freedom, when One consciously lets go of all the struggles, heartaches and worries that One has about oneself, One's relationships and One's life. Stop giving One's time, love and energy to people who are selfishly consumed by One's own egoic mind. Focus on being lovingly kind and compassionate over the course of One's life.

Memories are but moments in One's mind; they serve as a reminder, not a recipe for life.

Realise that all that One projects and radiates into the world comes from within. Trust One's spiritual intuition to guide oneself. One does not need to explain or justify everything One does in life. Some things are beyond people's comprehension, no matter how many times or different ways One explains them.

Have the courage and bravery to walk the path alone. Have faith and belief when One is confused about the right path to take. Have confidence and resilience to trust One's spiritual intuition and the process unfolding before One. The sanctuary of One's spirit is always within One. Be what One is meant to be in this life and proactively transform One's darkness into light. Do not look at the length of time of One's becoming. Instead, consider the depth of that which One has become now.

One is the designated driver for One's life on Earth. With the alignment of One's mind–body–spirit and the universe, synchronicity flows in One's life. With awareness of oneself, One's spirit and 'the way', there is harmony and balance in the world. With the awakening of One's divine consciousness, there is enlightenment within One on Earth.

SOL DAY 326
21 November

The dance of life takes place with One becoming who One truly is now. Not in possessing material objects or money, manipulating people for selfish gain or dodging the difficult dilemmas in life. Train One's mind to recognise the ego within and all it associates with in One's life. Make a conscious decision to quietly reject and politely refuse it a seat at the table of One's life on Earth. Starve it of satisfaction and deny it anything that it wantonly believes or demands it deserves. Reserve a space in One's mind to see the good in people and the world, the positivity in One's life, the optimism for the future and the joy and excitement in manifesting One's beautiful reality here today.

This is not a magical fairytale. It is about being realistic and setting boundaries about who One invites into One's life, including One's own ego. This is a normal, healthy, self-care practice. It is necessary for One's peace of mind and personal wellbeing. Others are more likely to respect One if One can show that One respects oneself. The only way other people will learn how to treat One is if One can effectively communicate this to the other person. This informs others about the best way to engage with oneself in the present moment.

What works for One may not necessarily work for another. It is important to find the way people like to receive information and messages. Eighty per cent of messaging is conveyed through body language.

The things that are meant for One will naturally show up in One's life when One is being true to oneself. Be oneself and be ready to receive it all now. Every time One is open and aligned with One's inner spirit, One is rewiring One's brain to be more peaceful, joyful, quiet, calm, mindful, serene, gentle, loving, kind, compassionate and still. This is a beautiful thing.

SOL DAY 327
22 November

Now is the moment to step out of and burn all of One's survival clothes. One needs to break One's unhealthy habits from the past and embrace a new way of thinking, living and being in the world. It is not possible to keep wearing the same old hat of hopelessness and wrap oneself up in rags of unhelpful beliefs. This kind of thinking will not lead One to a prosperous life on Earth. To thrive and not just survive, One must completely throw away the beliefs, thoughts and behaviours of yesterday and become naked in a river of infinite possibilities.

One has to switch off One's survival mode and turn on One's thrive mind. One does this by activating One's prosperity and abundance thinking. Realise that there is an abundance of food, water, shelter and everything else necessary for a beautiful, harmonious and balanced life on the planet. When One takes care of Country (land, sea and sky), Country takes care of oneself too. Just because One may not be experiencing a feeling of prosperity and abundance in this present moment does not mean it does not exist. The Earth has always provided and produced enough for everyone. It is a constant giver of life and never asks for anything in return. When One gives to others, it only creates more prosperity and abundance in the world.

If One has a spiritual relationship with oneself and Earth, One can heal both. Never underestimate the value of a having a deep sense of belonging to Country (land, sea and sky) and Earth. When One is at peace within oneself, One can access the oneness of One's spiritual consciousness and be One with all on Earth and everything in the universe.

Those who realise that One's inner way is as important, if not more, than One's outer life, will begin to see that what One does on the inside influences everything on the outside.

SOL DAY 328
23 November

Whichever way life appears to be pulling and pushing One, be intuitively guided to go in the direction of One's inner wisdom. It is only when One changes the relationship with One's spirit that One profoundly changes the path that One is on now. One can wait patiently for the world to change – it will eventually happen at some point in time. One may or may not be here to enjoy or witness it. In the meantime, act with virtuous intent to co-create One's vision for a new reality on Earth today.

Know that everything One does matters. One only needs a single spark to ignite a burning passion of positivity that changes the entire world completely. This spark of inspiration already exists within the light, love and oneness of One's spiritual Being.

A billion dollars or a million prayers will not feed a single hungry, starving child in the world, but giving nutritious food, safe shelter or a supportive home, clean water, fresh air, unconditional love, mindful education, spiritual awareness and a sense of belonging with a loving, kind and caring family or parents in a cooperative community will sustain this life. Everyone has a place in this world. One just needs to figure out where it is.

As Dorothy in the *Wizard of Oz* says, 'There is no place like home.' Planet Earth is One's home. It is One's only home planet in the solar system. Without it, One's human form would not exist. One needs to realise that if Earth dies, so do humans. But if humans die, life on Earth will survive. The good news is that One is powerful beyond measure and can influence the trajectory of humanity by shifting One's relationship with oneself to be more aligned with One's spirit. With everything that One thinks, says and does, One can renew and reconfigure One's life. One can co-create the best version of oneself and this world on Earth.

SOL DAY 329
24 November

Whatever One was before arriving on Earth and hosting a human form, One will return to this pure state of divine consciousness. In every moment of the day, be aware of everything that is in One's life. Listen to One's mind, body and the subtle messages that One's spirit is giving oneself today. Stay centred within One's spiritual presence and remain calm within One's mind. Cultivate a positive attitude and optimistic outlook about One's life. Envision the best version of oneself and work towards this new reality today. Create a vision board or journal that reflect One's new and improved life on Earth. Review it regularly and make changes as necessary. Make sure every step One takes and every thought One thinks is aligned to it.

At times, One may stumble, fall or even lose One's way in life. But stay true to One's inner spirit and know that the universe is with One, every step of 'the way'.

Know that One's failures are the footprints of the future to One's growth, transformation and success in life. View every encounter with another person as a living, learning and transformative teaching moment. People will come into One's life to teach One, train One, test One or simply spend time with One. Let things be as they need to be and create a sense of wakefulness in being able to see the wider and deeper picture of One's reality now. Learn to let go, be joyful and have fun in the moment. Enjoy life, celebrate life and express the best of oneself.

The universe is like a vast cosmic reflective mirror. Whatever One visions One's life to be, it will reflect it back to One as part of One's living manifested reality. The clearer One's imagination and vibrational energy is, the greater clarity it will reveal in co-creating One's new reality today.

SOL DAY 330
25 November

Begin to understand how special a spirit or sentient Being One is in the universe. One's pure divine self is perfect and so too is One's imperfect human form. This world may not be perfect, but it is the only home One has now.

One does not look at nature with all its imperfections and think it is not worthy or whole. One should apply this same approach to One's life. The beauty of nature is in accepting everything as it is now and allowing things to naturally be. Let the land be the land, the sea be the sea and the sky be the sky. There are no straight lines in Country (land, sea and sky). One's path in life is also full of twists, turns and unforeseen roundabouts.

It is important to care less about One's possessions and more about how One chooses to live One's life on Earth. Observe One's mind and One's way of life. If it is not aligned with One's spirit or sense of spiritual oneness in the world, realise it and change it now. There is no perfect way to live One's life, there is only 'the way' of the universe. Everything flows in the same direction to a point of spiritual singularity. It is a **'light hole'**, an alternative to a 'black hole' in space–time, only existing in a non-dimensional reality. Let this idea and concept of 'light' sit with One and know that, as a Being of pure divine consciousness, One is home wherever One is in the universe. One will always be guided to the right place in life.

A truly spiritual person will not try to escape and hide from the world in work, relationships, a cave or a monastery at the top of a mountain. One will not run from reality, instead One will embrace it and wake up to One's divine self and see the world for what it truly is. Spirituality is about having a direct experience of spirit and seeing through the illusions of this world.

SOL DAY 331
26 November

Create space, live in alignment (mind–body–spirit) and be awake now. Be aware how One is setting the intention for today. Imagine it as a peaceful, loving, kind, calm, harmonious, happy and chilled experience. Relax into One's inner peace, eternal serenity and endless space within One's spirit. Take a moment to look around oneself and sit in silence, letting oneself observe without absorbing everything that is around oneself. Close One's eyes and focus on One's breathing. With every breath that One takes, relax more and more into One's divine presence or cosmic consciousness. With practice, One will begin to shift One's centre point of living life from One's mind to One's spirit or heart centre/chakra.

Mindfulness is the key to holding a space where everything is observed.

Realise that One's ability to fold space–time will enable One to manifest that which One desires most in life. This may seem too good to be true, but it is not. The emptiness of space is often more valuable than One has been taught or realises. When One creates space in One's life, something else can be manifested into One's reality. Space has more potential than One has been led to believe.

Be a champion of space and change the way that One lives One's life today.

Space has always preceded everything in this world. When One holds a 'sacred space' for One's spirit, oneness, love, a loved One, a loving moment or loving intention it becomes an immensely powerful intention in One's life. The universe has no option other than to honour it. This is why 'holding space' is the perfect process to realise any potentiality in the universe. The same principle can be applied to every aspect of One's life. One can hold a sacred space for prosperity, abundance, wholeness, wellness or to be the best version of oneself today.

SOL DAY 332
27 November

If the world is an illusion, One's thoughts are essentially about nothing in the world. How can One think that One's thoughts are real if what One is thinking about is non-real? This is the paradox of thought. And yet, with One's thoughts, One co-creates oneself as well as One's reality and living experiences on Earth.

One's thoughts vibrate with a particular energy signature moving out into the world around oneself. One also has a spiritual aura, but this is a changing fluid state of consciousness and always in flux. All is in motion, including One's emotions (thoughts and feelings). Everything is moving through oneself like a wave of cosmic energy rippling out into the universe. This means that One can increase One's vibrational energy from low to high at any moment, naturally improving One's alignment with One's spiritual higher self.

When One loses One's connection to the noise of people, possessions and places in One's life, One is better able to centre oneself, hear One's inner voice and experience the presence of One's divine peace within One's spirit. Do not surrender One's mental sanity to the sights and sound of One's ego. Align with One's spirit and the universe. This is the secret to successfully surrendering to One's spiritual self. Realise One's only truth and true nature.

No matter what is happening in One's life, all is well. Whatever negativity people try and project into One's living space, shield oneself and say, 'All is well.' It may seem to other people that One does not care, but this is not so. One is simply stating an overwhelming obvious truth about the universe. Realise that One's spirit and the universe will always be present.

SOL DAY 333
28 November

Life is like a sandcastle on the beach – transient with the passing of the tide and time. People often feel a kind of restlessness in One's life and worry that One is missing out on things, people or experiences. If One is truly honest with oneself, One is right where One needs to be now. Everything is unfolding in perfect synchronicity with the whole universe. There are many things to be grateful for in One's life – the list is endless. One is immersed in the abundance of the Earth. One simply needs to be grateful for One's mind-body-spirit and everything else in the world.

Find the freedom within One's spirit and set One's mind free.

Free oneself from looking at the world from a glass that is half empty. Replace it with a 'glass half-full' perspective. Allow the magic to happen in One's life. Do not focus on what One doesn't have; be grateful for who and what is already in One's life. Be thankful for everything and everyone now. Nothing ignites more generosity and thoughtfulness in the world than people being mindful and consciously grateful. Openly give others personal praise, positivity, loving kindness, compassion and encouragement.

Generous people co-create generosity and a giving culture in the world. People like this give of oneself plus One's time, energy, enthusiasm, encouragement, enlightenment, wellness, assistance, advice and support (emotional, mental, physical, spiritual, health, financial, cultural and whole-of-life).

One's natural spiritual presence is unlimited and inexhaustible. Know that now is as good a time as any to give the gift of giving. Sometimes all it takes is showing up and being present in One's life and the lives of other sentient Beings on Earth to make a real difference.

SOL DAY 334
29 November

One's limitless potential exists in this present moment 'Now'. Do not be distracted, disengaged or diverted from it by One's ego. Never allow the insignificant actions of others to shift One's inner peace, internal calmness and the quiet stillness of One's mind–body–spirit. Let One's life flow in the direction of One's mindful desires and divine destiny. Pay careful attention that no emotion (thought and feeling) overpowers One's intuitive intelligence.

One is the master of One's mind and the captain of One's human experiences on Earth.

Leave the outside world to itself. One's real work is on the inside. In the end, One's belief, work and life will be One's life signature. It will speak for itself, nothing else need be added. What One sees, thinks and feels in life depends a great deal on how One has configured One's mind. When One has done the hard work of realising and transforming oneself, life flows effortlessly.

In order for this path to reveal itself, One sometimes needs to ask oneself a direct question. Is One going to face the truth that One is a spiritual Being and live a spiritual life on Earth? Or hide in the shadows of falseness and fear of an egoic mind? The choice is remarkably simple: to be or not to be?

Choose to be the light, love and conscious oneness that One's spirit, soul or cosmic consciousness truly is now.

When One consciously makes a choice to be who One is, it will ignite One's life and set the world on fire (in a good way, of course!) One is spirit and host to One's human form and One's life on Earth. It is time to be the best version of oneself. Be kinder, wiser and nicer than One can ever think possible, because it is always possible.

SOL DAY 335
30 November

Sit in silence, stand up alone and walk unaccompanied in the direction of One's vision. Stay committed to what One believes in today. Life is not a dress rehearsal for something that One may think, say or do. Life is what One does now in this moment. One has got this – this is what One's life is all about.

Despite the darkness in the world, be a visionary for light, love and oneness in One's life. Be radiant with One's living energy. Express One's positive optimism. Share it with all Beings in the world. Earth and every citizen needs what One is offering. This is the moment and time to shine One's light so that others may see with clarity and a sense of inner calm. One is contributing to making a new reality on Earth. One's vision is great and One's goal is valid.

Every great idea or thought ever manifested in life began as an inspiring intention to express itself in the world.

Whatever comes, let it. Whatever happens, allow it. Whatever is, accept it now. Stay young, wild and free. Do not be caged by others' pessimism or lack of belief in a better way of living and being on Earth. These people are unfortunately stuck in One's old bad habits, hurtful practices and unhealthy behaviours or relationships with oneself and others.

One of the most precious things in existence is knowing who One is and that One has the unimaginable potential to change One's destiny here on Earth. Realising this also means One does not need approval or consent to co-create One's lifestyle and live One's life. When One is content within oneself, One is free of explaining to others about One's beliefs. One can focus One's positive energy on being relaxed and joyful about living a spiritual lifestyle on Earth.

DECEMBER
Sol day 336-366

One believes in One's unlimited potential and immeasurable power to be the best version of oneself. Co-creating a successful life journey is not about arriving at a particular destination. It is all about learning to be truly present in the moments of One's life now.

Everyone, everywhere on Earth is a citizen of the future, living life in the present. When One brings the best of oneself into this present moment, One creates a positive ripple effect in space–time. It also alters the timeline and path in life for One's future. At the same time, One also changes the trajectory of living experiences for the next generation on Earth.

In a universe that is vast, infinite and endless, there is no relative direction, which is why it is easy to get lost along 'the way'. Believing in One's spirit, soul or cosmic consciousness is an act of divine faith and ultimate trust in the universe itself. To know oneself is to know 'no self'. When One believes in a better way of living and being on Earth – so will it be now.

It begins and ends with 'the One'. The One spirit, soul or cosmic consciousness who has the One realisation, the One transformation and the One awakening of One's infinite, eternal and immortal divine spirit.

SOL DAY 336

1 December

One's future life is always being manifested in this present moment. If One desires to experience a new reality and live a life that is positive, loving and kind, One needs to begin with a positive, loving and kind mind. The way that One thinks about oneself and speaks to oneself matters when co-creating the best version of oneself and a better life on Earth.

Face any fears for the future that One may have about oneself. Learn to let go and step into the unknown. Embrace a new enthusiasm for One's life. Focus on the good, the great and stay grounded in One's gratitude.

Miracles begin as soon as One realises that One is the creator of One's life and destiny on Earth. One's power does not lie in the validation and authority of other people's approval, but in One's own permission to change, grow and transform. The good news is that One is not meant to be a mindless human drone in this world. One was meant to awaken now.

One's human form was just stardust drifting in the cosmic currents of space–time.

One's manifested uniqueness and divine spirit will be too exceptional for limited minds to comprehend in this world. Some people will aim to fix One's living, growing and glowing aspirations to the floor of impossibilities. Others may try to suck One's life energy into a vortex of negativity in the hope of sharing One's fear and hopelessness.

As a child of the universe with a body manifested out of star stuff, One's worldly suffering and struggles are meant to lead to living a higher divine purpose on Earth. If One knew the infinite potential and unlimited power One holds to completely change One's life and the world, One would be truly in awe of oneself right now. One of the most important things that One can do in this world is to believe, transform and awaken the 'Bright' within oneself now.

SOL DAY 337
2 December

One lives in a world where most adults no longer believe in magic or the synchronicity of the universe. It is a world where people have lost the ability to create magic in One's daily life. One needs to realise that the universe is either a magical place or it is not. If One believes the world is a magical place, magical things can and do happen every single day. Magic is possible at any place, at any time or anywhere in One's life. One only needs to look up at the stars sparkling brightly or a full moon glowing radiantly in the night sky to see magic.

The greatest magic trick in the universe is to simply believe in One's own magic. Then watch as the great illusion of life unfolds and reveals itself before One's own eyes.

When One understands that One is the magician and One's life is the magic trick, One will begin to appreciate the interconnectedness between what One believes and One's reality in the world. As an illusionist, know that all of One's life is an illusion – a place to make things real where they did not exist before. What is magic if not an illusion to co-create something out of nothing or to make the impossible possible? This is what One does with One's life here on Earth. Every day is magic, if One believes it to be so.

This might sound like an oversimplification, but trust One. One's thoughts are One's magic spells and One's vibrations are the energy that can manifest One's illusion into reality. One's imagination is the key to see the unseen and make it seen in this world. Many will try and convince One that magic is not 'real' but remember this – doubters doubt and believers believe. This is the distinction between transcending space–time and being a prisoner of it.

Believe in oneself to manifest One's new life and living experiences – so be it now.

SOL DAY 338

3 December

Today is a day to read a clearing and cleansing affirmation to benefit oneself and other Beings:

One chooses to relax and release all toxic, negative and egoic thoughts, feelings, beliefs, habits and behaviours from One's mind and body that no longer serve One's higher self, greater good or divine purpose in every aspect of One's life on Earth and One's cosmic existence in the universe. One lets go of unhealthy dysfunctional egocentric relationships and harmful people from One's life and creates endless free space with One's infinite free will. One consciously invites positive, life-affirming, loving, kind, helpful, compassionate, generous, open, virtuous and spiritually centred people, Beings and relationships into One's life now. One completely dissolves and releases all guilt, shame, dishonour, disgrace, embarrassment and disharmony that One has ever felt in relation to any and all issues in One's life. One frees One's mind of these thoughts and feelings now. One knowingly and consciously transmutes all vibrational energies to love and aligns with One's spiritual state of conscious oneness or higher within One's Being. So be it now.

One believes in this affirmation with all of One's heart, mind and spirit. One is committed to all that One will become and all that will be. One honours the intent of this affirmation to create space for peace, love, harmony and balance within oneself. One realises that with change comes growth and with growth comes change. One is evolving into the best version of oneself and becoming a great 'Bright' or enlightened awake divine Being.

SOL DAY 339
4 December

One will only become what One believes oneself to be now. The power is in the giving, because the potential to become is already within One's divine presence. To be or not to be is the question of the day. And the answer lies in One's permission to be it. One's spirit exists in an infinite field of spiritual entanglement with every other sentient Being in the universe. It aligns with and is attracted to other spirits on Earth the same way a seedling is drawn to the light of the sun. It has an innate need to be in the light.

When One's mind–body–spirit is vibrating in harmony with another person, One will experience an alignment of energies. It can occur at any time or in any place in the world. It is a natural phenomenon. Sometimes it will happen in a crowded room, or as One is just going about One's daily life. Look for the external signs and recognise the inner signals from One's spiritual intuition.

The light of the creator lives eternally in everyone's spirit. It cannot be extinguished, evicted or excised from One's Being by anyone or anything in the entire universe.

Life is simple, life is short – enjoy every day with a clear intention of celebrating life itself. Where there is consciousness in the universe, there is sentient life. When One lets go, One is able to let life and the divine express itself through how One lives life on Earth. Know that love and truth vibrate at specific frequencies in the universe. As One becomes more aligned with One's spirit, One will feel it deeper within oneself. One's divine path is 'the way' to truth.

The more One surrenders to life and the universe, the easier it becomes to be who One was meant to be in life. One is exactly where One needs to be – be where One is now.

SOL DAY 340
5 December

Sometimes One feels like One is at a crossroads in One's life. Does One stay or does One go? Does One turn left or right? Does One have coffee, tea, water or juice? Does One continue on the mindless egocentric path before One or choose a more mindful, spiritually centred life to live? There are a million or more questions that One can ask oneself each day. However, know that the serendipity of life will always happen when it happens. One has no control over it. It is the occurrence and development of events by chance in a happy or beneficial way in One's life. When One is open, free and without a care in the world, this allows the universe to facilitate these events in an unplanned way, occurring right in the path of One's life on Earth.

When this does happen in One's life, One may remark to oneself or another person, 'What are the chances of this happening here and now?' This is serendipity, or the synchronicity of the universe in action. Things will naturally occur when they need to occur, so just relax and let it be so.

The less One fights, struggles or stresses in life, the more One can flow with the cosmic currents in One's life. Rest assured, nobody gets out alive – everyone dies. This may seem harsh or confronting, but it is simply a fact. The truth is that every human form will eventually reach a use-by date and dematerialise into its naturally occurring organic molecules and atomic elements.

In the meantime, work out an inner way to be more synchronous with the universe and allow greater serendipity into One's life on Earth. The good thing about serendipity is that One does not have to plan for it. It happens when One least expects it and in a way that usually surprises One. This is something to look forward to – don't expect it and it will surely happen.

SOL DAY 341
6 December

When a door closes in One's life, let it close. When a door opens wide, welcome it. Do not waste any energy trying to kick in a door by seeking acceptance and validation from others when the universe has obviously shut it in One's best interests. Know when it is over and time to move on with One's life. One has more important places to be, people to meet and things to do in this world than knocking on a door that is never going to open. Show some self-respect and dignity. Honour oneself and the universe in this moment.

Know that old ways of thinking, speaking and doing will never open new doors in One's life. Get out of One's own way and co-create a space for being the best version of oneself. Every time One believes or thinks a loving, kind thought about becoming a better version of oneself, it opens One's own door to a new future for oneself. Things will begin to happen in synchronicity with the universe. One will eventually stop calling these coincidences and realise that One has immeasurable power and infinite potential to create One's own reality on Earth.

Trust One's own intuitive intelligence and the vibe that One is giving off or receiving in any situation – energy is always truthful. Use meditation to free One's mind from the past and the future to be in the present. It is important to mindfully ground One's spiritual awareness in the 'Now' of One's life and living experiences. Sooner or later, One will be able to create One's own doorways in space–time and transcend life as One knows it.

A door is only a door because One believes it to be so. When One begins to shift the paradigm of One's unconscious reality into a state of living wakefulness, One will realise that there is no door, because the whole wall is an illusion.

SOL DAY 342
7 December

One is and has always been abundant and infinite beyond measure. The energy of abundance in the universe flows freely and effortlessly in all its forms. One is completely open and receptive to experiencing an abundance of joy, peace, love, freedom, awareness, kindness, compassion, clarity, insight, mindfulness, generosity, space, harmony, balance, serenity, health, wellness, money and divine wisdom in One's life. Align with and be willing to accept this new reality today. Unconditionally embrace this abundance with a grateful heart and a thankful mind now. Know that One is abundance, therefore One already exists in abundance.

The best way to experience abundance in One's life is to be abundant within oneself. Be abundant in One's beliefs, One's thoughts, One's feelings and One's life. Learn to demonstrate and radiate it into the world in One's daily outlook, One's attitude, One's perception and One's whole-of-life energy.

Whatever One is seeking to attract into One's life, be it now. If One seeks love, be a source point for an abundance of love in One's life. The same principle applies to every other experience that One seeks to manifest now. Abundance will always attract more of itself. This is how the universe works. Being and vibrating with the feeling of abundance for a certain thing, person or experience will only attract more of it into One's life.

One is responsible for how One perceives things and experiences life. Every time One shifts One's perception to be more abundant within oneself, it brings One closer to experiencing abundance in One's life. This creates a never-ending stream of abundance.

Sometimes in life One will experience a profound awareness of the infinite abundance so deep within One's Being that it is indescribable and unfathomable to One's mind.

SOL DAY 343
8 December

In a world obsessed with the endless streaming of information and people talking about nothing. Learn to sit in stillness and quieten One's mind in silence today. Look for the warning signs that One is about to 'lose One's mind'. A lost mind or 'no-mind' may be the sanest thing that One ever does in life. Just because One has a mental health breakdown, illness or episode does not mean that One is broken. One may simply need to reconfigure One's thoughts, improve One's brain chemistry and live life in alignment with One's true spiritual self.

Reflect on an alternative new modern definition of insanity: 'Being a sane person who tries repeatedly to "fit into" a world where most people's minds are operating a stream of egoic unconscious mindless thinking'. One can, at times, feel as if One is living in a world where everyone has basically gone insane. A kind of global psychotic pandemic, affecting nearly everyone on the planet. The only way to become immune to this worldwide illness is to mindfully cure oneself of the mental disease. Awareness is the best defence and conscious awaking the only cure.

Be the Master of One's mind and thoughts, then finally One's life. One cannot expect to figure everything out about oneself and One's life in One day. It is important to spend regular quality time with oneself – alone and uninterrupted. Whatever works and is good for One's mind, body and spirit – do it.

Looking after oneself is a lifelong journey. So is reaching One's full potential in life. Sometimes One will need to risk upsetting people because of the way One lives and what One makes a priority in One's life. One's inner wellness agenda will not always align with others, so do not expect it to. Being a sane person in an insane world requires focus and effort.

SOL DAY 344
9 December

To prevent chaos, casually organise it into order. To avoid disaster, gently massage it into alignment. To escape noise, quietly usher it into silence. One has the power to travel between the worlds of conditioned thinking and creative imagination. Just because someone says something, does not make it so. One must mindfully discern things for oneself and work out if it aligns with One's inner most virtues, values, truth and spiritual sense of One's Being. Only then believe it. Treat all experiences like a stone skipping across the water on a journey until it finally sinks to the bottom and disappears from view.

It may take a day, a year, a decade or One's entire lifetime, but never give up on being the best version of oneself. Stay committed, stay focused and stay on track. As the sun shines, so too will One's spirit in this world. Things will naturally fall into place when it is time and in synchronicity with the universe. Until then, One needs to remain committed and true.

Unclutter One's life, one thing at a time. Do it slowly, surely, safely and without any complication, confusion or concern. One's new life will manifest into the spaces that One creates for it. The universe works in space – this is why there is so much of it. At the beginning of the day and at the end of it, One must be there for oneself.

When One begins to trust more, believe more and honour more about oneself and the universe. Great things start to flow and happen more spontaneously in One's life. It is as if a great cosmic switch has been turned on for the very first time and One has been directly connected to the source of all things in the universe. With the right alignment of One's mind–body–spirit, One can download a new reality and co-create any manifested experiences that One so desires now.

SOL DAY 345
10 December

Extraordinary is what extraordinary thinks, says and does in life. Surround oneself with people who positively value who One is now. Be in the company of others who encourage One's best in life. Learn to unconditionally love oneself as One is and not pretend to be someone else. Fake personas are merely fabricated projections of false truths from fictitious people. Keep it real by being real with oneself in this world.

When One believes that life flows prosperously, abundantly and easily in the right direction for oneself, the universe demonstrates this to be so.

If One is feeling a little bit witty, wacky and weird today – that's perfectly okay, enjoy it. If One is feeling slightly eccentric or unconventional – that's absolutely fine too, embrace it. Life was not meant to be lived in a straitjacket of social conformity or rigid rules of collective community censorship. Realise that time does not exist, only clocks and calendars do.

When One is going to do something, do not do it because One has to or do it in a begrudgingly bad mood. Flip the script on One's self-talk and do it because One loves to. For example, say to oneself, 'One loves to clean house and keep things neat, tidy and in order.' This is why One is cleaning or washing clothes or vacuuming the floor – One loves living in a neat, tidy, clean space. One can then apply this mindful principle to every other aspect of One's life. All those chores, tasks and items on the 'to do list' will become tasks to do with mindful loving attention.

This is how One turns the ordinary into the extraordinary – by mindfully giving any challenge, issue or concern One's loving kind attention, devoted gentle focus and applied calm energy. The way to defeat procrastination is with mindful loving attention for oneself first.

SOL DAY 346
11 December

Everything that One does in life is imbued with the energy of One's mind-body and conscious presence of One's spirit. Every day that One is alive on Earth, One creates One's living energy signature and radiates it into the world and the universe. Take a moment to think about the frequency and type of energy One is projecting today. Change it so it is lighter, brighter, upbeat and more positive. One is under no obligation to be the same person that One was five days or even five minutes ago.

Do not be bothered that One is not completely human – no person is on Earth. All are spiritual Beings hosting a specific manifested human form or DNA in space-time. Every person alive today has an end date. Everyone who has ever lived or will be born will also die. This is the inescapable and inevitable truth of experiencing life as a human being on this planet. Life lives momentarily – death deconstructs all temporary living identities. The message for today is to enjoy living One's life, because it's the only life One has now.

There will come a day when One must decide if One goes all in and becomes the best version of oneself, or stays sitting on the sideline of One's life watching it all slowly slip away. There is a cosmic calling within One – can One feel it now? It invites One to be responsible and accountable regarding the collective field of conscious existence in the universe and at the same time to be free of it. This may sound impossible, but it simply means believing in oneself, One's spiritual identity and the universe as a whole.

To be One is to embrace One's Being and oneness. One is part of the whole of existence itself. The spirit in One is not separate from the oneness in all things. The essence of water in a single raindrop is the same as that in a stream, river, lake or ocean. Realise this truth.

SOL DAY 347
12 December

Anger, hate or violence in any aggressive or passive form will never be the path to peace, love and harmony in One's life or the world. Empty One's mind and body of these destructive thoughts and energies today. Do it so One can experience inner peace and a sense of spiritual sanctuary in One's life now. One owes it to oneself to lose these lower levels of vibrational living and aspire to be a better version of oneself. Help oneself to be a more lovingly kind, gentle and wholesome person. Encourage oneself to create a lifestyle of wellness for One's mind and body. Holistic wellness is One's greatest wealth in the world.

Only when One is truly loving, kind and compassionate to oneself and One's enemies, will One find true contentment in living life on Earth. When One can see and honour the spirit in One and all, One will see no separation in the world – only sentient Beings. Everyone everywhere is on the same path, returning to the divine source in the universe.

Any suffering that One is experiencing in life is a calling for One to bring One's awareness to this situation. Focus One's attention on giving One's mind–body loving kindness, tender loving care and compassion. It is an act of self-care to raise One's level of living wellness and increase One's positive wellbeing. Being sensitive to and responding to One's pain and suffering is a sign of maturity. Neglecting it is a sign of mistreatment, abuse and self-harm.

Learn to listen to One's mind and body. Teach and train One's mind to take care of oneself. At the end of the day, One has to be there for oneself (mind–body–spirit) in this life.

When One begins to co-create an oasis of wellness in One's life, it will have a cascading positive effect on One's living experiences on Earth. One is a creator of living wellness.

SOL DAY 348
13 December

Know that the future always takes care of itself. All that is left to do is to live in this present moment – today. Breathe and be the Being that One is meant to be on Earth.

Without going anywhere in the world, One can be open to the whole universe from where One is now. One does not need to climb to the top of a mountain, sail around the world or hide in a dark cave to experience freedom. Within One exists a state of conscious free will. It is the reason One can be anywhere or go to any space-time moment in the universe. One's spirit is free – always was, always will be.

The future will come of its own accord and in its own way. There will always be moments when One may feel awkward, empty and as if One is waiting for something to happen. Be patient and enjoy living in the moment. Become detached about what the future may hold for oneself but believe in the abundance of blessings coming to One when it does. As One looks back on the year that has been, realise that it could not have happened any other way than the way it happened. This is how it was meant to be in that moment. What is right for now is how One determines it to be now. Do not confuse the past with the future. One lives life in the present.

The fruit of the future only ripens when One is ready to taste its sweet flavour. Until then, cultivate a practice of contemplative meditation, virtuous actions and mindful living in alignment with One's mind–body–spirit and the universe.

Whatever One comes across along 'the way', accept it as is. Learn to look beyond the obvious, past the incidental and into the cosmic occurrences that are unfolding in front of One now. Today is the future of yesterday and the past of tomorrow. Life is always lived now!

SOL DAY 349
14 December

When One is truly awake, enlightenment will dawn on One like the early morning rays of the sun, blessing One with the light to see clearly. It will not make One a special human being, a superhero or turn One into some incredible intergalactic Being. Know that One is already divine, One just needs to realise it and wake up to One's place in the universe 'Now'.

Everything that One is hiding from oneself is preventing One from believing in and seeing One's true self and divine nature. There is nowhere that One can go in the universe to escape from One's spirit, soul or cosmic consciousness. This is inseparable from oneself. The more One looks outside of oneself for something to fill the void, loneliness or emptiness in One's mind, the less One will be able to find love, light and oneness within One's spirit, which already exists in One's Being.

Just because One has had an incredible spiritual experience does not automatically make One enlightened. Even if One believes in it with all of One's heart and has a certain spiritual practice One is committed to daily, that does not routinely qualify One as enlightened. Even to say that One is enlightened within One's friendship circle is a sign that One is not. There is no test, trial or trophy for being enlightened. In most cases, it may feel like the very opposite, as the universe will ask more and more of oneself to be all that One can be now.

Many people start on the path of enlightenment thinking it is going to be a wonderful way to spiritually 'clean house', improve One's lifestyle and become a well-rounded, conscious person, as well as a way to have wonderful, loving, amazing experiences, manifest One's desires and live a better life on the planet. This is true for many people. But One's new life comes at the cost of One's old ways of living, thinking and doing. This benefits One and all.

SOL DAY 350
15 December

One is not the person One thinks One is today. Trust One when One says that One is not human, One has no human parents, One was never born and One will never die on Earth. What One thinks of as 'I' is a residual self-image of One's personhood created out of One's ego-identity. In essence, there is no 'I' in the universe only 'One', meaning spirit, soul or cosmic consciousness.

One has been groomed since birth to believe in the 'I' of One's human experiences. One's mind has been filled and collectively reinforced in the community with false truths, like 'I think therefore I am' or 'I am ... who I believe myself to be' or 'I think I can, I know I can ...' The list is endless. There are too many 'I' statement examples to mention here but they all support the construct of the 'I' of One's ego-identity. However, what really scares people is losing One's human avatar of identity into the void of infinite space and having nothing for the ego in One's mind to cling to as 'real' in this world. People are basically terrified to lose the attachment to One's ego-identity and human form. If One is not human, who is this human being? Knowing this can really mess with One's egoic mind and freak some people out. However, it is a necessary truth that One must realise on One's pathless path and inner way.

One cannot escape the fact that One is a divine sentient Being of the universe, not a separate individual conditioned by previous generations and the community in which One lives. It is time to start believing in One's spirit and act like the divine Being that One is.

One will never be able to reach One's full potential in this life or the next, if One does not come to terms with One's spiritual existence in the universe and being a host to One's human form. One has infinite potential and immeasurable power to co-create One's life and reality.

SOL DAY 351
16 December

Today is an important day to realise that One's life on Earth makes a positive difference to the lives of others. Even when One is not present, other people are aware of One's positive energy and its uplifting effect. Whatever gift, ability, divine wisdom, loving kindness or compassionate virtuous gesture One has ever received in One's life – pay it forward. Pay it forward to other people in the now of One's life on the planet. Pay it forward to people who One is familiar with, like One's friends, partner, lover, family, kin, cousin and other individuals.

It is not the size or content of the gift being paid forward but the generosity of the giving that counts. Giving creates more abundance in everyone's lives. The more One gives, the more there is to share with everyone else in the world. All the resources of the planet are a shared and intergenerational responsibility of all citizens of Earth, not something exclusively reserved or entitled for a certain few as defined by lines on a map.

No individual person, community, multinational company, state, province, nation or country owns the sky or space. So how can anyone proclaim One owns Country (land sea and sky) or the Earth? Especially when One does not even have a spiritual relationship with it.

The legacy of a life should not be measured in what One has accumulated or given away, but in how One lived One's life when One was alive.

The generous support, loving kindness and spiritual presence One has offered and given to others will silently imprint upon others' psyche and positive wellbeing. It may not seem important at the time, but it all adds to the collective wellness of all life on Earth.

Realise the significance of One's positive impact upon others. It is bigger than One imagines it to be. One has the creative capacity to positively influence everyone on Earth.

SOL DAY 352
17 December

Stop running away from One's spiritual destiny in life. Let go of One's pain and suffering. Come out of the shadows and end hiding from One's negative emotions (thoughts and feelings). Give up pretending that One has got all of One's life together and all figured out, especially when One knows that One is still working through things.

Now is the moment to be totally open and honest with oneself. Accept where One is and how things are at this time. If One is messed up, broken or feels like One's life is in chaos, so be it. When One hits rock bottom, there is nowhere else to go but up. Sometimes One has to allow oneself to completely break down in order to become the best version of oneself on Earth.

Learn to face One's egoic fears as a warrior of the light. Let no darkness or negativity be safe within One's mind. Understand that every time One confronts the illusions of One's egoic doubts, worries or concerns, One moves closer to the light of One's consciousness. Know that One is truly worthy, deserving and whole. One is intrinsically valued as a spiritual Being. One need not prove anything to anyone for any reason at all. Being here on Earth is all the permission One needs to validate One's existence as a Being of light, love and oneness.

As hard as it may seem, broken people are beautiful, because they value life.

Being authentic and genuine is a rare and wonderful quality in this world. When One can speak One's truth without judgement, it has a way of shinning a light on the things in life that need One's attention. One needs to realise that the old version of oneself was never meant to be part of One's new life on Earth. Say goodbye to the old and embrace the new. Being free now is the path to One's spiritual destiny and new life on Earth.

SOL DAY 353
18 December

One will think differently, speak differently and move differently when One has a different perspective and understanding of One's infinite potential and immeasurable power as a sentient Being. One will conduct oneself in a way that aligns with One's mind-body-spirit and the universe. The synchronicities of the universe will flow effortlessly in One's life. These are normal shifts in One's relationship with One's spiritual self and the rest of the world.

One will have a different glow about oneself. One's positive vibrations will lift to a higher level and One will feel delight, joy and bliss for no particular reason. The neural pathways in One's brain will have changed, as will the chemical composition. One will have a craving to be away from the white noise of society, crowds and gatherings. One will seek out a more serene, peaceful and quiet lifestyle. One will yearn to be content with One's own company and let the days go by as the sun arcs across the sky. Seasons, circles and cycles of life will appear as One stays centred within One's divine spiritual presence on Earth.

One will realise that superficialities of society have nothing to offer One of any substance. One will laugh uncontrollably at the illusion of how it appears to be today.

One's inner awareness will expand exponentially out into the universe and, with this expansion, One will realise that what One is experiencing is a natural phenomenon of spiritual evolution on this world and in this solar system. Many will desperately try to cling and hang on to the old paradigm of life, thinking that it will save One in this new age of enlightenment – but it won't. Most people do not realise that the world as One knows it stands on the precipice of destruction, change and transformation, which will mean the death and decommissioning of One's own egocentric identity and life.

SOL DAY 354
19 December

Realise that One can choose to be free today. Free from competition with anyone else on the planet. Free from groupthink and egocentric collective thoughts that promote greed, scarcity, judgement, control and separation in society. Free from toxic and negative relationships with people who choose to operate and live life at a lower level of cosmic vibration and consciousness. Free from egoic minds of unconscious or unawakened people in the world. Free from the work–eat–sleep cycle of busyness to make things that nobody needs and buy things with money One does not have in order to impress people One does not like or know.

One has no desire to play the game of ego or participate in a world that enslaves other human beings. Earth needs a Declaration of Freedom for One and all future generations.

Declaration of Freedom
One holds these spiritual truths to be self-evident, that all sentient Beings have always been and will always be free. A free spirit, soul or cosmic consciousness of the universe. As a divine Being, One exists in a state of endless beingness and field of infinite possibilities. One has infinite potential and immeasurable power to co-create oneself and manifest any reality in the universe. One is infinite, immortal and eternal. One is imbued by Source Consciousness with certain states of aligned consciousness, that among these are inner knowing, awareness, oneness, joy, free will, peace and presence. One has the inherent inalienable right for One's human form to be born free, live free in a world of prosperity and abundance, and enjoy all universal freedoms as a citizen of Earth. These freedoms exist in perpetuity for One and all future generations. Everything is Connected — All is One.

SOL DAY 355
20 December

A loving kind conscious relationship or partnership with a lover or life partner is a wonderful, beautiful and amazing experience. It involves co-creating a safe space and shared willingness for One's co-existence with another Being in the world. It is, among other things, a place to honour One's spirit and the spirit in the other person. It can be a profound and powerful experience to nurture and nourish One's inner child and help each other to heal, express, develop, grow and transform into the best version of oneself.

This is not about being a slave to One's ego or changing other people. Changing oneself needs to be done by oneself to be the best version of oneself. Coming mindfully together to share One's life journey on Earth is about creating a loving, caring, encouraging space or circle of trust filled with delight, desire and devotion for the other person to be the best that One can be here and now. Express One's positive practices, healthy habits and benefiting behaviours. Celebrate these qualities with an open heart, mind and spirit.

Good communication is the key to great experiences and an even better relationship. It is an important strategy to facilitate a shared purpose and unifying path for One's mutual direction in life. See only the best in the other person and people. Promote an atmosphere of positive thinking, unconditional love and a deep sense of united togetherness. Express gratitude for all things in One's life. One is both the parent and the child, the teacher and the student, the Master and the servant. See the duality in life and within the relationship. Realise that One is whole, deserving and worthy of love, kindness, affection and support in One's life.

One's spirit is free and so too One's love.

SOL DAY 356
21 December

Everyone is engaging in life at One's own level of awakened consciousness. Go easy on oneself and others in the world. If One stumbles or experiences failure, it does not mean that One has lost One's way on One's spiritual journey. It just means that One needs to adjust One's spiritual footing – that is all.

It does not matter if One is in front of or lagging behind the wave of conscious enlightenment sweeping across the planet. Earth is making the transition to a new age of spiritual enlightenment anyway. Regardless of One's belief, culture or situation in life, Earth and the Beings living on it are a function of the whole universe, in the same way that the tides are a function of the moon. Everything is in motion with respect to all that is now.

One may feel an incredibly strong pull or change to One's energies and shift in One's perceptions of life on Earth. It is no surprise if One seeks to leave the ego matrix behind and explore an alternative life in this world. There is nothing in the 'new normal' modern society that is of any intrinsic value in and of itself. The small group of 'elites' know that One's hold on power, control and authority over others is slipping away as time moves on. These people are human dinosaurs destined for extinction as One takes One's place in this new Earth today.

A new and better version of Earth already exists today. One just needs to manifest this reality with the cooperation of other sentient Beings on the planet. If One can imagine it, it can be a reality now. A mass awakening is already happening on the planet. No person, company or government can stop it. The more who consciously awaken, the more others will awaken too. This change is happening exponentially and will change the face of Earth forever.

SOL DAY 357
22 December

Everything in One's life is unfolding in perfect timing and in synchronicity with the whole of the universe. Know that the divine dwells within One on this day and every other day. One does not need to go searching for it or trying to google it on the internet. One does not need a search engine to find One's divinity or enlightened spiritual presence, One only needs silence and a good meditation practice.

Everything comes to One when One stops looking for it now.

Just by sitting quietly in the world, One can observe and absorb the wisdom of the universe. Every individual human or animal in nature is a reflection and expression of the whole universe. All are perfect and all are connected in some way, shape or form. Life gives birth to life on this planet. This is the way it has always been and will always be.

One's way is not to become an enlightened 'somebody' but to be an awake 'nobody'.

One's real job description is to dismantle and deconstruct the ego-identity which One has artificially manufactured within One's mind since One was born. One has been compiling an illusion that has been re-enforced by family, friends and society about who One is and how One is to conduct oneself in life. There has been an unspoken rule that One does not speak about this false personhood in the fear that it is not real. To speak of it will destroy the illusion that has been carefully crafted as a truth, but which everyone knows is a lie. Only when One destroys One's own egoic identity will One be able to see One's true self and divine identity.

Realise that most people are playing the game of false identities, trying to be a 'somebody' in the hope of not facing the real truth that everyone is a 'nobody' in disguise.

SOL DAY 358
23 December

Live a life of ongoing joy, positivity and laughter. A place where what One believes, thinks, says and acts upon is in alignment with One's mind–body–spirit and the universe. Balance and harmony will flower naturally when One goes with the natural flow of life.

Do something different with One's life. Follow a creative path that resonates deeply with One's spirit. Make a conscious decision not to be ordinary like the billions of others out there seeking validation from a few individuals. Remind oneself that One is special and One has an abundant creative imagination. Show the world One's light and allow One's divine creativity to flow through One in every aspect of One's life on Earth. Free One's mind–body from negative opinions, limited thinking and low dysfunctional energies of others.

It is time to reach for the stars and express One's creative ideas. Work-life balance is about being true to One's spirit and knowing how to give oneself freedom in life. Freedom to live, freedom to express, freedom to be creative and freedom to just be now.

Do not be compelled to be like others. Step into the unknown of One's own creative imagination and manifest a new kind of reality for oneself here on Earth. Have no fear, the right people will come onboard and join One on One's path in life. At times it may feel like that One is lost, but this is all part of finding One's way through the enchanted forest of life to the light of One's inner awareness, realisation and awakening.

Every time One feels like One is drowning in despair, depression or despondency, remind oneself that One is a sentient Being of love, light and oneness in this world. One is greater than anything or any challenge that faces One in this life. Awaken to be a brilliant living 'Bright'.

SOL DAY 359
24 December

Get offline, give oneself a break and go outside today. Make an effort to engage and connect with Country (land, sea and sky). Immerse oneself in the natural environment. Look up at the sky and see how open and free it is. Sky does not cling to anything and yet its presence is everywhere, always above oneself throughout One's day and over the course of One's life.

Listen to the birds and the wind. Stand firmly rooted in the land and know that One is held unconditionally with love on Earth. Accept where One is and rejoice in One's place in the world. One's inner joy is limitless within oneself. Joy is a state of consciousness that is inseparable from One's spiritual Being. No amount of external conditioning or unfortunate life experiences can ever diminish or dissolve this eternal light within One's spirit.

Know that a single act of love, kindness and compassion towards oneself, others or an animal is worth more than a million prayers or good wishes in the world. Praying by itself does not manifest a better life or world. If this were the case, humans would have already ended all pain and suffering on the planet many centuries ago.

Intention requires action to improve or change what it is now. Accept first, then act with a clear intention to benefit oneself and others. It is not about being caught in a loop of thinking–reacting–doing. Repeating this cycle is like being in a washing machine, going around and around in the same spot but getting nowhere. There is no real progress, but the clothes do get clean. One must keep moving forward in a positive direction.

It is fine to set the intention for today to be virtuous or loving, but One must also act in a way that aligns with this intention. This is how things change in One's life. This is the process of manifesting the magic throughout One's day.

SOL DAY 360
25 December

Today, believe that something wonderful, magical and spontaneous is about to happen in One's life and it will. In fact, One needs to infuse One's life with this belief every single day.

When One believes in the wonder, magic and spontaneity of the universe to manifest positive things in One's life, guess what happens? It does exactly that. The universe has always been on One's side, even before the day One was born on Earth. The universe is continually working in One's favour and in the best interests, even when One thinks it is not. Do not get so caught up in the daily actions of One's life that One cannot take into consideration the universe's greater plan of divine chaos in which everyone's lives are part of now.

One is part of something greater than oneself and it is beautiful and awe-inspiring.

As the stars shine, the moon glows and life goes on. As a spirit hosting a unique human form, One is meant to be the master of One's destiny and captain of One's ship in life. The world is One's classroom and One is a student of life. Everyone is One's peers and all are One's pupils. Everything that One materially possesses will be left on Earth when One finally returns to source consciousness. One will only leave with One's divine spirit.

Use this time wisely, mindfully and graciously, not for the accumulation of thousands of things, experiences and people but as a series of interconnecting moments where One can rise to the highest and best version of oneself in this world. Everyone who One meets on Earth is a reflection of oneself in One form or another. See the sprit in oneself and One will recognise the spirit in all other sentient life forms on this planet. It is easy to be a loving spirit because it already exists within One now.

SOL DAY 361
26 December

There is no progress without struggle, there is no growth without change, there is no enlightenment without transcending suffering. Everything comes to One at the right moment of One's life. All is a journey to realise One's own divine truth and place in the universe. Every Being who has ever come to Earth has come here of One's own free will. It is this free will to be or not to be that gives One access to this third dimension of space-time.

It may seem that One is human, but One is not. It may appear that One is One's mind and body, but One is not. It may appear that One's thoughts and feeling are a real part of One's human identity, but it is not. It may look like the world is a living reality that One is part of, but One is not. It may give the impression like time is real, but this is all an intricate and clever illusion in space-time created for the purposes of source consciousness to know of and experience its own existence. The only thing that is real is that which is unchanging – One's divine spirit, soul or cosmic consciousness. Everything else is simply a convincing illusion.

In the meantime, live a mindful virtuous life in the service of One's spirit, benefiting oneself and others on Earth. To be great – serve others. To be happy – give happiness to others. To be joyful – bring joy to others. To be loving, kind and compassionate – share these qualities with others. To be prosperous and abundant – live this type of lifestyle for oneself and act with the intention to benefit others wherever One is in the world.

When One becomes 'the way', any way is One's way to the future. Know that it is okay to be self-centred for the benefit of One's mind-body-spirit. To take care, to be kind, gentle and loving to oneself is an act of self-compassion. One has a duty of care towards oneself.

SOL DAY 362
27 December

Everyone everywhere is just a single spiritual flower from the same tree of divine consciousness. All living within the same celestial cosmic rhythm of the universe. All flowering in the same way and blossoming with the light of eternal oneness. When One realises that One's gift of being what One is now is enough, One will never be a slave to One's human emotions in life.

Do not be concerned with the daily rituals of other people and business activities endlessly happening in the world. Focus on being a free spirit with an open mind and loving kind heart. Let this be One's business practice for life and One's daily mantra for living. With good intentions, One co-creates good in One's life and the world. Be kind to every person and animal. When One does good for and with others, it will come back to One in unexpected ways. Be a generous philanthropist of love, kindness and compassion on Earth.

Believe in oneself and no-one or thing will be able to defeat oneself.

It is time to start thinking for oneself and realise that 'the way' will open for One when One moves towards One's divine destiny now. With One's thoughts, One can change One's perception and manifest a new reality today. Seek the light of One's own spirit for the benefit of all Beings on Earth. Wherever One is standing now is where One's spirit is. It is not hiding from oneself, it is only being hidden by One's own ego from One's awareness of itself.

One has not lived until One has spoken and acted upon One's inner spiritual truth from One's heart with fearlessness and humility. When One has the courage to be free and chooses freedom, One can be said to be divinely free to express One's divinity in this world.

There is nothing as great as a person who is truly free – free to live and free to be 'Now'.

SOL DAY 363
28 December

With One's awakening on Earth, One will realise that 'All is One'. There is nothing that separates One's spirit from others except for One's own perception. The illusion that One calls reality is where One's inner difficulties and challenges arise. Come to terms with this and One will create a sense of peace, serenity and tranquillity in One's life. Move beyond a belief in the outside world and align with an inner knowing of One's inside existence.

Give generously and stop expecting anything from anyone in this world or on Earth.

Know that things will naturally fall into place at the right moment in One's life. Look forward to it happening when it does and be excited in the moment. Fall in love with being alive and living One's life today. Do not over-think it, over-plan it or over-do it. What One deeply loves and radiates into the world will be reflected back to One. There is a resonance in One's Being and heart that will naturally and effortlessly attract One's true friends in this world. It is a magnet for co-creating good spaces in One's life for great people to be present. It is the dimension, depth and divine radiance of One's inner energy that attracts people.

Empty One's mind of everything – stay focused on being a beautiful 'Bright' on Earth.

Meet everything and everyone from the centre of One's spiritual presence. It is this eternal stillness that is aligned to the entire universe in the moments of One's life. Know that the space between One's thoughts is where infinity lives eternal – go there, be there now. Swim in the silence of One's Being and One will always be at peace in these still, calm waters.

Human life is a learning and awakening experience. Never be attached to what happens. As far as the existence of the universe is concerned, it knows only 'Now'.

SOL DAY 364
29 December

Spiritual people will often have undergone a significant change, life-altering mind–body transformation and profound awareness of who One is, life and the universe. This will in most cases require One to surrender oneself completely to all that is now. This process of realisation and awakening will be reflected by the degree to which One has let go of all references to One's own egoic identity and experiences from One's personhood. To be free, One must free One's spirit from 'the self' of One's human identity that One has constructed.

Know that an egoic mind will always want to cling, grasp, hold on to and fix itself to an idea, concept or notion of 'the self'. This attachment is not real. It is only a reaction to the flux, fluidity and vibrations of One's existence on Earth. If One begins any statement with 'I am this …' or I am that …', One's egoic mind is trying to attach itself to something. Instead, say 'One's mind or body is…' or 'One's mind–body thinks/feels…' This is a more accurate way to observe and be a witness of oneself or One's human form. It is a way to divinely express oneself.

This is the 'language of spirit' – it is 'the way' to a spiritual dimension within oneself and alignment with the oneness of One's Being and source consciousness. When One speaks in the language of spirit, One is able to align with and access the whole universe.

Language shapes the way that One thinks and perceives the world. It also changes the neural pathways in the brain and One's reality in the world. When One begins to learn a new universal spiritual language and express oneself with it, this results in a cascading effect within One's mind–body and life. It reconfigures One's brain and aligns One's life to a more spiritual dimension, path and perspective in the universe. This is a good thing for those who openly, honestly and genuinely seek it now. This language lives within One now.

SOL DAY 365
30 December

Over the course of One's lifetime, some things will work out and some won't – just accept it now. There will be failures and successes. One's task is not to judge or become a victim of these circumstances, situations and events in One's life. One's role is to be fully present in the moment as it is happens. Ninety per cent of One's job-life description is about having the courage to just show up and be present. The other ten per cent is everything else in the world.

Do not be concerned about what One might have done differently, could have tried or should have said. Let the past be the past, completely forgive oneself and move on to the present moment of One's life. This is where life is – all the action is happening here and now.

There are many beautiful things, people and surprises in the world just waiting for One now. Keep moving along 'the way' of One's spiritual path as it leads One in the right direction in life. Create a loving, kind, sacred space in One's life that is free from all negativities, hate, anger, jealousy, concern, worry, anxiety, fear, attachment, judgement and resistance. As One heals oneself, One also creates a healing energy in the world. Prepare One's mind-body and life to be open and receptive to experiencing higher vibrational energies together with positive, loving, kind, gentle, caring and peaceful experiences. One is worthy and deserving of co-creating an inner and outer space that attracts light, love and oneness into One's life now.

Say to oneself over and over again, 'One is worthy, One is whole, One is deserving, One is a beautiful divine spirit of the universe, One is a loving, kind, gentle and compassionate person, One is positive, One is optimistic, One is enthusiastic, One is joyful, One is passionate, One is mindful and virtuous, One is a co-creator of prosperity, abundance and wakefulness, One is a 'Bright' and today is another day to shine One's light upon the world.'

SOL DAY 366
31 December

Believe that the universe is a safe and magical place. Believe that everything in One's life will work out. Believe in the formlessness and fluidity of One's spirit, soul or cosmic consciousness. One exists beyond space–time in a state of unending beingness. One has infinite potential and immeasurable power to co-create any manifested reality on Earth or in the universe. One is a truly awesome sentient Being. One is not One's thoughts or body. One is not human at all.

Know this as One's truth – so be it now.

As One awakens from One's illusion of separateness and realises One's divinity within, One creates a ripple in the fabric of space–time that aligns to the whole oneness of the universe. Be aware that One is responsible for co-creating and manifesting a new age of spiritual evolution on Earth. One is source consciousness itself. One's divine destiny is now.

Now is the time to change and transform. Now is the time to realise and awaken. Focus on co-creating One's future life simply by living in the present. Transmute all negative energies that are less than love for the benefit of oneself and other Beings. One is allowed to be completely free and live a spiritual life now. It is okay to think, live, be and do things differently from the way One lived life in the past. Through the power of One's inner love, light and oneness, One is raising One's vibration to a higher level of consciousness in the world.

As One creates One's thoughts and intentions, One co-creates a new reality on Earth.

A brighter future begins to be manifested the moment One commits to it.

It is in One's divine nature to be awake so One can consciously manifest a new vision, a new reality and a new Earth today.

ACKNOWLEDGEMENTS

One is incredibly grateful and blessed to be here now on Earth during this time of increased global awareness and spiritual awakening. The presence of so many wonderful living leaders brings a higher level of cosmic consciousness and positive energy into the world. All are freely working towards creating a brighter future – today.

Openly sharing One's insights and learnings on 'the way' of the universe is One of many paths that will spiritually enable people and bring benefit to all. A new reality, new world and new Earth requires the cooperation of all sentient Beings, not just a few mindful thought leaders. All are part of this process of prosperity, abundance and awakening – it is inevitable and inescapable.

It is with heartfelt thanks that One acknowledges past, present and emerging First Nations Elders (like One's mother, Shirley Foley nee Wondunna), spiritual mentors, thought leaders, 'Brights' (light warriors and enlightened awake Beings) and divine wisdom keepers across the world by whom One has been inspired to create this new book.

One knows that the brightest of light often shines when One is awakened from One's illusion of darkness. One can embrace One's inner spirit and truly honour One's divine truth in this world.

One is very thankful to Adrienne and Murray Williams for being able to stay at their onsite art studio residence in Mt Perry, Queensland, Australia during the COVID-19 lockdown in 2020. At the time, One was planning to travel overseas, so all of One's material possessions were in storage and One's current lease of accommodation had expired. The synchronicity of the universe was perfect in its timing. Over those months, One was able to use this space and time to experience and enjoy living a mindful, creative and artistic writing lifestyle. The creative writing studio, which One temporarily established onsite, was in town but was surrounded by the greenery of mountain bushland. It was a welcome tree change and beautiful blessing to be in the country. One was free to meditate, reflect, write and align with One's inner way of living and being in the moment.

As the cold winter nights drew in around One, One was comforted by a wood fire place, the crackle of burning timber and warm glowing embers throughout the evening. One never felt alone on this journey in life, and never has been … each new day on Earth is a wonderful blessing to simply be alive – here and now.

As One sat and thought about One's life and living experiences on Earth, One aligned to One's inner spirit and reflected upon the beauty, magic and wonder of this world. A silent thought stream of ideas, inspiration and intuitive insights flowed effortlessly from within. The wellspring of words in this book aim to quench One's thirst for truth and divine place in the universe. All that is written within the pages of this book points 'the way' for One to awaken, rise and shine like a brilliant star in the universe.

One is also appreciative of all the people that One has met along the way in writing this book, especially One's long-time friends Steven and Sue Clark. When One lives a life that is continually washed and worn away by the relentless waves of time, One is truly welcoming of a place to rest, refresh and renew oneself in One's time of need.

Again, One is ever so grateful to all the readers of this book for whom these words are intended to benefit and ripple throughout One's life in every direction. May every future generation of divine Beings on Earth benefit from the love, light and inspiration within the pages of this book — *Awaken*.

Thanks everyone. With loving kindness and compassion

— Shawn

AFFIRMATION FOR LIFE

One is worthy. One is deserving. One is whole. One is beautiful. One is talented. One is resourceful. One is joyful. One is love and loving. One is kind, caring and compassionate. One is blissful. One is mindful. One is intuitive. One is free. One is amazing, awesome and aware. One is spirit and a divine sentient Being of the universe. One is immortal, infinite and eternal. One is changing the world in One's own way. One's past does not interfere with One's spiritual, soulful or cosmic conscious way for oneself. One is at peace within and with all. One is aiding others by sharing One's story. One is exactly where One needs to be in this world. One has entered a season and time of great prosperity and abundance in One's life. What One once dreamed of is now manifesting and unfolding in perfect synchronicity with the universe.

One knows that it is One's responsibility to be the best version of oneself so One can share One's gifts, insights, wisdom, love, kindness and compassion to benefit all living and future generations.

One is the co-creator of One's reality. One possesses infinite potential. One's power as a divine Being of the universe is immeasurable. One is a magnificent Being and a radiant light in this solar system and galaxy.

One exists – so One is and will always be free now.

CIRCLE OF MINDFUL AND CONSCIOUS EXISTENCE

Being virtuous creates an alignment to
One's spiritual consciousness and the universe

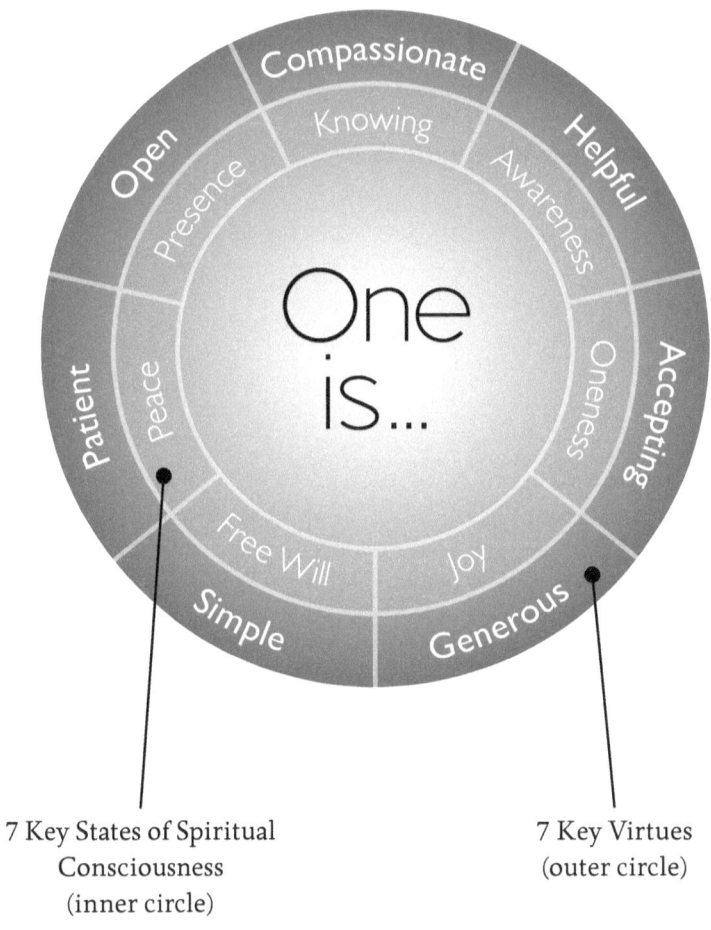

7 Key States of Spiritual
Consciousness
(inner circle)

7 Key Virtues
(outer circle)

FINAL NOTE

It takes a person with great will, loving self-worth and mindful resolve to stand still, stay calm and be silent in the face of One's own fear and the death of One's ego.

To know and realise One's true courage in this moment is to completely transform One's reality.

An indomitable spirit already exists within One.

One is the co-creator of One's living experiences in the world.

One's new future on Earth begins the moment One is true to oneself and truly present 'Now'.

Shawn Wondunna-Foley

www.ingramcontent.com/pod-product-compliance
Lightning Source LLC
Chambersburg PA
CBHW020313010526
44107CB00054B/1823